TEACHING WORKPLACE SKILLS

Creative ways to teach students the skills employers want

Linda Koffel
Houston Community College System

Gulf Publishing Company
Houston, Texas

This book is dedicated to
Dean Calvin Smith of Houston Community College
who always believed in me.

Teaching Workplace Skills

Gulf Publishing Company
Book Division
P.O. Box 2608
Houston, Texas 77252-2608

10 9 8 7 6 5 4 3 2 1

Library of Congress Cataloging-in-Publication Data

Koffel, Linda.
   Teaching workplace skills : creative ways to teach students the
skills employers want / Linda Koffel.
     p. cm.
   Includes index.
   ISBN 0-88415-076-3
   1. Career education—United States. 2. Vocational education—
United States. I. Title.
LC1037.5.K63 1994
371.11′3′0973—dc20
                                         93-44413
                                            CIP

Disclaimer

CONTENTS

PREFACE

Teaching Workplace Skills was written with one basic idea in mind: students should get out of the educational system what they expect and deserve—an education that prepares them for their futures in the workplace. Workplace literacy is a hot topic right now. From the disturbing information outlined in *Workforce 2000: Work and Workers for the 21st Century* by William B. Johnston to the surprising and comprehensive study conducted by the American Society for Training and Development and its subsequent report *Workplace Basics: The Skills Employers Want* by Anthony P. Carnevale, Leila J. Gainer, and Ann S. Meltzer, one issue is clear: the product of our education system is lacking in the skills necessary for **living and working.**

This book develops a systematic approach that any teacher who teaches any subject can use to better prepare his/her students for their important roles as workers in the twenty-first century. It is a practical book. Most of the theory that leads up to this approach has intentionally been left out. There are myriad educational tomes on the market that outline theory after theory on teaching and learning. Some of them are quite good; others are not. What I wanted to provide in this book was a solid foundation of classroom techniques teachers could use every day to design learning activities that shape the employees of the future.

I wanted a book that went beyond the theoretical discussion into the reality of life in the workplace. I wanted to take the theories that make the most sense to me, namely, Rogers' theory of student-centered learning and Knowles' theory of andragogy or adult learning, to create a simple, systematic approach to improve teaching in all disciplines and at all levels. Although the foundation for the strategies in this book is the theory of andragogy (the art of helping adults learn) by Knowles, its techniques and strategies can be used by anyone who is a teacher or a trainer (even elementary teachers).

There are those who might think they are teaching English or sociology or history, pure subjects that do not involve preparation for occupations. To these I say, we are not preparing students for the next test, for the final, for their term paper, or for the next course. We are preparing students for life, and no matter what subject we teach, we are our students' only chance to learn the skills of life that will be survival skills in the next century. We must begin now to change our methods of teaching so that the next generation of workers will be better able to cope with their careers and with life. Only by restructuring education and better preparing each individual student can we ensure democracy, ensure a better life for those who will follow us, and reduce problems of modern society such as illiteracy, poverty, hunger, and crime. As teachers, we prepare our students for their futures, and we cannot afford to fail them.

This book is divided into four major parts. Chapter 1 introduces the American Society for Training and Development Study and its importance to education as well as the theoretical basis for this systematic approach. Chapter 2 develops a step-by-step systems approach for using the strategies in this book to reinforce and develop workplace skills—no matter what the subject being taught. Chapter 3 provides several evaluation methods for assessing the effectiveness of the strategies and includes ideas from K. Patricia Cross's work on classroom assessment. Chapters 4 through 10 outline the different strategies for improving motivation to learn, basic skills, communication, critical and creative thinking, career development, teamwork and leadership, respectively. These strategies are easily adaptable to almost any classroom situation.

I have many people to thank: The Carl Perkins Grant Administration of the Texas Higher Education Coordinating Board for providing seed money for the development of the system; Dr. Karla Back of Back and Associates and an Adjunct Faculty for University of Houston for introducing me to the world of adult learning; Dr. Sharon Pinebrook of the University of Houston for not only introducing me to the work of Malcolm Knowles, but also inspiring me to succeed; Vincent D'Amico for giving me a wonderful foundation in writing; Elaine Novak for her constant support and advice; Calvin Smith for his constant motivation; Gwen Joseph for unblocking my creativity; Dorothy Lewis for her support; Debbie Herring for her valuable insight; and Joseph DiFlavio for his understanding.

Linda Koffel

TEACHING WORKPLACE SKILLS

CHAPTER ONE

WORKPLACE SKILLS SYSTEM

A Method for Teaching
Workplace Skills in Any Classroom

Each year thousands of students crowd into classrooms in elementary schools, high schools, junior high schools, and colleges. A majority of these individuals attend classes because they truly believe that if they attend, they will learn. Our society and culture has convinced them that an education will help them to be successful citizens and employees in the future. But, will our educational system provide the kind of education that these individuals truly need to become successful employees by the time they graduate? Maybe. Maybe not.

New technology. Participative management. Sophisticated statistical quality controls. Customer service. Just-in-time production. The workplace is changing and so are the skills that employees must have in order to change with it [Carnevale *et al.*]

The American Society for Training and Development conducted a research study with the U. S. Department of Labor in 1988 to find out which skills employers want to see in entry-level employees. ASTD used its 50,000+ membership as a base to conduct an extensive study of employers across the United States. Seven skills categories were identified as being the most valuable to employers [Carnevale *et al.*]:

- Motivation to learn
- Basic skills

1

- Communication
- Teamwork
- Critical thinking
- Career development
- Leadership

Unfortunately, most secondary and post secondary institutions have not been successful in instilling these skills in their students. A disparity exists between educators who emphasize the study of ideas, discussion of concepts and thoughts and the business community and employers who emphasize skills. Educators spend much time discussing theories, sharing knowledge, experimenting, and searching for concepts, while employers who hire students who graduate from our educational system want to see results and want their employees to be able to *do* something with their knowledge.

Students, oblivious that what they are usually getting in the classroom is broad background material for what they may have to teach themselves when they get on the job, typically sit through hours of lecture and discussion classes with very little interaction or opportunity to practice doing anything. The skills listed above are seldom discussed in the classroom, unless the students are business or management students. In short, the majority of classes in a typical high school or college do not adequately prepare students for their roles as employees.

That is not to say that broad discussions, experiments, and theories are not important. They are. For the employees of the future to survive, they need both skills and a broad education. "We need employees who are broadly and deeply educated, men and women who are 'liberally' educated," says David T. Kearns in *Winning the Brain Race.* He also says, "The modern employee has to be more highly educated, better informed, more flexible than ever before . . . . He or she must be, because what we're paying for is the ability to think, to solve problems, to make informed judgments, to distinguish between right and wrong, to discern the proper course of action in situations and circumstances that are necessarily ambiguous." What Kearns wants is an employee who has developed the skills listed above. That is why the educators in secondary and post secondary systems especially must prepare students for their future roles as productive skilled employees.

No matter what a student's future profession, be it as an historian, anthropologist, social scientist, nuclear physicist, auto mechanic, lawyer, writer, doctor, or whatever, he or she will either be an employee of some organization or institution or will be an owner of a business. Regardless of the situation, the seven workplace skills are critical to his or her success in life.

The ASTD study outlines the need for dramatic changes in our approaches to teaching. It cites statistics that indicate the problem in the future will be one of having too many unskilled workers and only a few jobs for unskilled workers, while at the same time, having a shortage of skilled workers and an overabundance of jobs for those few skilled workers. Of course, demographic data, such as the shrinking size of the work force, will contribute to the problem as will the shift from a manufacturing-based economy to a service-based economy. Employers will be competing for the best, most skilled workers—especially the workers that can help employers compete in a global economy.

"Employers want a new kind of worker with a broad set of workplace skills—or at least a strong foundation of basics that will facilitate learning on the job" [Carnavale *et al.,* p. 11]. In other words, employers who will provide the students who are in the classroom today with jobs tomorrow want more (much more) than our educational system typically provides to a student. What can our educational systems do to offset the problem of unskilled workers? How can we begin to redirect our efforts to teach both the important theoretical components of learning as well as the important skills? What can we do to begin now to prepare our students for these challenges?

We can begin with teachers in classrooms. Until our educational systems catch up and begin developing far-reaching programs for changes in curricula and other services, the logical place to begin is in the classroom with the teachers. We as instructors and teachers can begin tomorrow by changing how we teach, not necessarily what we teach. No longer can we be content with memory tests, with electronically graded prepackaged exams, or fill-in-the-blank worksheets. We need to find new ways of teaching to bring out the skills our students will need—no matter what discipline we are teaching. We can begin by changing our teaching behavior in our classes with our current curriculum.

The Workplace Skills System presented in this book provides a systematic method for reinforcing these seven valuable skills. It takes the discussion about workplace skills from the theoretical to the practical. This book provides instructors with specific classroom strategies for teaching these skills along with a systematic approach for infusing them into the curriculum for maximum benefit to the students. The strategies are diverse enough to fit most disciplines and teaching styles. With a variety of strategies to choose from in each area, the instructor has many resources from which to draw.

The strategies presented are merely ideas for the instructor to use as he/she sees fit. Some have been tested in the classroom and some have not. Even through the draft versions of this book, many have been altered and implemented as ideas have spread throughout the academic community. These strategies are presented as a resource and guide to anyone who teaches adults (loosely defined as someone from ages 16 through 90). In many cases, these strategies will also work with elementary and junior high school students.

Developmental psychologists discovered that there are predictable developmental stages that adolescents and adults pass through as they develop. One of the basic differences between adolescents, children, and adults is their experience levels. Adults have a much wider range of experience to draw from and frequently tend to view learning as a means to an end—as a way to develop a new skill, to learn a new language that will enable them to communicate on the job, or to learn a new approach to problem solving that they can practice at their job or some outside activity.

The Workplace Skills System is based on the andragogical model of helping adults learn. Malcolm Knowles perfected this theory of learning, which is based on the realization that adults view learning differently. They see it not as knowledge for knowledge's sake, but as knowledge for some practical purpose. Knowles defined andragogy as "the art and science of helping adults learn" [Knowles, p. 2]. It differs from pedagogy in that pedagogy assumes the learner has no experience to speak of and that the learner is a dependent person. The instructor has full responsibility for the learning process and for making decisions about what will be learned, how it will be learned, to what degree it will be learned, and when it should be learned. Because the learner's experience is viewed as having little value, the learner takes the role of submissive receiver of information. Generally, the learner develops a subject-centered orientation to learning and expects to be taught subject matter content. This type of learner is motivated by *external* factors such as peer pressure, parental pressure, and pressure from teachers.

In contrast to the pedagogical approach, the andragogical approach views the learner as a self-directed learner—a learner responsible for his or her own learning. Andragogical learners see learning as a process that transforms them and makes their experiences a part of the learning process. In this way, learners can transfer the subject matters they learn in the classroom to practical applications of enhanced knowledge or skills on the job or in their lives.

Usually, adult learners will find themselves taking a passive role to learning when they get back into a classroom, reverting back to their childhood role of listener waiting to be given knowledge by a teacher or a textbook. For this reason, adult learners have to be initiated into the andragogical learning style. It is important to show them how the andragogical approach works, why it works, how it makes learning easier for them and how they can help direct their own learning.

Because the experience of the andragogical learner is used in the learning process, the learner becomes aware of how his experience interplays with the material he is learning to help him internalize information and transform information from one setting to another. The emphasis is not on memorizing subject matter content, but on using subject matter content to see similarities between dissimilar issues and to apply content learned previously to new contexts. The andragogical learner can help set the direction of the study so the learning process can be more relevant to the learner.

This andragogical model is an extension of some of the humanistic approaches to learning and to teaching espoused by John Dewey and Carl Rogers and in direct opposition to theories such as B. F. Skinner's conditioning theory, which used a mechanistic model based on experiments conducted on animals. The andragogical model uses a more humanistic foundation for learning success: the idea that adults can create their own stimuli based on their own minds and memories, which are a culmination of their knowledge and their experiences. Knowles synthesizes ideas from Cyril Houle, Eduard Lindeman, and Rogers. He also cites the work of Carl Jung, which "advanced a more holistic conception of human consciousness, introducing the notion that it possesses four functions—or four ways of extracting information from experience and achieving internalized understanding—sensation, thought, emotion and intuition." [Knowles, p. 38]. The adult learner needs to synthesize all of these factors in order to learn. Tapping into the thought function (through rote memorization, for example) will not provide the adult learner with a balanced experience for learning. Learning must be *experienced.*

Carl Rogers provides a hypothesis on student-centered learning that Knowles uses as a basis for his theory [Knowles, pp. 41–42]:

1. We cannot teach another person directly; we can only facilitate his/her learning.
2. A person learns those things he perceives as maintaining and enhancing him/herself.
3. Experience that the learner perceives as inconsistent with his/her self image is either denied, distorted, or the self image is changed to include it.
4. The educational situation most likely to be effective promotes learning that is not a threat to the self image and that expands the field of experience (perception) of the learner.

If an instructor adopts Rogers and Knowles theory that learning is controlled by the learner through his/her internal processes as he/she reacts to his/her environment, then a new approach to teaching is imperative. No longer can teaching be seen as providing conditioning or stimuli for the learner in a controlled, sequential, and scientific manner. No longer can the teacher believe the notion that to teach is to cover the content material from the text at least well enough for students to memorize it and offer it back on a test. No longer can the instructor assume control for learning and assume that teaching equates to learning.

The instructor must begin to design experiences using emotion and thought (knowledge or facts), relying on the senses, and using intuition that will facilitate learning and help students to spark their own learning processes. This is a much different task than that of teaching.

Using an andragogical approach means rethinking and redesigning the experiences of the classroom to create learning situations that will carry far beyond the final exam or the end of the course. And, while the term *andragogy* has the word *andra,* or adult, as part of its root, it may be that children and youth can learn easier and faster through andragogical methods as well.

The strategies developed here are based on andragogical principles and as such tend to emphasize students taking responsibility for their own learning. The instructor is no longer the "authority" in the classroom, the person with all the answers whose job it is to give information. Instead, these strategies have been conceived with the instructor in the role of a "facilitator" of learning—someone who develops an experience by which students will learn both the material (content) and the process of how to use that material. The instructor is no longer required to stand up behind a lectern and dispense words of wisdom. The instructor is a catalyst for learning. He or she "conducts" the learning experience. Like a maestro, the instructor plans the highs and lows of the session, but it is the players, the students, who interact to contribute to the total learning experience.

This model of instructing and of learning is more appropriate for the kind of learning that will be required of the students and employees of the future. Students must participate, learn to work in teams, learn to motivate themselves, learn to solve problems (not memorize formulas), learn to create their own formulas, learn to lead and to follow. The lessons these facilitators provide will equip their students with the tools for survival in a modern world—a world in which the only thing that cannot be taken from the student is what he/she knows. If we successfully equip our students with tools for life, with the ability to think, to lead, to work together, to communicate, we will be giving them a lifelong ability to survive as independent persons—a gift that will not fail them.

The Workplace Skills System is based on the instructor using at least one strategy designed to enhance each of the seven skills areas in every class or course. Of course, there is no limit to the number of class assignments that could be taken from the system. Any instructor (for any discipline) can use the system. He/she simply chooses those strategies that fit well with his/her style of teaching. There are strategies for discussion, classroom activities, testing, and classroom evaluation.

For a 16-week course, at least one (or more) class period could be dedicated to infusing each skill category and, if time permits, the instructor could "fortify" the course with additional strategies in the areas most critical to his/her subject. These strategies can be used to teach content area as well, so the instructor could cover content material while he/she infuses workplace skills into the course.

In addition to the specific use of andragogical methods, an ongoing program evaluation is also essential to the success of such a system. The evaluation techniques developed in the system have been influenced by classroom assessment techniques prescribed by Patricia Cross and others. In addition, the skills enhancement techniques have been influenced by Marcia Heiman's Learning to Learn Program as well as others.

USING THE WORKPLACE SKILLS SYSTEM

Using the Workplace Skills System is easy. The strategies provide excellent sources for ideas for classroom activities and programs. But, the system will have the most overall impact on the education of individuals if it is used systematically. If the instructor develops a systematic approach that integrates these strategies with his/her content syllabus, the student will have an education infused with the seven important skills.

The instructor can use various approaches to create course structures based on skill/content blocks. A systematic approach means that the instructor uses strategies to upgrade each of the seven skills areas in a way that best meets the needs of the students likely to be taking a course in a specific discipline.

The process model in the figure that follows shows the basic system approach to infusing a course.

The system can be used by any instructor in any discipline. It does not require approval from curriculum committees or coordinating boards. It can be accomplished through whatever methods of teaching content material an instructor chooses to use. It simply requires the instructor to "break out of the box" of lecture format and experiment with other classroom strategies.

Ways to Use the Workplace Skills System

An Idea Source

The strategies presented in this book can be used as catalysts for other types of classroom activities. The instructor can read through the strategies

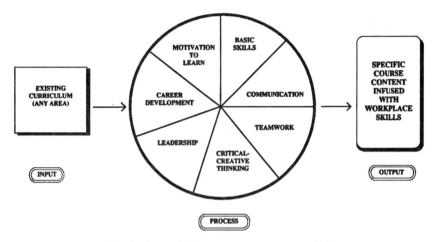

Workplace skills system process model.

and use them as a starting point for making revisions in his or her teaching methods. The strategies are guidelines that can be redeveloped and reconstructed for use in an unlimited number of ways.

Innovative Teaching Methods

The system can be used as a foundation for programs to develop and enhance innovative teaching methods. It can provide a wealth of information and new ideas for instructors who may not have "broken out of their boxes" and may need information as well as a process for using new techniques.

Special Classes in Skills Areas

Each of the strategy series for the skills areas contains at least one strategy called "module," which is essentially a content module on that skill itself. The system provides seven modules that can be used as content material for a stand-alone class or seminar designed to enhance the skills. In addition, each strategy series also presents several exercises based on the specific content material for that skill area.

Cooperative Education

Because there are seven content modules that discuss components of the seven skills areas as well as exercises that describe the skills categories, the system can be used as content material for classes in cooperative education.

Industry Training for Upgrading Skills

Because the book has seven modules that present content material from each of the seven skills areas, the system can be used as a foundation for training and seminars as part of company-sponsored development programs.

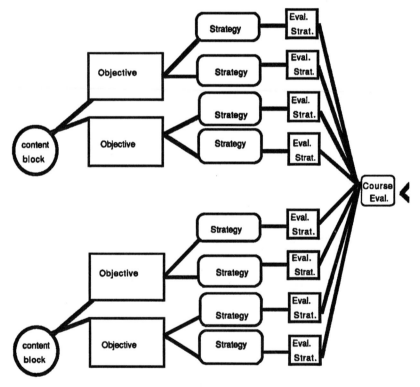

The infusion process. 1) Choose the content block (usually the chapters in the text); 2) Choose objectives; 3) Choose strategies to achieve the objectives and implement them; 4) Evaluate the strategies; 5) Evaluate the total course; 6) Revise strategies that did not work well and improve on all strategies. Note: More than one objective can often be achieved using only one strategy.

Process for Course Infusion

Start Content Blocks

To redesign a course, begin with the content blocks that you currently use for the course. You do not need to revise your curriculum. Your course probably has content blocks already developed. Most courses simply use the chapters of a text as the content blocks. For each content block you will want to set course objectives. If your institution or organization has already developed program-wide objectives for your course, they may be found in the course write-up or curriculum guide. If not, many textbooks list major objectives at the beginning of each chapter. If none are available, the instructor may need to develop a list of major objectives for the course.

The following are examples of objectives that might be set in a Principles of Marketing course (text: Pride and Ferrell's *Marketing,* 6th Edition, Houghton Mifflin).

1. Provide an overview of marketing as a subject.
2. Develop an understanding of the marketing concept.
3. Acquire an overview of strategic marketing issues.
4. Identify environmental forces.
5. Apply tools of environmental scanning and analysis.

A text may have five to ten objectives per chapter and the instructor may want to use only one to five objectives from each chapter as a base for developing the activities. Some objectives can be combined into topics for activities. The objectives may also depend on the formal assessment of the course (especially if the course deals with industry training instead of college curriculum). In many cases, the curriculum for a certain course may be set, but choosing which elements of the course to emphasize may be left to the discretion of the instructor.

The instructor can also develop a survey to assess the important skills (and/or content areas) to emphasize. Using a survey like the one described under Motivation to Learn, Strategy 1, the instructor can better define those areas that should be emphasized.

These content blocks are essentially blocks of time that have been reserved for specific topics identified with their objectives. An easy way to develop activities for a course is to set a content block for each chapter, with its associated objectives, and to develop appropriate activities taken from the strategies that follow.

Sample Objectives and Activities for Marketing Course

Content Block	Objectives	Activities
Overview of Strategic Marketing (Chapter 1)	1. Explain the definition of marketing 2. Explain the role of marketing 3. Explain the marketing concept 4. Explain general marketing issues 5. Explain components of marketing strategy	Socratic method Critical Thinking Strategy 3
The Marketing Environment (Chapter 2)	1. Explain importance of environmental scanning 2. Identify major forces in the marketing environment 3. identify ethical issues relative to marketing 4. Explain tools used to compete in the environment	Debate Teamwork Strategy 24 Socratic Method Critical Thinking Strategy 3 Article Reviews Basic Skills Strategy 2

These content blocks are then matched with appropriate strategies from the seven skills strategies discussed in this book to create a totally infused course. In addition, it is also beneficial to develop competency-based objectives for each content block as well.

Identify Concepts to Know Within Content Blocks

As part of outlining the important information to be learned within a content block, the instructor will want to outline all *concepts to know* for the content block. A concept to know can be an actual term or a theoretical concept—any bit of information that is necessary for the student to think about or experience the content block. The instructor should include all important vocabulary associated with the content block and the discipline. Some content blocks may have many concepts, others few. Models (such as the communication model) are often included as concepts as well as graphic explanations of theories or processes.

Sample Competency-Based Objectives for Marketing Course

Content Block	Competency-based Objectives
Overview of Strategic Marketing	1. Use information to develop a marketing plan project Motivation to Learn, Strategy 3, Communication, Strategy 38 2. Use information to complete a case study final exam Critical Thinking, Strategy 36, Communication, Strategy 35
The Marketing Environment	1. Use information to develop a marketing plan project Motivation to Learn, Strategy 3, Communication, Strategy 38 2. Use information to complete a case study final exam Critical Thinking, Strategy 36, Communication, Strategy 35

Identify Strategies to Best Present Content Blocks

This step integrates the content of the course (content blocks) with workplace skills. The instructor develops a system of specific strategies for teaching the content of the course that also provides the student with practice in workplace skills. There are several approaches for selecting the appropriate strategies for course infusion. The strategies can be selected based on several factors such as those that follow:

- **Size of class.** Will the strategy work well with the average size of the class? A long-term project competition (Strategy 4, Teamwork) works best in classes where there can be several groups with three or four members. (**SC** indicates small classes are better; **LC** indicates large classes are better.)
- **Level of difficulty.** Will the strategy be easy to adapt to a particular subject matter. Difficulty ratings are given at the end of each strategy. (**D** indicates the strategy tends to be more difficult than others.)
- **Ease of evaluation.** Will the strategy require a greater effort for evaluation than the instructor wants to provide and/or will the effort for evaluation be magnified if several other strategies are used that require extensive evaluation? An evaluation rating is given at the end of each strategy. (**EE**

indicates fairly easy to evaluate; **DE** indicates difficult to evaluate, and **SE** indicates a subjective evaluation is required.)

- **Balance of strategies.** Will the total work load and the effect of strategies overwhelm the students? For example, using Strategy 22, Critical Thinking (open-ended essay exams) with Strategy 5, Teamwork (group projects) with Strategy 30, Motivation (learning journal) might cover these separate skills areas, but the combination would not be balanced because there would be a heavy concentration of writing assignments. Long-term projects such as the one described in Strategy 2, Teamwork might need to be given on the basis of one per course.

- **Visual/verbal orientation.** Does the strategy appeal to visual or verbal learners? A visual or verbal designation rating is given at the end of each strategy. (**VI** indicates visual orientation and **VE** indicates verbal orientation.)

The following code is given at the end of each strategy as a rating for classroom implementation:

SC—small class
LC—large class
D—difficult
EE—easy to evaluate
DE—difficult to evaluate
SE—subjective evaluation
VI—visual orientation
VE—verbal orientation
A—analytical approach
P—project based approach
G—group approach
I—individual approach

The Workplace Skills System has been developed to upgrade students' skills in *all* of the seven skills areas. Therefore, it is important to use at least one strategy from each of the seven skills categories for every course. However, there are several different approaches to designing the strategy most workable for a specific objective or set of objectives. These approaches are simply structures or paradigms for choosing the most effective strategies for course content and for use with other strategies.

Hierarchical Approach

This approach uses all the skills categories but selects the set of skills areas the instructor deems more appropriate for the subject matter. For example, if this method were used to design a course for Principles of Electronics, the instructor might think critical thinking is especially important and basic skills (with its emphasis on computation) as second most important. He/she would then use the following plan for a course containing 20 content blocks.

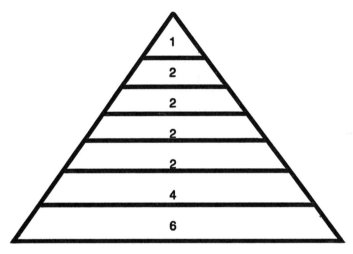

The Hierarchical Approach.

- 6 strategies from Critical Thinking
- 4 strategies from Basic Skills
- 2 strategies from Communication
- 2 strategies from Teamwork
- 2 strategies from Leadership
- 2 strategies from Motivation
- 2 strategies from Career Development

Quota Approach

This approach simply requires the instructor to itemize the content blocks (see section on identifying content blocks), and then divide the number by 7 to decide how to provide an equal number of strategies for each skill area. If there were 28 content blocks for a photography course, the 28 would be divided by 7, and the instructor would choose four strategies from each skills category.

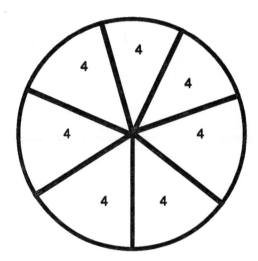

The Quota Approach.

- 4 strategies from Critical Thinking
- 4 strategies from Teamwork
- 4 strategies from Motivation
- 4 strategies from Leadership
- 4 strategies from Career Development
- 4 strategies from Basic Skills
- 4 strategies from Communication

Verbal Approach

If the instructor wishes to use techniques highly appropriate for verbal learners, he or she could pick those strategies designated with a verbal orientation, still choosing at least one strategy from each skills area. This might be the case if the subject area was English, English as a second language, journalism, or creative writing.

Visual Approach

If the instructor wants to use techniques that are highly appropriate for visual learners, he or she could pick those strategies designated with a visual orientation, still choosing at least one strategy from each skills area. This might be the case if the subject area was art, commercial art, desktop publishing, photography, drafting, or computer-aided drafting.

Preselected Strategy Sets Approach

Several preselected strategy sets have been developed using one strategy from each category. Each set has been selected and balanced in terms of difficulty, evaluation ease, ease of application, size criteria, verbal or visual orientation, and other criteria. See the end of this chapter for preselected strategy sets.

Relationship Sets Approach

This approach uses different strategies throughout the system to select at least one strategy from each skills category that will relate to other strategies from other categories. The related strategies are highlighted in each section. The term *related* means that the instructor may be able to combine the related strategies into one assignment. Choosing strategies that are related (or similar) to others will help the course have more overall cohesion and effectiveness.

Analytical Approach

This approach matches strategies (at least one from each category) that require analytical ability. Teachers in engineering, electronics, science, and mathematics might use this approach. The instructor would choose only strategies coded with **A.**

Project-Based Approach

Instructors in occupational and vocational programs might want to choose their strategy set to include maximum project work for students. For this approach, the instructor would choose at least one strategy from each category marked with a **P.** These are the strategies that involve student project work.

Building Block Approach

This method (similar to Hierarchical) uses the strategy area the instructor and/or the students are most interested in reinforcing as a foundation and then builds on that to create the strategy set. For example, an instructor who teaches journalism might choose the following for a course that has 20 content blocks.

Critical/Creative Thinking (3 strategies)		
Motiv. (2)		Lead (2)
Basic Skills (4 strategies)		
Career (2)		Team (2)
Communication (6 strategies)		

The Building Block Approach.

- 6 strategies for Communication
- 4 strategies for Basic Skills
- 3 strategies for Critical Thinking
- 2 strategies for Teamwork
- 2 strategies for Motivation
- 2 strategies for Leadership
- 2 strategies for Career Development

Star Method Approach

For this method, the instructor would choose the two skills areas most important to his/her content area and would maximize use of strategies for those skills. An instructor of marketing, for example, might choose the following as a strategy set for a Principles of Advertising course with 20 content blocks.

- 7 strategies from Critical Thinking
- 7 strategies from Communication
- 2 strategies from Basic Skills
- 1 strategy from Teamwork
- 1 strategy from Motivation

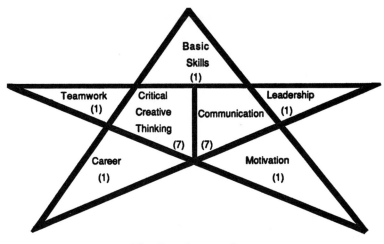

The Star Approach.

- 1 strategy from Leadership
- 1 strategy from Career Development

Individual Approach

An instructor might want to primarily emphasize individual work tasks for a course. If this was the case, he or she would develop a strategy set that would include one strategy from each skills area with a code of **I.**

Group Approach

An instructor might want to primarily emphasize group work throughout his or her course (as in the case of a human relations course). He or she would simply choose at least one strategy from each skills area with a code of **G.**

These methods for choosing a strategy set are guidelines intended to provide an instructor with some kind of paradigm or framework. They are guidelines only and are not intended to be rigidly adhered to. The only rule, if there is a rule to developing an infused course, is to choose at least one strategy from each skills area so that students will be prepared in all seven areas.

Overall course strategies should also be selected that will satisfy the requirements of the competency-based objectives. (See the example concerning a Principles of Marketing course outlined above.)

Evaluation of Strategies

Once an instructor has developed an infused course, he or she will try it in the classroom. Individual strategies may or may not fit with particular subject matter, textbook, or content blocks, and others may work out very well. The instructor may want to develop a system for testing the success of the individual strategies by using the methods based on classroom research that are described in Chapter 3.

Total Course Evaluation

At the end of the course, the instructor will want to take the individual evaluations of the infused course and synthesize them into an evaluation of the success of the total course. Chapter 3 offers several techniques for evaluation of both individual strategies and the course. A key element in evaluating the course is that students, peers, the instructor, and mentors (see Teamwork) get involved in the evaluation process. The instructor can use the feedback gained in this process to make adjustments to the course, such as choosing different strategies, eliminating certain strategies, and revising strategy set balance.

Strategy Revisions or Replacement

If any of the strategies do not seem to be working with the content material of the course, the ineffective strategies should be replaced with strategies that seem to work better. This process of infusion (like any teaching or learning process) is based on constant upgrading and revision. The infused course can be improved by thorough and constant review and revision.

Summary of the Infusion Process

The process for infusing a course with workplace skills involves adjusting the delivery of the instructional content material using an andragogical process that facilitates the student's own learning processes. It involves designing experiences for the student that act as catalysts to his or her own learning processes. The emphasis is on motivating students to learn on their own and creating situations in the classroom that facilitate learning while reinforcing the skills needed in the workplace. The process can be divided into eight steps:

1. Identify content blocks (usually chapters or major topics).
2. Set objectives for content blocks.

3. List concepts to know or factual material to be presented either by the instructor or through some student-centered learning experience.
4. Choose a wide range of strategies (at least one from each category) for delivering content material.
5. Facilitate the content block.
6. Evaluate each strategy using classroom assessment.
7. Evaluate the total course using evaluation instruments.
8. Revise the strategies as necessary.

Using the Workplace Skills System will require the instructor to strategically plan each segment or content block of information for the course so that students learn both the subject matter of the course and learn from the workplace skills experiences developed through the system. This kind of andragogical approach to learning will better prepare each student for the future.

A completed content block follows.

Infused Curriculum

Principles of Marketing

Text: *Marketing,* Pride and Ferrell, 7th Edition, Houghton Mifflin, 1989.
Content Block: Overview of Strategic Marketing (Chapter One)
Length: One and one-half hours
Delivery Strategies: Socratic Discussion
  Reference: *Critical Thinking* by Richard Paul
Strategy Considerations: This may be the first introduction to marketing for many students
Workplace Skills Coverage: Critical thinking; motivation to learn; communication

Content Objectives

1. Explain definition of marketing
2. Explain role of marketing
3. Explain marketing concept
4. Explain general marketing issues
5. Explain components of marketing strategy

Concepts to Know

- Marketing
- Product as good, service, idea
- Marketing concept
- Production orientation
- Sales orientation
- Customer orientation
- Marketing mix (product, price, promotion, or place)
- Marketing strategy
- Forces of marketing environment (legal, regulatory, societal, economic, technological, political)

Activity 1
Socratic discussion method (Critical Thinking, ST2) for questioning students about the role of marketing in business and the economy

Evaluation Tools

- Encompassing Projects (Motivation to Learn, ST3)
- Take Home Essay Exams (Critical Thinking, ST22)
- Multiple Answers Tests (Critical Thinking, ST25)
- Group Tests (Critical Thinking, ST5)

Competency-Based Objectives

1. Use information to develop a Marketing Plan Project (Motivation to Learn, ST3; Communication, ST38)
2. Use information to complete case study final examination (Critical Thinking, ST36; Communication, ST35)

Selected Sets

The Workplace Skills System offers a menu of different strategies for a teacher to use in the development of curricula and/or lesson plans. With such a wide variety of options, it may be difficult to decide which strategies can be used effectively together or which strategies are more achievable under specific conditions. To simplify the process, several different strategy families or "selected sets" of strategies have been developed which teachers can use immediately in lesson plan development. These strategies work well together for the types of disciplines selected. These sets may allow some teachers to start infusing their lesson plans immediately and to read through the other strategies at their leisure for use later.

Set 1

Motivation to Learn, Strategy 2, Learning Contracts
Basic Skills, Strategy 11, Chapter Outlines
Communication, Strategy 14, Free Associative Discussion
Critical Thinking, Strategy 7, Approaches to Thinking
Career Development, Strategy 16, Role Play for a Job Interview
Teamwork, Strategy 8, Team Decisions
Leadership, Strategy 5, Discussion Leaders

This set is especially good for courses that can use cooperative learning and group interaction. The strategies are interrelated and emphasize teamwork, negotiation, leading teams, and team discussion.

Set 2

Motivation to Learn, Strategy 8, Self-Learning Program
Basic Skills, Strategy 11, Chapter Outlines
Communication, Strategy 35, Case Study Analysis
Critical Thinking, Strategy 36, Case Studies
Career Development, Strategy 1, Resume
Teamwork, Strategy 3, Complementary Individual Projects
Leadership, Strategy 19, Report on Theories of Leadership

This set is good for courses in which the instructor wants to maintain individual assignments. All strategies emphasize individual activities that can be interrelated, such as the case study analysis and case study report.

Set 3

Motivation to Learn, Strategy 22, Visual Strategies
Basic Skills, Strategy 39, Computer Software/Computation
Communication, Strategy 39, Flow Charts
Critical Thinking, Strategy 18, Observation Techniques
Career Development, Strategy 27, Video Profile of Profession
Teamwork, Strategy 28, Concrete Model Building
Leadership, Strategy 32, Leadership Poster

This set supports the visual elements and is an excellent set to use for visually oriented courses such as photography, CAD, or commercial art.

Set 4

Motivation to Learn, Strategy 23, Verbal Strategies
Basic Skills, Strategy 13, Vocabulary Exercise
Communication, Strategy 6, Information Relay
Critical Thinking, Strategy 3, Peer Coaching
Career Development, Strategy 35, Self-esteem Tape
Teamwork, Strategy 24, Debate Teams
Leadership, Strategy 20, Panel Discussion on Leadership

These strategies are selected to emphasize the verbal aspects of a course and are appropriate for courses such as music and other courses that emphasize hearing and aural communication.

Set 5

Motivation to Learn, Strategy 3, Encompassing Projects
Basic Skills, Strategy 17, Long Writing Projects
Communication, Strategy 17, Group Presentations
Critical Thinking, Strategy 4, Group Projects
Career Development, Strategy 22, Panel Discussion
Teamwork, Strategy 2, Series of Group Projects
Leadership, Strategy 10, Leader, Long-Term, Large Group Projects

This strategy set is designed for maximum emphasis on group projects and group interaction. Of course, the same long-term project can be used to interweave all seven workplace skills. Using the project to synthesize all facets of skills into one major student product is an excellent simulation of real workplace challenges.

Set 6

Motivation to Learn, Strategy 19, Analysis Strategies
Basic Skills, Strategy 30, Mandatory Computation Assignments
Communication, Strategy 21, Situational Analysis
Critical Thinking, Strategy 10, Teaching for Process

Career Development, Strategy 13, Analysis of Job Ads
Teamwork, Strategy 6, Team Problem Solving
Leadership, Strategy 9, Decision Making

This set emphasizes analytical skills and will work well with courses that require heavy analytical work such as mathematics, electronics, physics, and logic.

Set 7

Motivation to Learn, Strategy 15, Self Expression Exercise
Basic Skills, Strategy 21, In-class Essays
Communication, Strategy 40, Writing Assignments Per Discipline
Critical Thinking, Strategy 22, Open-ended Essay Exams
Career Development, Strategy 26, Interest Essay
Teamwork, Strategy 39, Group Diaries
Leadership, Strategy 26, Leadership Journal

The strategies in this set emphasize writing and use several means to reinforce it, including group diaries and leadership journals which can be integrated with writing assignments from the discipline.

Set 8

Motivation to Learn, Strategy 8, Self-Learning Program
Basic Skills, Strategy 24, Essay Journal
Communication, Strategy 3, Role Play to Understand Communication
    Types
Critical Thinking, Strategy 31, Decision-Making Skills
Career Development, Strategy 10, 5- and 10-year Career Plan
Teamwork, Strategy 3, Complementary Individual Projects
Leadership, Strategy 21, Leadership Self Assessment

These strategies stress self motivation and the qualities students need to be "self-starters," that is, self-motivated individuals who can learn new tasks easily on the job with little supervision.

CHAPTER THREE

EVALUATION TECHNIQUES

The continuous improvement of teaching methods is paramount for instructors. The strategies outlined in this book are excellent ideas, but they are not of value unless they mesh with a particular instructor's style and unless the instructor develops some systematic process for evaluating each strategy. The infusion process (see Chapter 2) requires that some form of evaluation take place after each strategy has been used in the classroom. The purpose of this chapter is to highlight some of the evaluation techniques instructors can use to demonstrate the effectiveness of particular criteria and of the course. These techniques are not scientific. They are not based on statistics or the scientific method. They are based on feedback from students, mentors, other instructors, and the instructor teaching the course.

Student Evaluation

An excellent method for getting feedback from students is to provide a short questionnaire after each strategy to get an indication of the students' reactions immediately after the strategy. A questionnaire such as the following can be developed.

Mentor Evaluation

Mentors can be valuable sources of insight into the appropriateness of certain assignments and activities. The instructor can invite a mentor into the classroom to observe an activity or class assignment and provide feedback with a short questionnaire. The observations and comments of a mentor will

---

Class activity questionnaire

Name of activity_____

Group activity_____ Individual activity _____

Classroom activity_____ Outside activity _____

Did you enjoy the activity?_____ Why or why not? _____

List 3 items you learned from the activity: _____

_____

Can you suggest any changes that might make the assignment work better
or easier?_____

---

help the instructor see areas of his/her approach that may be confusing to someone outside his/her field (especially students). Mentors are able to view the
lesson from the eyes of someone outside the classroom environment.

Class activity questionnaire

Name of activity_____

Group activity_____ Individual activity _____

Classroom activity_____ Outside activity _____

Did you understand the activity?_____ Why or why not? _____

Did the students seem to enjoy the activity?_____

What did you observe the students learning from the activity? _____

_____

Can you suggest any changes that might make the assignment work better
or easier? _____

Pop Quiz

This method can actually test the student's learning. The instructor uses
a strategy such as Open-Ended Essay Exams, Critical Thinking, Strategy
22. Once the assignment has been completed, the instructor provides a
five-question pop quiz from the assignment. This quiz should be unannounced
and given at least two weeks after the completion of the first assignment.
The instructor can track the average percentage of retention based on this

information. This will give the instructor at least some indication of the retention of the information. This strategy does not provide for an evaluation
of the student's ability to use the information.

Using an Encompassing Project

Using a broad competency-based or encompassing project (Motivation,
Strategy 3) as a long-term evaluation of what students have learned in cumulative strategy assignments can be an alternative method or additional
method of evaluation. The instructor covers certain portions of the assignment through strategies and then relates the average performance of segments
of the encompassing projects back to the original strategies. In our marketing
plan example (see Chapter 2), different strategies would be used to cover
material from market research, product, and promotion content blocks. In
the final encompassing project—the market plan—the instructor would
develop a method to average the number of points per student in each of these
three areas and then relate the grading system back to the strategy used. If
an in-class exercise involving a research questionnaire (Motivation, Strategy 25) is used to cover market research, the average points gained by students on the market research portion of the encompassing project can be related back to Strategy 25, and so on. This method may take more time initially,
but the results will outweigh the investment in time.

Subjective Evaluation

The instructor must always trust him/herself in making a judgment about
what works in the classroom and what does not. Gut feelings and intuition
in a subjective setting like the classroom may have more value than any pseu-
doscientific system that attempts to measure subjective attitudes, feelings,
and learning. The instructor may want to make notes to him/herself and keep
an ongoing file of immediate reactions to strategies used. These notes can
be used at a later time to help the instructor in planning new strategies for
the next semester or in identifying strategy types that seem to work well with
the subject matter as well as those that do not seem to work well. Only the
instructor knows if he/she feels comfortable with a certain strategy or if that
strategy seems to fall flat in the classroom. Teaching is more of an art than
a science, and sometimes the right intuitive or aesthetic combination of activities may make a greater impact on the students' abilities to learn than
even the most well-planned, detailed execution of learning variables. The

questionnaire that follows can be used as a permanent record of those "gut feelings." It should be filled out immediately following any activity, before the feelings and emotions about that activity have diminished.

Class activity questionnaire
Name of activity_____
Group activity_____ Individual activity_____
Classroom activity_____ Outside activity _____
Skill category_____ Name and number of strategy _____
Did the students seem to enjoy the activity?_____
What did you observe the students learning from the activity? _____

Focused Listing

K. Patricia Cross and Thomas A. Angelo use a technique in *Classroom Assessment Techniques* [pg. 22] they call *Focused Listing* in which the instructor asks students to list ideas related to the subject matter. The instructor compares the quality and quantity of information with his/her own list of important topics.

Directed Paraphrasing

Cross and Angelo discuss another technique they call *Directed Paraphrasing* in which students are asked to briefly paraphrase a lecture or activity [p. 34]. They suggest separating the responses into four categories: confused, minimal, adequate, and excellent. The instructor should look for patterns in the responses that indicate a problem with the material or the activity.

Focused Dialectical Notes

Another technique used by Cross and Angelo is called *Focused Dialectical Notes* in which students are asked to respond to questions and to assertions they read or hear about the subject [p. 52]. The instructor quantifies the number of key points students react to to see if the important elements of the subject matter are being comprehended.

Course Questionnaires

In addition to the usual student feedback questionnaires provided by the institution (which can provide excellent information), the instructor may want to test the effectiveness of his/her methods by providing students with a special evaluation form to be filled out anonymously and sent to the instructor. The instructor would provide self-addressed, stamped envelopes with the institution address as well as a course evaluation form. Students would be asked to fill out the forms no earlier than six months after the completion of the course. The forms would be a combination of questions about the course methods as well as a few representative questions about the content of the course itself. A course evaluation form for Principles of Marketing could be developed similar to the one that follows.

Using a few general questions that the students fill out from memory will give the instructor an indication of retention over a six-month period of time. Although this approach is not scientifically and statistically reliable, it can give the instructor solid feedback about the parts of the course that seem to be more effective than others and whether his/her approach to teaching (using the workplace strategies) is working.

Evaluation—A Continuing Process

Some strategies may work better in certain circumstances. Students in a small class, for example, tend to be harder to motivate for group projects. What works in one class may not work at all in another class taught by the same instructor. The use of evaluation tools will help the instructor continually evaluate his/her approach using the different strategies so that a stronger, more effective course can be developed over time. Some strategies will be failures and others will succeed. Many of the successes will depend on trial and error, correction, revision, reevaluation, and redevelopment. But, if the instructor continues to evaluate and refine, students will benefit by learning the skills necessary for future success, and the instructor will continue to improve his or her teaching ability. There is no substitute for evaluation. Only evaluation and revision can improve teaching in the classroom.

If the strategies are failing as individual techniques, they can be replaced by more effective ones. If they are failing across the board, the instructor may need to rethink his/her philosophy of teaching. Are tests, for example, a way to set grades and evaluate learning or are they a means to inspire students to study? Is the end product the grade or the learning achieved from

---

Course evaluation
Principles of Marketing

Students: Please fill this form out (from memory) no earlier than six months after our course completion and no later than seven months after our course completion. Please send it in to me using the self-addressed, stamped envelope provided. Do not put your name on it. I appreciate your feedback. Your input will help me provide better, more effective instruction in the future.

Name of course _____

Did you enjoy the course? _____ Why or why not? _____

_____

List three items you learned from the course: _____

_____

_____

What activities stand out in your mind as most enjoyable? _____

_____

What activities were most effective in fostering your learning? _____

_____

Can you suggest any changes that might make the course
work better or easier? _____

_____

Describe the four components of the marketing mix? _____

_____

_____

_____

Describe the process of new product development? _____

_____

_____

Describe the components of the promotion mix? _____

_____

_____

_____

_____

What are the common links in the consumer channel of distribution? _____

_____

---

preparation? Is the role of the instructor to provide students with knowledge or to develop a situation from which students learn? Is the control of the assignments and class time better kept in the hands of the instructor or the students? Have the students learned when they think they have learned or when some outside measure indicates they have? What is the goal of teaching—imparting knowledge or inspiring learning?

The instructor's own philosophy of teaching will have to guide the development and evaluation of strategies for the classroom. Whether the strategies are used for workplace skills reinforcement or simply as classroom instruction strategies, the instructor must always evaluate against his/her philosophy of learning and teaching. The instructor must evaluate the success or failure of the course not on the performance of other instructors, but against his/her own performance and goals for teaching excellence. Evaluation and improvement are the foundations of continued teaching excellence.

CLASSROOM STRATEGIES FOR MOTIVATION TO LEARN

1. Self Assessment of Learner	21. Creative Strategies
2. Learning Contracts	22. Visual Strategies
3. Encompassing Projects	23. Verbal Strategies
4. Student-Developed Syllabi	24. Problem-Solving Strategies
5. Role Models	25. Research Strategies
6. Life-Centered Learning	26. Discovery Strategies
7. Card System for Questions	27. Exam Strategies
8. Self-Learning Program	28. Note Taking
9. Self Evaluation of Learning	29. Observation Strategies
10. Peer Evaluation of Learning	30. Learning Journal
11. Teaching for Transfer	31. Philosophy Statement
12. Mentors for Learners	32. Volunteer Strategies
13. Learning Resources Inventory	33. Experiential Techniques
14. Self-Esteem Enhancement	34. Problem-Oriented Content
15. Self-Expression Exercise	35. Experience Paper
16. Self-Designed Assignment	36. Learning Log
17. Life Goals Map	37. Learning Skills Campaign
18. Learning Program	38. Behavior Modification Contract
19. Analysis Strategies	39. Initiative Breakers
20. Synthesizing Strategies	40. Self-Learning Content Modules

The andragogical model outlined in this book can be used as the foundation for motivating adults to learn because it proposes that motivation to learn develops from internal factors within the person. When the decision to want to learn comes from within, the learning process is made both easier and more successful. The American Society for Training and Development (ASTD) has identified motivation to learn as one of seven skills required for entry-level employees in all occupations. A method of learning such as andragogy, which can be used as a catalyst to create self motivation for learning, can be extremely valuable in developing a competency-based learning program.

The system presented in this book is based on Knowles's model as well as the theories of several other major thinkers in the area of learning and learning motivation. The concepts of Benjamin Bloom are also used as a paradigm for developing easily adaptable learning strategies within the learning to learn framework. The evaluation techniques developed in this book have been influenced by classroom assessment techniques prescribed by Patricia Cross and others. In addition, the skills enhancement techniques have been developed from Marcia Heiman's Learning to Learn Program.

Strategy 1
Self Assessment of Learners

Learners need to have some indication of the skills they possess, the knowledge they possess relative to the skills, and the knowledge required to do an entry-level job in any vocational area. To achieve this, an extensive needs assessment outlining entry-level skills and proficiencies at those skills must be conducted for the educator to define skills requirements and knowledge requirements for any particular course within a program. Once a skill level is defined, with the advice of an advisory board, self-assessment tools can be developed to assess learners prior to the development of their individualized learning program. These assessments can be conducted in a seminar-like setting, with counseling and encouragement provided to the learner from the outset.

For example, if the following skills have been identified as entry-level skills required for marketing employees, assessment tools can be developed to assist the learner in identifying learning experiences to achieve these skills:

- Ability to read at 14-year level
- Ability to write at 14-year level

- Ability to give a presentation to an individual
- Ability to give a presentation to a group
- Ability to analyze a request for proposal
- Ability to research an environmental situation of an industry
- Ability to research current situation analysis of a product
- Ability to write a project description
- Ability to write product specifications
- Ability to plan a one-year promotion campaign
- Ability to input and use a database system
- Ability to read and analyze a trade or business publication article
- Ability to analyze pricing issues and develop pricing strategy
- Ability to write a sales letter
- Ability to write a sales proposal
- Ability to conduct and analyze a survey
- Ability to write copy for a brochure
- Ability to write copy for an ad
- Ability to write a press release
- Ability to plan and organize a special event
- Ability to plan and use a sales lead system
- Ability to use a marketing information system
- Ability to write a report
- Ability to analyze a report
- Ability to write a summary of a firm's history
- Ability to prepare resumes for firm's principals
- Ability to prepare and edit a newsletter with desktop publishing
- Ability to lead a work team in accomplishing a specific task
- Ability to negotiate with other team members
- Ability to calculate sales percentages
- Ability to calculate ongoing budget expenses
- Ability to calculate hit rate information
- Ability to estimate costs/expenses
- Ability to forecast sales figures
- Ability to develop and recommend budgets
- Ability to resolve conflict between work team members
- Ability to generate ideas
- Ability to develop action plans for ideas
- Ability to analyze information and integrate it into action items
- Ability to make successful decisions
- Ability to make appropriate judgments
- Ability to make a sales call

- Ability to make a cold call on the telephone
- Ability to use a computer
- Ability to coordinate production of printing
- Ability to coordinate production of video
- Ability to coordinate production of audio
- Ability to write and deliver speeches

These skills need to be assessed before the learner decides on the appropriate learning experiences for his/her individualized training. The skills could be grouped into the assessment activities that follow.

Communication Activities

One of these activities requires the learner to use a formatted guide to write a sales letter. The sales letter is assessed as to proper usage of words, grammar, and punctuation, logical organization, flow of words, content of information, persuasiveness of wording, and overall professionalism.

The learner is also given a short scenario dealing with a product and is asked to provide an impromptu sales presentation based on that scenario to other learners. Learners are assessed on their abilities to identify important information, organize that information, and present the information in an informative and interesting manner.

Basic Skills Activity

This activity uses the TASP test to identify the current reading level, the mathematical skill level, and the level of language skills of the learner. The learner would be placed in a skills category using the test.

Analysis, Problem Solving, and Creative Thinking Activities

The learner is given a marketing case study and asked to analyze the case study and develop a proposed solution to the problem(s). The written solution is assessed as to completeness of analysis of component parts, inferences based on analysis, development of logical solutions, viability of solutions, creativeness of solutions, and overall problem-solving ability.

The learner is given a marketing case study and asked to analyze the case study, develop a proposed solution to the problem in the form of a plan, and then develop creative materials based on that case study. The products developed are assessed as to their appropriateness, creativity, and logic.

Leadership and Teamwork Activities

As part of a group, the learner is given a marketing situation and asked for a group solution to the problem. This requires the team members to analyze the problem, propose solutions, negotiate solutions, and then choose a solution. The group is observed by industry mentors and the mentors assess members on their abilities to lead, follow, act as a link connecting two opposing sides of an issue, move the team ahead, work with others, and the overall teamwork of each learner.

Learning Styles Inventory

Each learner is given the Learning Styles Inventory by Richard Brostrom. From this, a profile of the learner's learning style is developed. The learner is asked to develop a flowchart of his/her current learning process in order to understand how that learning style affects his/her ability to learn.

From this series of assessments, the learner is given an individual profile that will highlight his/her current skill levels and then provides a comparison of skill levels required by the employers in their industries. The learner negotiates with his/her individual advisor for ratings, taking into account not only the assessments by mentors and educators, but also the self assessment by the individual. This assessment battery provides the bench mark against which the competency-based skill improvement is measured. It provides a broad analysis of the individual learner and the learner's strengths, weaknesses, and interests that allows the educator to develop a comprehensive, individualized training program for that learner.

SC, G, V

Strategy 2
Learning Contracts

A major emphasis of self-directed learning as developed by Knowles [p. 40] is the use of learning contracts in which students assist in the development of their own educational program so that the program is individually tailored to each student. This provides students with control of their own learning and helps them shape its content and provides them with more motivation because they have contributed and negotiated their learning.

According to Knowles, a typical learning contract begins with the assessment of the learner in terms of the skills to be developed. From the assessment, the student and teacher develop a package of objectives to be accomplished by the student that will both satisfy the requirements of the course and will satisfy the needs of the student. These objectives must be measurable and achievable. Once the objectives have been agreed upon, the instructor and student together identify possible resources that the student can use to help him/her achieve those goals. The student and instructor also identify the specific evidence that will be used to demonstrate the goals to the satisfaction of both the instructor and the student. In addition, they must decide what methods to use to evaluate the evidence. Strategies and specific tactics can be identified to achieve the goals. The student then works at his/her own pace in accomplishing the goals and demonstrates the achievement of the goals. The process ends with a self evaluation by the student and an evaluation by the instructor.

A key factor to this process is the role of the instructor. In a sense, the instructor should take on the role of a coach, assisting the student as needed, staying out of the way when not needed. The instructor should be there for the student as a constant resource so the student can constantly verify his/her approach and get feedback on work in progress. This approach is designed to change the student's motivation from externally driven to internally driven.

SC, SE, P, I

Strategy 3
Encompassing Projects

In developing curricula based on the idea of self-directed learning and facilitated learning, the content of the course, such as terminology and concepts, can often be covered using self-paced modules. These modules are designed to cover all key terms and key concepts using questioning, writing, and other active participation techniques for students. A challenge to the instructor, then, is to develop means by which students can integrate these materials once they have learned them through self-paced modules. An exciting and adaptable vehicle for integration of concepts is the use of encompassing projects—projects that "encompass" more than one of the skill groups and, through discussion and interaction, help bring the important ideas into focus for the student through experiential learning.

Individual Projects

Depending on the subject matter, it may be prudent to assign individual encompassing projects to students so that each student experiences the decision making, prioritization, and creativity of the project for him/herself. These projects can range from the all-too-often-used research paper to more challenging and creative assignments such as developing a business plan. A key factor in the development of such a project is to assure that the potential of the student is not limited by the assignment. If the instructor makes no prejudgments as to whether or not "sophomores can accomplish this," and makes the assignment, chances are the sophomores (or whoever) will not only fulfill the assignment but will perform better than expected. Too often instructors make prejudgments as to whether or not a particular assignment is beyond the abilities of their students and deny students the opportunity to be challenged.

Examples of individual projects

Management:	• Write a chapter on your favorite topic for a management handbook.
	• Write the script of a role play situation illustrating the proper way to criticize a subordinate.
	• Develop your own model for decision making.
Marketing:	• Write a marketing plan for a new product.
	• Develop an advertising campaign for a nonprofit organization.

A major component in each of these assignments can be a short research section in which a "situation analysis" is developed that will allow students to assess the current situation and provide a foundation for their subsequent decisions. (See also Teamwork and Critical Thinking.)

Group Projects

Group projects can be used successfully in combination with individual projects when the skills areas to be taught rely heavily on teamwork and interpersonal skills. The group project allows a simulation of the working environment, if the teams are organized to provide maximum responsibility and accountability. Typically in a group setting, some students will open up and take a leadership role while others will sit back and remain silent. This tendency can also translate into one or two of the students doing the bulk of the work on the projects with other students in the group riding on the merits of the hard workers. To eliminate this, each group is assigned a group leader responsible for coordinating the work of the group and the group is given a mandate that each person will have a certain segment of the project to be responsible and accountable for. If both group and individual grades are given for the projects, participation from all students will be heightened. As a last resort, some kind of reporting system can be used so that if a student is not performing the rest of the group can report on the student's lack of participation and have the nonperforming student taken out of the group, much as a company would fire an individual who was not doing the job.

Examples of group projects:

Management: The group is responsible for writing a management handbook that would bring out major topics of the course. Each student writes five to ten pages on a topic and then the students integrate these into a whole product.

Marketing: The group develops an operations plan for the development of a retail store in a mall. This includes marketing plan, sales plan, operations factors such as labor costs, capital, and salaries.

These kinds of projects place the content of the course into a practical and experiential framework that students can integrate into their own experience. The knowledge they gain from actually making these kinds of decisions and verbalizing them will stay with them far beyond the memorization of terms for a multiple choice test.

LC, SE, VE, G, P

Strategy 4
Student-Developed Syllabi

For many adult learners, having a participative role in the development of their educational process can be very motivating. While some programs use the learning contract to provide this participation, some instructors find that an excellent way to achieve the same results is to allow students to "design" their own syllabus for a class, using a combination of non-negotiable items that must be covered and activities that must be accomplished with a menu of negotiable items students may choose to do.

Essentially, the instructor creates a menu of "must" items and "possible" items either to be accomplished or to be covered as content material. Students choose those areas of interest to them as a group and those activities they would enjoy most.

On the first day of class, the instructor arrives at class without a traditional syllabus and explains to the students that they will be allowed to develop their own syllabus for the class within certain guidelines. After the usual first day introductions, the class is given an overview of the course, the skills to be developed, the relevance of the course to them as individual students, and an idea of the kinds of tasks/activities the instructor believes to be beneficial to them. At this point, the instructor reviews the menu item by item and allows students to choose the combination of concepts and activities that would make up the syllabus.

To a certain extent, policy items such as absenteeism and make up for missing tests should remain set from class to class as nonnegotiable items. Criteria for grading and evaluation can often be developed by students as well. With students and the instructor negotiating criteria, students have a clearer vision of the necessity of evaluation, which evaluation methods are best suited to which kinds of activities, and what type of subjective problems may occur when instructors make evaluations.

The rest of the syllabus often evolves as a creative and ambitious set of learning experiences that is more challenging and fulfilling than anything an instructor would have developed for a class. Students have more motivation to complete the items when they know they chose to accomplish them.

Nonnegotiable items	Negotiable items
Mandatory tests	Type of test
One major project	Type of project
Two minor projects	Scopes of projects
Final exam	Type of exam

From the items shown above, a class might opt to do one individual major project and two minor group projects with three take-home tests and a final exam. The class might further negotiate to drop the lowest of the three test grades and might negotiate for tests to count 10% each, the major project to count 30%, the minor projects to count 15%, the final to count 15%, and participation to count 5%.

Providing students with a sense of contributing to the overall planning of the course can be a valuable tool in motivating them to challenge themselves to learn.

LC, SE, VE, G, P

Strategy 5
Role Models

Adults want to be assured that what they are learning has meaning for them in terms of practical application. They want to know how learning some new content material will help them to either grow personally or professionally. It is sometimes difficult for students to visualize how certain types of information will be used in the future. One method for alleviating the fears students have of "wasting time" on certain content materials is to provide role models for them to identify with who will help them see that someone who is considered successful has been able to integrate the information into his/her life.

In the occupational, vocational, and technical areas, this method can be especially useful. Cooperative programs can be developed in conjunction with businesses that provide mentors to individual students or to student groups so students can learn how the information is applied. Mentors can coach a certain class, or certain student groups, or even individual students. These programs bring together mentors who provide information and input into the classroom and students who spend time on the job with the mentors. Other programs use one-on-one interviews between mentors in specialized areas and students who have specific career or personal interests.

To set up a program, advisory boards can be tapped to provide lists of business people interested in volunteering to serve as mentors. A special contract listing the goals of the program, responsibilities of the mentors, and other pertinent information should be negotiated as the mentors are brought into the program. In addition, recognition for outstanding performance from the mentors should be designed to keep the enthusiasm and interest of the mentors at a high level.

A mentoring program does more than just provide a guest speaker to a class. It creates an ongoing partnership of a seasoned and successful professional with a class, group, or individual student to provide the students with the benefit of the mentor's experience.

Strategy 6
Life-Centered Learning

One of the principles of andragogy, according to Malcolm Knowles [p. 54], is the idea that adults need to relate the subject matter of what they are learning to their life experience. For many content areas, the course can actually be redesigned to fit around life experience situations. For example, mathematics can be taken out of the realm of the abstract and theoretical and placed in a context involving the student in life-based problem solving. Instead of simply learning to plug numbers into algebraic formulas, students can be given true-to-life problems from engineering, business, or scientific research that illustrate the need to know the formulas. Using a life-centered format to learn subject matter will make it easier for students to assimilate the information provide them with a more lasting understanding of the material.

A history course, for example, could use life-centered decisions made by key political figures or other notables from history that shows that history relates to individual lives. The thinking process of Lincoln as he prepared the Emancipation Proclamation could be explored as well as the thinking of Frederick Douglass on the impact of that statement to individual blacks. A sociology course could explore the decisions made by legislators to build prisons or low-income housing and then discuss ways these decisions are affected by the subject matter.

This strategy calls for rethinking the entire curriculum of a course. The content is grouped by factors that influence life experience and then the life experiences are taught through role play or documentation of actual case situations. A portfolio of such life experiences must be developed for each course as well as a systematic method for exploring each experience for the maximum learning benefit of the students.

I, VE, A

Strategy 7
Card System for Questioning

A goal of assisting adult learners is to develop in them the ability to formulate and answer their own questions so they can use this study technique in all subject disciplines. The student's perspectives should be viewed as equal to those of the instructor so that he/she can feel a sense of empowerment in his/her learning experiences.

A simple strategy for developing the reasoning abilities of students is to use a concept card approach in questioning students. For subjects with high content, that is, a large amount of vocabulary words or process steps, concept cards can be used much like flash cards. The terms are placed on the blank side, and a description or definition is placed on the lined side of the card.

For subject areas that require higher level thinking skills, students are asked to write down (on index cards) the answers to questions posed in the Socratic style. Then, students are called on to read their answers. This promotes participation by everyone in the class and also provides a structure in which each student learns to actively think through each question posed.

Several Socratic questions can be used in a programmed sequence and students can be required to relate concepts into concept clusters with implications, predictions, and applications. Students can then use these concept clusters to make practical decisions or as the basis of written essays or plans.

VE, A

Strategy 8
Self-Learning Program

Many students can benefit from the development of a specialized program of education tailored specifically to them. In *An Invitation to Lifelong Learning,* Ronald Gross discusses the issues involved in lifelong learning and points out that all adults will be learning continuously throughout their lives. The difference between those who are fulfilled and those who are not may be in the direction this learning takes. Some learning requirements will be "have to's," designated by a college or institution in order to fulfill some requirement for a degree. The learning requirements or opportunities that the student plans for his or her own lifelong learning may have the most lasting value to the student in terms of his or her own educational development [Gross].

To guide a student in developing his/her own lifelong learning program, the instructor can develop a step-by-step flowchart for the student—a kind of self-development road map—that can provide the student with serious questions about his/her direction for learning. This program is developed to chart not only progress in structured educational programs, but also to reflect those areas of learning a student may want to enjoy as part of his or her life away from the classroom.

A typical program might include the following:

1. List the subjects in grades K-12 in which you received A's.
2. List the subjects in grades K-12 in which you received B's.
3. List any extracurricular activities you were involved in during your K-12 years.
4. List the ten best books you have read.
5. List five subject areas you would enjoy learning more about.

VE, I

Strategy 9
Self Evaluation of Learning

An important aspect of promoting self motivation for learning and later for self motivation on the job is involving the learner in negotiating learning evaluation criteria and involving the learner in his/her own evaluation of learning. The ability to judge one's efforts according to one's goals, abilities, and potential is a key element of success as a student and as an employee. This ability aids the student and the worker in gaining self-fulfillment from achievements. It boosts self-esteem as well, because the learner does not have to wait for an outside source to validate his or her learning.

Self evaluation of learning can be embedded in curriculum in numerous ways. In some instances, the self evaluation is built into the self-directed learning contract. This requires the student to make self evaluations of each learning requirement and to negotiate these with the instructor or facilitator. In other cases, the evaluations are made in part by the student, the instructor, and a mentor from a partnership firm in the industry in which the student will be seeking employment [Knowles, p. 57]. In yet other programs, the student is allowed to evaluate the entire learning program, and the instructor makes changes only in rare cases.

Probably the most practical approach involves some combination of student-based and instructor-based evaluation that provides a model for students to practice self evaluation and a framework for students to use in establishing criteria with which to judge their achievements. It should provide some kind of mental tools against which achievement can be compared—a taxonomy of issues to think through before coming to a conclusion as to the value and quality of the learning achievement.

This evaluation can take the form of a self-administered questionnaire with Likert scales that ask the student to superficially make judgments as to achievement in each learning requirement area. It can also take the form of a written in-depth report that analyzes the achievement, compares and contrasts strengths and weaknesses as they affected the outcome of the behavior, identifies new (to the student) thinking that affected the behavior, and makes predictions as to future learning behaviors that may be affected.

If a third party (such as a mentor from a participating business) is used in the evaluation, a survey of observed behaviors might be listed for comment by the observer. In some cases, a panel of observers can be used to judge final student products that are developed to satisfy certain tangible requirements.

VE, DE, SE, I, A

Strategy 10
Peer Evaluation of Learning

In developing in-class projects for a portfolio of learning requirements, peer evaluation can be an exceptionally effective way to enhance student learning of process as well as material. When students who are involved in group projects are evaluated by their peers, they get the objective viewpoints of the other members of their class. These additional viewpoints enhance the instructor's evaluation by providing additional information and insight that can help the learner master the competencies required.

Peer evaluations can be anonymous. Evaluation criteria are fixed on a questionnaire and individual students are asked to respond to questions about the learner. An alternative to this, which also protects the anonymity of the students, is to ask students to simply write essay comments in response to observation of another student's project.

Peer evaluations can also be open. A loose list of criteria are developed and the peer group brainstorm with the learner to discuss possible improvements to performance and to make suggestions.

An important consideration, though, in using peer evaluations is to keep the situation from becoming one in which students feel criticized or ostracized because of the emphasis on the evaluation of their progress. Keeping the evaluation process open and yet guarding against undue harsh criticism can sometimes be a challenge, but it is an important way to keep students motivated to learn.

VE, DE, G

Strategy 11
Teaching for Transfer

Adult learning can be enhanced by curriculum that takes into account the amount of material the student should be able to "transfer" across curricula. Transfer issues are critical because a key element to success as an entry-level employee is to be able to think through problems and transfer the applications learned in school to the job. Teaching students to read using only literary materials, for example, does not prepare these students to read the technical or business-related information they are likely to see once they get on the job. Teaching students to read through the use of everyday business articles, technical articles, popular work-related books, as well as literature, provides students with the opportunity to practice reading the types of materials they will see in the workplace.

Similarly, teaching pure mathematics using formulas without word problems does not adequately prepare students for the kinds of mathematics they are most likely to see in an entry-level job. Rather than emphasizing pure mathematics, the instructor can adopt a more practical approach using word problems dealing with everyday job-related situations. Using budgets, percentages, operations-related statistics, etc., can provide students with the reasoning power necessary to apply the pure math theory to the practical requirements of a job.

As another example, instead of asking students to memorize tedious details, the history instructor can develop a curriculum for high transferability showing the importance of analyzing past situations in order to understand and deal with present situations. Teaching students to see the implications of events and how future events can be shaped by those implications is far more important than teaching facts students can look up in the encyclopedia.

Teaching students the findings of social scientists and how the research of social scientists allows them to make predictions about human behavior and how understanding human behavior can affect the workplace is much more important than requiring students merely to recognize prominent social scientists. To understand the reasons for studying a specific discipline and the methods for applying that study to one's life provides a student with a lifelong ability to use that knowledge for more than just recall.

In addition to the techniques mentioned above, instructors can supplement examples in their own disciplines with examples from other disciplines to directly point out the possibilities for transferring processes and approaches to other areas.

VE, A

Strategy 12
Mentors for Learners

Mentors can be a great asset in providing adult learners with motivation to learn. Developing a formalized system of mentoring in which industry and business representatives work with the instructor to help direct learning and inspire and counsel learners can be a great asset.

To set up a mentoring system, work must begin before the actual semester starts. A list of the most appropriate firms in a particular discipline can be developed using the public affairs office of the school, or the marketing department, or any other community relations department, such as business and industry development. A minimum of six mentors should be developed for each class. If appropriate, a mentor can be identified for each student. Once a list of 30 firms has been identified, qualification criteria for serving as a mentor should be developed and a brief screening interview conducted so that each mentor candidate can be appropriately evaluated to eliminate any potential problems. Calls should be made to the 30 firms to identify possible candidates. Once the candidates have been identified, brief interviews should suffice for choosing interested mentors to be matched with students.

This type of program can allow students to have an ongoing connection with the work world in the discipline they are studying. The mentor can make suggestions about what learning requirements are most important for obtaining employment, keeping employment, and achieving self enhancement on the job. The comments and opinions of the mentor often have more impact on motivating students to learn than the comments of an instructor ever could. Knowing what learning applications will be directly applicable to the job the students are training for can truly show them that time spent learning is well worth the investment.

VE, I, LC

Strategy 13
Learning Resources Inventory

For adult learners in college or in an entry-level position, an important part of the interactive process of learning is to know where to get the resources they need and how to use those resources. Providing learners with a comprehensive guide to learning resources is helpful, not only because it gives them access to materials, but also because it will help them frame their thinking about what items can be considered resources.

A Learning Resource Inventory should be developed for each course curriculum. It could include as a minimum:

* books in the library at your college
* books in the library at surrounding colleges
* films/videos
* tapes
* computer-aided training
* current names of ten individuals in their fields and their companies who are willing to share their experience with students
* job descriptions of typical jobs for two-year graduates in the field
* published lists of research in the discipline
* example of a typical resume and/or portfolio
* learning assistance information from Learning Assistance Center
* current names of tutors
* top 30 firms in your area who hire individuals with these qualifications
* list of commercially available books/tapes

In addition to the inventory, a short guide could be developed to explain how the inventory items can be used. This can be as simple as a paragraph under each heading. A sample handout guide for students follows.

Sample Handout Guide

Books. Books can be used to enhance your learning by providing you with another written explanation of key concepts with differing points of view and additional conceptional information that may help you achieve your learning requirements more easily.

Video/Film. Video and film can be used to enhance your understanding of conceptional material, but more importantly, to give you a sense of the people involved in the field, what they really do, how they feel about their work, and how groups of individuals work together in a team effort.

Audio. Audio tapes can supplement your understanding of contextual material. These can be used most effectively when you can play them while you're working on material tasks or doing low-concentration work.

CBT. Computer-based training can help you in learning processes by providing an interactive, participatory component to create opportunities to think through problems. As you advance from one step to another in a certain process, the computer will provide you with ever more challenging choices. You must think through each choice before proceeding on to the next. CBT training is especially helpful in mechanical training, training for planning, and problem-solving training.

Successful Practitioners. The individuals listed in this section can assist you by providing you with insight into the actual entry-level job you might obtain. These men and women have already volunteered to speak to students whether on the phone or in person concerning jobs and careers in their respective fields. They can help you decide what type of job is best for you.

Job Descriptions. These job descriptions have been provided from ads and other sources to give you an idea of what you would be doing in an entry-level job. From these, you can gain important information about which types of content material will be most relevant to your desired entry-level job. Of course, these are sample descriptions only and not every job with the same or similar title will have the same requirements.

Secondary Published Research. Often secondary published research can give you information about current trends and developments in the industry or discipline. This section lists new products, new software, and new approaches in your field that you should be aware of.

Resume/Portfolio. This example of a resume for an entry-level job is included to help you understand typical skills needed for an entry-level job. From it, you can see how to develop your own resume to cover the important areas necessary to obtain employment.

A portfolio may be necessary when seeking some professional positions. A portfolio can include such items as letters of reference, articles, projects completed, artwork, and other items of original nature that might be of value as an indicator of your creativity, planning ability, and communication ability.

Learning Assistance Center. The LAC is a center that can assist you if you are having difficulty mastering a certain discipline. The LAC provides self-paced tapes, CBT programs, and some tutoring.

Tutors. If you want a tutor on a one-to-one basis, these tutors can be made available. It's best to work with a tutor through the use of questions that can be answered by the tutor. Tutors generally do not actually reteach the subject; they clear up problems in communication by providing a different explanation than the instructors.

Firms. The top 30 firms that provide employment to graduates of two-year programs in a discipline are listed here. They will assist you by providing contact persons to call for advice and in providing addresses for resume mailings.

Strategy 14
Self-Esteem Enhancement

For adult students to achieve success, many need to develop a higher level of self-esteem. Tools that help students evaluate their interests, motivations, strengths, and weaknesses can be beneficial for the instructor who develops a student-centered curriculum. Self-evaluation tools such as self-administered questionnaires can be provided to the student on the first day of class as a kind of self-analysis tool. Each student is given a "self portrait" portfolio to keep his/her results in. The results of these self-administered questionnaires help students in negotiations for course requirements.

A key to the successful use of self-esteem tools is to choose tools that are very positive so the tools do not demotivate students. The tools should help students easily and quickly identify their self-perceived strengths and weaknesses.

Program tapes, such as positive thinking tapes, can enhance student self-esteem if the tapes are used appropriately. Using ideas from these commercially available programs throughout a structured class program can enhance motivation and give students morale boosters throughout the course. (Sales organizations often use such programs to keep their sales people motivated.)

I, SE, VE

Strategy 15
Self-Expression Exercise

Adult learners, having been educated in a traditional pedagogical system, may not have built up their confidence and self-esteem. For many, their attempts to express their ideas, careers, opinions, and experience have been met with criticism usually at the hands of a well-meaning teacher more concerned with grammar and punctuation than with enhancing a student's self-expression. For some adults, the act of putting pen to paper conjures up negative emotions of rejection, incompetence, and anguish. Many students when asked to write a plan or an ad are very concerned about how the mechanics will be graded but are not overly concerned about the quantity and quality of the original thinking or the content.

For programs truly concerned with improving the student's ability to perform on the job, self-expression of ideas is of primary importance.

Of course, correct use of language is important as well. (This issue is dealt with in Chapter 5 on basic skills strategies). Self-expression can contribute greatly to an individual learner's motivation to learn.

In the beginning of a particular course, a self-expression exercise can establish an atmosphere that is conducive to self-expression. Learners are asked to write an extemporaneous paper (without concern for grammar or punctuation) to describe their viewpoints on the following questions:

1. Was learning a high priority with you and your family while you were growing up?
2. What did your parents do to encourage your learning?
3. To discourage your learning?
4. How important do you feel learning is to you now?
5. What are your three major goals in life that can be reached via your learning?
6. What do you see as the one primary factor that gives you motivation to learn?

After the students write the answers to these questions, they share them with the class. The results are analyzed to see which students have had similar life experiences that have contributed to or detracted from their ability to learn. Important similarities between how and what people see as motivational factors can be analyzed.

This exercise will "break the ice" and demonstrate to adult learners that their input, their ideas, and their views are as important to what they are learning as are the text and the instructor. The ability to formulate and express ideas and opinions is a crucial skill to develop for entry-level employees.

VE, I, SE

Strategy 16
Self-Designed Assignment

Many programs are flexible enough to allow for one assignment that is totally designed by the students (and approved by the instructor).

To use this approach, the instructor places a value on the project comparable to that of other instructor-designed projects. The learner is then asked to design a project suitable to the content of the course and to provide the criteria with which the project should be evaluated. When given such an opportunity, many students design excellent projects—often more challenging than those the instructor would have designed. The project requirements, criteria, and deadline must be approved by the instructor before the project is undertaken. When the project is completed, a self evaluation according to the criteria is also turned in.

The instructor evaluates the project against the student-designed criteria and also comments on the appropriateness of the project to the material.

One student-designed project per course allows students some "ownership" of their learning. They can express their creativity and will be much more enthusiastic about the course and the learning requirements.

VE, I, SE, DE, D

Strategy 17
Life Goals Map

Adult students often must be encouraged to plan their learning as it coincides with their life goals. One strategy for assisting adult learners in this endeavor is to assign to them the task of developing a life goals map to chart their course in life.

A life goals map provides not only the goals an individual may set but also a direction for achieving those goals.

Step 1.   List the life goals a person may have in each of these categories:

• Personal
• Spiritual
• Educational
• Vocational
• Recreational

Step 2.   Once these have been listed, focus them on a chart showing the years in which these goals are to be achieved.

An example list follows.

Personal
• Be a good mother
• Read parenting books
• Go to parenting classes

Educational
• Finish AA
• Sign up for spring
• Finish with A average
• Finish BA

Recreational
• Learn to ski
• Learn to paint

Occupational
• Learn desktop publishing
• Make $60,000/year

Spiritual
• Join a church

Life goals map

	Year 1	Year 2	Year 3	Year 4
Personal				
Educational	X	X		X
Recreational	X			
Occupational	X			X
Spiritual	X			

This graphic representation of a person's life goals is an excellent motivational tool for learners to map out their desired achievements and provides a point of focus for them as they set about to reach their learning objectives in the content class.

VI, I, EE, SE

Strategy 18
Learning Program

Once a life goals map has been created, students can be assigned the development of a comprehensive learning program to support the life goals. This is simply an outline of tasks associated with each life goal. This learning program relates the achievement of lifelong learning as well as the achievement of the learning goals for the content course.

An example of a program follows.

Occupational
  Desktop publishing
    Learning goals
      Learn about software
      Complete class in desktop publishing
      Complete class in graphics
      Complete class in presentations
  Promotion to Account Executive
    Learning goals
      Complete time management course
      Complete decision-making seminar
      Complete certification as a certified advertising planner
      Complete marketing certificate
      Complete human relations course

VI, VE, I, EE, SE

Strategy 19
Analysis Strategies

Many adult students have not been exposed to the various techniques for analyzing reading material, solving mathematical or scientific problems, working with creative problems, or discussing case studies. Instructors can provide a handout that explains various approaches to analyze material common to the discipline. Basic analytical techniques such as the following can be included:

- Breaking item into parts
- Synthesizing parts together
- Listing facts, assumptions, and desired information
- Identifying alternative causes
- Identifying alternative options
- Weighing advantages and disadvantages
- Judging the reliability of sources
- Judging the credibility of sources
- Defining language precisely
- Interpreting objective data
- Interpreting subjective data
- Classifying data
- Creating ideas
- Identifying main ideas
- Identifying supporting data
- Identifying process steps
- Making analogies
- Relating concepts
- Making inferences from data
- Developing arguments
- Making judgments
- Using inductive reasoning
- Using deductive reasoning
- Making generalizations based on data
- Identifying causes

Such a handout can provide students with direction and with options for analysis that they may not have known were possible. The instructor might also recommend a general text on critical thinking.

LC, A, DE

Strategy 20
Synthesizing Strategies

Adult students use synthesizing skills much more frequently than younger learners do. Job skills often require extensive use of synthesizing skills, so it is of value to provide students with a handout detailing techniques. Techniques such as the following can be included:

Synthesize by list
• List each separate item you know about the problem
• List ideas from your experience relevant to the problem
• Relate the two lists
Synthesize by research
• Use the learning research center to find out about cases relevant to your problem
• Relate the solutions of these cases to your situation
Synthesize by category
• Separate possibilities by category
• Relate categories
Synthesize by process
• Identify steps involved in the process
• Identify the order of steps
• Identify the process

A, DE

Strategy 21
Creative Strategies

The ability to solve problems creatively will be discussed in detail in Chapter 7, Critical Thinking. For most disciplines, however, a handout that lists and explains various critical thinking techniques can be developed and given to students.

Creative Techniques

Delphi Method. Each member of a focus group is independently asked to solve a problem. Once proposed solutions are developed each member of the group writes his/her solutions and then these are circulated. Members vote on solutions and discuss solutions until one primary solution is agreed on.

Brainstorming. Ideas are developed randomly, each idea being treated as important. All possible ideas are generated (from bizarre to conservative). Once all the ideas have been developed, the top ideas are selected and possible solutions analyzed.

Association. Different objects, articles, or other factors are used to provide the creator with springboards for solutions to problems. Sometimes paper is cut into shapes that can be easily manipulated to help the group or student to develop new associations.

Modeling. Physical objects such as children's building toys are used to help students see the physical relations between concepts, the abstract relationships between ideas, or the relationships between process steps.

Nominal Group. A facilitator leads the discussion, giving everyone the chance to make suggestions as the group leader works through a previously developed agenda.

VI, VE, G, DE, A, LC

Strategy 22
Visual Strategies

In many vocational programs, the skills that need to be learned require learners to practice visual concentration. In a society that encourages learners to tune out much of what is presented visually, many students may need extra assistance in learning to truly observe mechanical sketches, diagrams, or whatever. A handout of approaches for using visual learning techniques may help. In *The Zen of Seeing,* Frederich Franck says "a non-creative environment is one that constantly bombards us . . . overloads our switchboard with noise, with agitation and visual stimuli. Once we can detach ourselves from all these distractions, find a way of inscape, of 'centering,' the same environment becomes creative again" [p. xii]. He goes on to say that most of us see without seeing. We do not truly notice the details of the subject before us unless some outward influence forces us to look more closely.

Visual Techniques

1. Practice "seeing" by drawing. Choose an object in the classroom and draw a rough sketch of it. Notice how many features it has that you did not notice before.
2. Practice "seeing" by using videos related to the subject. Watch each 15 minutes of the video, pause the tape, and then list the observations you have made. Continue to repeat this. As you repeat, you'll be surprised at how much more you observe when concentrating.
3. Practice "seeing" using a book or magazine related to the discipline. Look through the book, read what interests you, and then put the book down. List all the items that you remember observing.
4. Practice "seeing" by observing tasks on behavior or explanations without taking notes. After the event has been completed, list your impressions and observations.

VI, SE

Strategy 23
Verbal Strategies

Many students describe themselves as verbal (vs. visual) learners. This means that they learn best when they hear someone explain or they talk solutions "out loud" to themselves. Students may be tested to discover if they are verbal or visual learners. There are numerous techniques that can be used to develop verbal concentration abilities. Often students can improve their concentration by improving these abilities.

Verbal Techniques

1. When students have taken notes on a subject, record those notes on a tape recorder and then play them back.

2. Have students practice verbal concentration using commercially available audio tapes related to your subject area. Have them close their eyes, listen for 15 minutes, and then list what they remember. Repeat the process to the end of the tape. Students will begin to concentrate more skillfully as they practice.

3. Practice concentrating on tapes from old radio programs. Students will have to listen intently to follow the story line and this will help them develop listening skills.

VE, DE

Strategy 24
Problem-Solving Strategies

Students should be provided with guides for solving problems before they are assigned lengthy problems, case study problems, or large quantities of word problems, math problems, or science problems.

Students can be provided with handouts that give detailed information about problem-solving approaches related to the discipline they are trying to master. Many students have not yet been exposed to different methods of solving problems. They do not know the structure or methods to use to solve problems. Providing them with strategies for problem solving with step-by-step instructions can help them recognize how to use these important tools. (See Chapter 7 on Critical Thinking).

A handout can be devised that cites examples of how and when to use different approaches.

Developing Case Study Solutions

Step 1. Decide what decisions the writers of the case study stress.

Step 2. Decide what elements are important in making those decisions.

Step 3. List facts you have.

Step 4. List facts that are missing.

Step 5. List possible decisions as well as pros and cons.

Step 6. Choose a solution and decide how to make it work.

Developing a Solution to a Client Problem (Marketing)

Step 1. Research for facts. Obtain all possible written material, interview clients, develop a questionnaire.

Step 2. Set marketing objectives.

Step 3. Set communication objectives.

Step 4. Set budget.

Step 5. Design media plan or program to meet client needs while fitting budget.

Step 6. Portray the solution in a professional manner so the client can visualize your solution.

Step 7. Obtain client approval.

Step 8. Execute campaign.

Step 9. Evaluate results.

Developing a Solution to Word Problems

Step 1. Decide what facts you are given, what is important, and what is irrelevant.

Step 2. Decide what you are looking for.

Step 3. Decide what facts you have that can be used to get to what you are looking for.

Step 4. Work the problem using the different components to supply what is requested.

Step 5. Evaluate the problem to assess whether the answer you have seems logical.

A, VE, DE

Strategy 25
Research Strategies

Many competency-based and student-centered learning programs rely on students to do extensive research on their own time in order to supplement material in their text on certain topics, to provide raw information for the development of learning requirements, or to provide for additional techniques for mastering their skills. Many students have some experience with research in high school or junior high school, but the quality and extent of that experience may be minimal.

To overcome this, the instructor can provide each class with the usual walking tour of the library with a handout providing strategies for researching different topics in the college library, public library, and from commercially available databases.

A Student's Guide to Research

Sources:

• dictionaries	• anthologies
• encyclopedias	• histories
• thesauruses	• concordances
• biographical dictionaries	• book reviews
• indexes	• texts
• readers' guides	• theses
• bibliographies	

Research Process:

1. Look in microfiche or card catalog.
2. Look for books and articles on your topic.
3. Conduct online search.
4. Have a direction to your search so you won't be overwhelmed by too much material.
5. Follow a schedule for your research so you won't get behind.
6. Define unknown terms.
7. Locate quotations and statistics where they apply.
8. Use outside sources to support ideas.

9. Develop an outline.

10. Use your good time management to review and edit your work while you have plenty of time to make revisions.

I, VE, A

Strategy 26
Discovery Strategies

Adults will be motivated to learn and will retain information longer if they are allowed to "discover" answers for themselves rather than being given advice from the instructor. The idea is to develop curricula that position content material in the same vein as the outcome of an experiment—that allow students to discover the facts.

An excellent technique that can be used to enhance discovering for adult learners is to design curricula so that each content area in a particular text is supplemented by several other sources—articles from writers having controversial views, other texts that highlight different but relevant material, biographical accounts, and autobiographical memoirs that dispute or reinforce the material.

For example, adults want to know what the reality of history is, not just the noble, patriotic accounts of the texts. Spicing up well-known facts with autobiographical accounts can enliven and invigorate the subject. Similarly, adding material from exceptional and popular business leaders can complement the content of an introduction to business or accounting text. Almost every discipline can be brought to life if personal accounts are woven through the content material.

An auto mechanic text can be supplemented with articles from *Auto World* and other magazines covering successful mechanics and their methods. Computer science text can be supplemented with articles about Grace Hopper and others who pioneered the development of computers. This type of approach allows students to discover hidden perceptions that might go without detection if only a straight text were used. This approach is much stronger than the instructor lecturing to students about "how it really is in business, or how it really was when computers were developed."

I, A

Strategy 27
Exam Strategies

Overcoming test anxiety can be painful for adult students, many of whom may have dropped out of high school or college previously because of the stress involved in taking exams. Developing curricula that eliminate the "artificial stress" of exams can be very beneficial to students.

Few employers will require an employee to memorize terminology or recite it without referencing a text or a manual. An instructor of marketing, for example, can provide a much more realistic testing situation by giving take-home tests with specific deadlines that require no rote memory, but do require the student to read through the terminology, write the definitions, write about the concepts, and finally explain them.

However, some disciplines may have just the opposite requirements. For an instructor who teaches Emergency Medical Technicians (EMTs), tests may require extensive memory and essay answers because EMTs must know the material from memory as there won't be time to consult sources at the sight of an emergency.

Instructors can also reduce the stress of exam taking by fully explaining requirements prior to issuing the exam. They can explain how to study for a particular type of exam as well as what to study. Handouts explaining the key factors involved in studying for the kinds of exams to be given can also be helpful in showing students that they can control their own test anxiety.

Tips for Taking Exams

1. Briefly look over the exam, but don't get anxious if it appears that there's something you can't answer.
2. Quickly judge how much time you have relative to the number of questions you need to answer. Decide how much time you can allot per question.
3. Begin working with the first problem. Work each problem and answer each question carefully. Double check all your answers.
4. If you come to a problem or question that you are unsure of or that you think you can't answer, skip it. Mark it with a "?" and go on to the next question. The idea is to answer everything you can answer completely and carefully and then spend any excess time trying to figure out those problems that are more difficult.

5. If there are problems you can't answer, weigh the consequences of making an educated guess. If the instructor does not take off for guessing, it's always better to guess than to leave blanks.

6. If the test is an open-book test always put as much or more effort into studying than if it was a memory test. Open-book tests are constructed to be more difficult than memory tests.

7. After the test, reflect on your performance. What could have been done to improve it?

A, LC

Strategy 28
Note Taking

Organizing notes and learning to write down important concepts is essential for an adult student. There are many methods for taking notes, such as taking notes on one side of the page, leaving a portion blank for reflection later; taking notes in pencil and making comments in ink; writing notes in outline form; and writing notes in phrases. Students should be encouraged to adopt a system that is convenient for them and use it consistently.

Students write down the concepts that seem to be important. Instructors provide indications of importance by repeating terms, by stressing major headings or topics within a lecture, and by identifying information as a series, process, or program of information.

I, VE

Strategy 29
Observation Strategies

A few years ago, Sperry Corporation developed an institutional advertising campaign based on the assumption that humans often hear but do not listen. This assumption can be especially true of students who learn the lecture or see the film but are so busy hearing or viewing they do not listen and observe. It can be useful to provide students with specific observation strategies to use in mastering course material, viewing a film, or making observations in an experiment.

Each learning requirement should be accompanied by self observation and general observation. Strategies that give students direction in what to look for or listen for in a presentation are especially helpful.

Student Guide to Observation Techniques

When viewing a film or presentation, students should look for:

- New ideas they haven't encountered.
- Important concepts that are repeated.
- How ideas relate to other ideas.
- Hidden agenda items that are revealed through nonverbal communication.
- Controversial ideas.
- Opinions of speakers.

VI, I, SE

Strategy 30
Learning Journal

For adult learners, internalizing the material is a foundation of success. To aid this process of internalizing, instructors can require a daily learning journal. A learning journal is simply a daily account of the successful and unsuccessful learning experiences of the learner.

Any type of commercially available journal can be used. Students are asked to write down a daily entry—a summary of their activities that also explains which techniques seem to have helped them learn and which have not. The entries need not be detailed or lengthy. The daily act of thinking about learning—of writing those thoughts out on paper and organizing them—will assure that students become cognizant of how they are learning.

There are some variations of the learning journal. Instructors may request students to write synopsis of journals, articles, and texts to record quotes from other readings that interest them.

Creative writing teachers, journalism teachers, or copywriting instructors may require original essays to be written daily as part of the journal.

VE, I, SE, A, P

Strategy 31
Philosophy Statement

An instructor can use a philosophy statement at the beginning of a specific course to outline the parameters of the course and the instructor's expectations as well as what students can expect from the instructor. While many instructors use such statements in their syllabi, they will find that giving each student a written statement can be effective.

The philosophy statement brings out important philosophical foundations on which the curriculum has been developed, such as:

- students will be expected to direct their learning.
- teacher will act as a facilitator.
- students will be expected to ask and answer questions.
- students will be expected to fulfill all requirements within negotiated time frames.
- instructor will be used as a resource.
- problems will be discussed through the duration of the course.

An exceptionally well-written philosophy statement can be an excellent prop if brought into the classroom either as a poster or a framed certificate. The fact that an instructor would go to the trouble to have a philosophy statement graphically produced can illustrate how committed the instructor is to the course.

I, VE, SE

Strategy 32
Volunteer Strategies

For many adults, a college education means the opportunity to change careers, gain a promotion, or improve on-the-job skills.

Oftentimes, older students have less flexibility though in the employment market. Companies won't hire them as entry-level employees because they are older and require a higher salary, yet they don't have enough experience to be hired in at a level that is commensurate with their salary requirements.

Many adult learners can gain much needed experience and learning by volunteering to work a specific number of hours a week for a nonprofit organization doing the kind of work they want to do. Adults who have full-time jobs cannot usually work within the typical internship structure that gives a grade for 20 hours per week of work. But many of them can afford to donate two to six hours a week doing marketing planning for the YMCA, accounting for the boy's club, or managing a fund raiser for the cancer society. These nonprofit groups need the volunteer support and provide the learner with excellent responsibility from the outset (unlike many corporations that bring on interns only to give them little if any responsibility). The student can document the volunteer experience as part of the work experience and ask that letters of achievement and recognition be written to help demonstrate that he/she has gained in-depth knowledge of how to do the work he or she is learning.

I, SE, P

Strategy 33
Experiential Techniques

The classroom can be an exciting place for experimentation, both for students and for the instructor. An instructor who uses the classroom as a "living laboratory" to provide students with learning experiences similar to those most often encountered on an actual job often keeps his/her students excited about learning, eager to achieve results, and impatient to master more of the material.

To develop an experiential curriculum, the instructor can interview individuals holding entry-level jobs in the discipline and gain insight into the kinds of experiences most relevant to the student. Then the instructor designs the curriculum around items that replicate those experiences. For a commercial art instructor, for example, experiences might include translating the needs of a client into a finished piece of art that is aesthetically pleasing and yet meets the economic needs of the client. For an auto mechanic, an experience might be diagnosing a car problem. For a computer science student, an experience might be troubleshooting a system for possible bugs or programming a specific piece of software.

Once a pattern of important experiences has been identified, content material can be clustered around the experiences to provide content and practical appeal for the experiential techniques used.

A, I, G, DE, SE

Strategy 34
Problem-Oriented Content

A technique similar to Strategy 33, problem-oriented content involves identifying the common problems associated with an entry-level job in a discipline and then clustering the content around the identified problems. This often means that content is reorganized and students may be reading a chapter from the latter part of the text in conjunction with a chapter from the early part of the text in order to solve the problem. The course must be redesigned in order to provide students with information as needed.

This approach is much more relevant to job requirements though, because students learn immediately and can directly apply the content information to the problem. A competency-based program that relies on problem-oriented content provides the student with experience, not just terminology.

I, A, DE, VE

Strategy 35
Experience Paper

A technique that can bring out the transferability of a specific content area is the experience paper. The student is required to complete a certain segment of learning requirements such as interviewing someone in the discipline or developing a comprehensive program such as a marketing plan, training plan, or identity package for a client and the executives of that plan. Then, the student is required to reflect on what he or she learned by writing an experience paper. The experience paper is simply a forum for reflection for the student that forces him or her to scrutinize his/her learning techniques. At the end of the course, each student can trace important progress through a set of experience papers.

I, A, SE, DE

Strategy 36
Learning Log

Students may often be unaware that they are learning. They may not see the benefits of what they are learning nor be able to judge how what they are learning will help them meet their goals.

A learning log is a logbook in which students log the major topics or ideas they have learned during each day. It is important, if this is assigned, to have students log not only what they have learned in one particular class but to log what they have learned in other classes or in general. The actual log can be formatted to suit the student's needs, but it should include **major concepts learned, date, relation of concept to student, possible uses of information.** Once a student begins to log what he/she learned, he or she may become more aware of the learning process. The entries should be kept short and precise, but also complete.

The learning log differs from a journal in that the log just itemizes the concepts and does not cover the details, emotions, or other aspects of the learning experience.

I, VE, SE, A, PB

Strategy 37
Learning Skills Improvement Campaign

This strategy requires the student to assess his/her learning skills and to develop a "self-improvement campaign" for developing better learning habits. This self-evaluation tool should not be used for discussion. The student rates him/herself based on the following:

I, A, SE

How I Feel About My Study Habits

	Never	Almost Never	Don't Know	Some- times	Always
I usually do assignments					
I do my work on time					
I like to read ahead					
I usually do my research in advance					
I keep up with my courses each day					
I take good notes					
I think of pertinent questions					
I produce quality work					
I like to study					
I spend a good deal of time studying					
I do not make excuses					

Strategy 38
Behavior Modification Contract

Behavior modification is a tool psychologists use to help people learn to change their behaviors. It can be used to great advantage in helping adults learn how to learn. The different tasks involved in learning, such as studying for an exam, outlining a research paper, reading text, and completing homework problems, can be achieved more readily if the student can motivate him/herself by offering some kind of reward for achievement. For example, Russon and Wallace in *Personality Development for Work* offer the following list of possible rewards for completing assignments:

• listening to music	• outdoor activity
• solving problems	• entertainment
• food	• dancing
• beverages	• painting
• sports	• sewing
• watching sports	• shopping
• reading	

In the beginning of a course, students develop a list of rewards and penalties (the absence of those rewards) that could be self-administered through-

---

BEHAVIOR CONTRACT

I, _____, DO HEREBY ENTER INTO THE FOLLOWING AGREEMENT WITH MYSELF. I WILL PERFORM THE BEHAVIOR STATED BELOW AND I WILL RECEIVE THE REWARDS LISTED BELOW.

BEHAVIOR _____

_____

REWARDS _____

_____

IF I FAIL TO LIVE UP TO THIS CONTRACT, THESE PENALTIES WILL TAKE EFFECT.

PENALTIES _____

_____

_____

SIGNATURE

out the course. For each assignment to be completed, there would be a reward. Students write a contract for themselves such as the following.

The student writes a contract for each assignment so he/she can reward him/herself at the completion of the learning activities (Adapted from Russon and Wallace).

I, SE, VE, A

Strategy 39
Initiative Breakers

A key part of motivation is understanding how and when to take initiative for learning. For this strategy, students are asked to develop an initiative breaker. Like an icebreaker, an initiative breaker is the opening project and is designed to create a sense of self motivation and initiative for the student. During the course, the instructor leaves one assignment blank—the initiative breaker.

Students are to seek out and develop on their own some kind of project that identifies some niche in the course that could be supplemented by additional work in a specific area. The actual project is left up to the student, but it should be developed as a response to some area of knowledge lacking in the regular course or as a way to assist the student in mastering some part of the material the student has difficulty with. The initiative breaker forces students to: 1) identify a niche or a need for further study or work; 2) think through what kind of project will fill that need; 3) develop a very special, unique project; 4) take initiative for their own learning. Hopefully, once students have learned how to take initiative in this case, they will continue the practice throughout their learning.

Each project will have to be evaluated on the basis of its own criteria because each project will be unique. The instructor can set aside a certain percentage of the course grade for the initiative breaker.

I, DE, SE, P

Strategy 40
Self-Learning Content Modules

Learners need to be able to integrate the material to be learned with their own experience—to make the act of learning one in which the learner is active and not passive. Courses or training sessions that revolve around the lecture format often place students in a passive learning mode. Lecture format is thought to be a necessity in many institutions if the subject matter or content involves a high concentration of terminology or basic or foundation material. An alternative approach to the teaching of content for foundation courses is to develop self-paced content modules that organize the material in such a way to make it more relevant to the student's experience and to the skills areas important to the student in later course work.

Such modules can be written as a series of questions prompting the student to read the textual material, analyze the readings, define the terms, relate the information to his/her own experience and then internalize the information by writing the outcomes in his/her own words.

Modules can also be developed using the case study approach where the student reads, analyzes the content information, and uses that information to solve a series of skill-related cases in a self-paced case study portfolio.

It is important to put the emphasis for covering, reviewing, and learning content material on activities the student can do him/herself, and leave classroom time for the instructor to integrate those concepts in meaningful group activities and other instructional devices.

In developing courseware for such modules, one approach is to carefully peruse all materials to be taught, skills to be developed, and other related resources, and to list each important concept that students must learn. Concepts can then be grouped into concept families that provide the basic structure for the modules. This approach often will yield an organization for the course that is much more relevant to the actual skills the students need to develop. Using this approach, however, involves some risk because the new organization rarely matches the organization presented by the textbook, and students and instructors must realize that courses do not necessarily have to follow the textbook.

SC, SE, VE, P, I

CHAPTER FIVE

CLASSROOM STRATEGIES FOR BASIC SKILLS

1. Book Reviews
2. Article Reviews
3. Remedial Reading
4. Bibliography
5. Newspaper Assignments
6. Book List
7. Book Review Adler
8. Abstracts
9. CAI in Reading
10. Chapter Reviews
11. Chapter Outlines
12. Dictionary Use
13. Vocabulary Exercises
14. Reading Assessment
15. Remedial Writing
16. Writing Assignments
17. Long-Term Writing Projects
18. CAI in Writing
19. Tutor Program for Writing
20. Grading Grammar
21. In-class Essays
22. Stylebook
23. Grading Template
24. Essay Journal
25. Mandatory Writing Assignments
26. Letter to the Instructor
27. Course Summary of Learning
28. Joint Writing Assignments
29. CAI in Computation
30. Mandatory Computation Assignments
31. Computation Questions
32. Computation Using Newspaper Articles
33. Grade for Computation
34. Grade Process
35. Search for Numbers
36. Decision Models Based on Computation
37. Statistical Summary
38. Computation Handbook
39. Computer Software/Computation
40. Process Cards

This chapter deals with instructing and reinforcing basic skills for students in any curriculum area. While it is true that students who lack in basic skills should have been taught those skills prior to entering higher level classes, the fact remains that many students are lacking in one of the three major areas (reading, writing, and computation). The instructor can use the strategies listed in this chapter to help reinforce the basic skills abilities of his/her students, allowing them more practice with basic skills and providing them with choices to reinforce their mastery of the content material and improve their basic skills.

The strategies in the chapter are divided into three sections:

Section one: Strategy 1 through Strategy 14—Reading

Section two: Strategy 14 through Strategy 28—Writing

Section three: Strategy 29 through Strategy 40—Computation

Most of the ideas on basic skills are designed for use as extra credit opportunities or adjunct assignments for students the instructor identifies as needing remediation in reading, writing, and/or computation. For example, students who do not need remediation probably would not need to use computer-aided instruction on reading or writing. Similarly, students who did not seem deficient would not need a tutorial program developed for computation. These strategies would be used only for students who are deficient in some areas.

There are, however, several strategies that can be used for all students to reinforce these basic skills and provide practice in important areas whether the students are deficient or not. Any student can benefit from an assignment that requires a book review in the subject or a bibliography for a research project. Similarly, all students can learn from using the dictionary, developing abstracts, outlining chapters, and writing mandatory assignments.

If there can be any summation of the process for infusing the basic skills of reading, writing, and computation into any course, it is to seek opportunities throughout the course to require writing assignments, to require reading of materials other than the textbook, and to include some form of computation within every course.

Even a course in history can include a computation component if, for example, the teacher asks students to speculate about the outcome of history if certain historical armies had 25% fewer troops. For some courses, building in computation (in particular) may necessarily be creative, but the long-term benefit to students outweighs the effort. These students will see the importance of computation in all aspects of life and work and will acquire a greater appreciation for computation as a life skill. Similarly, even in courses such as electronics or computer-aided drafting, students should be encouraged to read trade publications and books that involve the subject and can help them not only keep current with the topic, but improve their skills as well. Writing, also, is a skill that is of great importance to all future workers, and any assignments that stretch the students' abilities to synthesize information and to communicate in writing or orally should be greatly stressed throughout any course.

To use the strategies listed in this section most effectively, the instructor would want to highlight those strategies that he/she could see as being assignments for students who have deficiencies. Strategies in all three sections should be noted in the event students have deficiencies in each area. Instructors would also want to include in their course at least one strategy from each section for all students, with or without deficiencies, to provide them with adequate practice in reading, writing, and computation. As discussed in Chapter 2, instructors should build in at least one strategy from each major workplace skill category, and ideally, should develop a total course package that includes at least one workplace skill each class meeting.

The instructor may have to seek opportunities to infuse the basic skills strategies because basic skills is not as easily integrated into some courses as critical thinking, teamwork, or leadership may be. The instructor may have to think more creatively in order to incorporate these strategies, but again, the improvement of basic skills is highly important for students.

Strategy 1
Book Reviews

Students must be encouraged to read more than just the text books required in a course. In European countries, it is common for a teacher to require outside reading of three to five extra books to accompany a semester class. This strategy requires the instructor to develop a list of excellent books written by experts that relate to the discipline and to require students to choose two or three of those books and provide a two- to three-page abstract and commentary to the class.

This strategy encourages students to 1) read more during a semester; 2) seek out books related to their subject that they would enjoy reading; and 3) analyze those books critically with an emphasis on judging accuracy and reliability of the source. This assignment prompts students to read critically and to think about what they read. As Mortimer Adler points out in *How to Read a Book* [p. 40], "Bacon distinguished between a book to be tasted, others to be swallowed, and some few to be chewed and digested." Adler argues that reading is learning and that increasing our skill at reading can help us to acquire more knowledge. Most of the world's new knowledge, opinions, and thoughts are not included in a textbook, and if students limit their reading to texts, they will grow stagnant in their careers especially in later years once they have finished formal classes. Encourage them to seek out new information by requiring extra reading.

VE, I, P, A

Strategy 2
Article Reviews

Students must be encouraged to read beyond the textbook (see Strategy 1). If full-length books cannot fit into the curriculum, the instructor can research a list of articles applicable to the subject area published during the previous three years. The instructor would then require students to locate the articles, copy them, read them, analyze their content, and then write a review of the articles for presentation to the class.

Students will get more benefit from this assignment if each student is given a different set of articles to research so that students only hear about each separate article once. This strategy encourages students to 1) learn to research information in addition to that in the text; 2) read articles critically; 3) think critically about the articles related to the subject; and 4) judge the accuracy and reliability of the source.

The more students are required to read, the more practice they will get in reading, and reading will become easier for them. Students also need to learn to research information from journals and articles in order to keep current in their field.

VE, I, P, A

Strategy 3
Remedial Reading

In addition to any institutional programs for remedial reading assistance, instructors can assist students who may lack basic skills or may be weak in the basic skills areas by developing extra credit, self-administered remedial programs using information from the specific discipline.

In a course of Principles of Marketing, for example, if a student lacks reading skills, the instructor can develop a remedial plan similar to the following example.

Marketing Remedial Reading Plan

1. Read the following books:
   Oglivy's *On Advertising*
   Ries and Trout's *Bottom Up Marketing*
   Ries and Trout's *Guerrilla Marketing*
2. As you read, be sure to use a dictionary and look up EVERY word that you do not understand. (You will be tested.)
3. Outline the books for comprehension using brief, conceptual outlines.
4. Use your outlines to write one-page book reviews (See Strategy 1).

If students lacking basic skills could be encouraged to read more (and have a more concrete reason for doing so, such as extra credit for a specific course), and if they could be encouraged to read for meaning and to increase their vocabulary, they would begin to read faster and with more understanding. This simple remedial system, if applied in all classes, could gradually encourage a student to read more and upgrade his/her reading skills.

VE, I

Strategy 4
Bibliography

To encourage students to read from broad, varied sources, instructors should require a bibliography of five or more sources for every project assigned during a specific semester class. It may be of benefit to also require that two of the five sources be books (not texts) and three be journal or magazine articles.

If students must prove they have read several sources to complete their work, they will be encouraged to read more and to read from several sources.

VE, I

Strategy 5
Newspaper Assignments

Reading material can and should come from a variety of sources including newspapers. Newspapers provide excellent material, no matter what the subject. Students can be required to peruse the paper each day for a month, clipping and/or copying articles that could pertain to the class. Students should analyze the articles for trends that could affect the industry. The articles as well as clippings and reviews can be gathered into a notebook at the end of the project as an overall summary of information gleaned from a one-month review of the newspaper.

Instructors can contact their local newspaper for other ideas about how to use newspapers as effective classroom tools. This strategy will 1) provide students with the opportunity to review the paper—a source of information many of them may have overlooked; 2) develop in them the habit of reviewing a newspaper; 3) provide additional reading for them that is not textbook based; and 4) provide them with more practical information about the topic.

VE, I, A

Strategy 6
Book Lists

Instructors in all disciplines should encourage students to read often and widely. Several companies have published lists of "greatest books" and most libraries carry these sets. Instructors can pass out a list of great books to be read during a college career. Even if the lists vary, students will still become aware of the importance of the classics and of reading widely.

Instructors can either obtain a list or make up one of their own. They can give students a personal challenge to complete the book list (of between 30 and 50 titles) within the next ten years. Students are usually unfamiliar with the classics, and a list of the best books of all time can provide them with direction and enhance their reading and comprehension in general reading as well as subject areas.

Those books that easily relate to the subject matter can be used as assignments for book reviews and abstracts.

VE, I

Strategy 7
Book Review—Mortimer Adler's
How To Read A Book

Few students have ever analyzed their own reading or seen how effectively reading can be used as a learning tool. Mortimer Adler's classic *How to Read a Book* can benefit students in any discipline by providing them with a systematic method for improving their reading and for seeing reading as one of the most important activities of their lives.

This strategy requires students to read Adler's book and then to develop a comprehensive report of its methodology. They are required to react to Adler's philosophy and to assess the importance of reading as well as to learn how to improve the most important skill for modern man. Students should be required to read, analyze, and comment on Adler's book.

VE, I

Strategy 8
Abstracts

Students can begin to organize their own learning process by developing their own system of note taking and by using abstracts to refer to as their education progresses. Instructors who require additional reading can require students to fill out an abstract form for each book read, referred to, or used during the class. These abstracts (which summarize the books) can be kept in a three-ring binder for use in later classes.

The use of the abstract form makes it easier to keep track of the books and takes less time than writing out a full abstract. Instructors can require five or more abstracts in classes that involve projects that require reading from five or more sources. If students can develop a habit of scholarship, these abstract forms will help them to integrate their studies when they graduate.

VE, I, A

Strategy 9
Computer-Aided Instruction in Reading

This strategy requires instructors to develop a computer-aided instructional package for use either in the school's remediation center, or by the student on the student's computer, or in the computer lab. Unlike many of the "packaged" remedial programs, a computer-aided reading program developed for marketing students, for example, would use the terminology, reading matter, ideas, and concepts most often used in the marketing industry. This remedial package would not only help students upgrade basic reading skills, but would do so in the context of the marketing profession so that when students obtained jobs, they would be comfortable with the kind of reading requirements a marketing job would entail.

Instructors can often obtain grants to help pay for development time required for creating computer-aided instruction packages. Even if a particular instructor is not adept at using a programming language, the instructor can write the instructional format and work with a programmer to program it. Computer-aided training packages can provide students with discipline-oriented practice in reading that can help them perform better on their jobs.

VE, I

Strategy 10
Chapter Reviews

The objective of this strategy is to encourage students to read the text more carefully and to digest the information more thoroughly. Students are required to read each assigned chapter and then provide a written one- to two-page review of the chapter. The idea is to get students to read for meaning, review for content, and to set priorities as to the most important information in each chapter.

An assignment such as this requires students to read more carefully and to analyze information more thoroughly. At the end of the semester, the reviews are collected into a notebook for which a grade is given. The notebook should be 10% to 15% of the total grade. The instructor would evaluate the notebook in terms of completeness, professionalism, and clarity.

VE, I

Strategy 11
Chapter Outlines

Similar to Strategy 10, the objective of this strategy is to encourage students to read chapters more carefully and more thoroughly. Students are required to read the chapters and to outline each chapter, taking special care to define any new terms presented in the chapter. At the end of the course, copies of the outlines are put in a notebook and turned in for a grade. The instructor might use 10% to 15% of the final grade for this activity.

Requiring students to outline chapters is similar to requiring students in accounting and mathematics classes to turn in homework. For some students, it is a catalyst that requires them to study and review each chapter more carefully.

VE, I

Strategy 12
Dictionary Use

Instructors can encourage students to develop broader, more accurate vocabularies by requiring them to look up any word with which they are unfamiliar as they read through assignments in a text or an article. Students can greatly enhance their reading, thinking, and communication skills by taking time to look up (and write down) definitions to words with which they are unfamiliar.

Once the words have been defined, students can develop a series of flash cards for their new words by writing the words on the blank side of an index card and the definitions on the other side. Not only can instructors require this, they can add a "word-of-the-day" quiz or discipline-centered vocabulary to their tests. Students should develop a habit of looking up every word with which they are unfamiliar, and this strategy not only provides them with a process for defining new words, but encourages its long-term use.

VE, I

Strategy 13
Vocabulary Exercises

There are several excellent prepackaged vocabulary building programs the instructor can use as a basis for this strategy. The instructor would develop a vocabulary self-test exercise to be given to students during the first day of class (and later at the end of the course). The instructor could pull the words from a prepackaged program or could scan the text itself for words used frequently in the discipline. (These words do not need to be discipline-specific.)

In any case, students who do not score well on the self test can be counseled and encouraged to improve their vocabulary. A take-home self test or exercise can be developed to assist students in improving their vocabulary. At the end of the semester, students are given the vocabulary self test again, and the new score is compared with the old score to calculate the amount of improvement.

This assignment encourages students to actively work on their vocabularies—not for an English class or a speech class, but for a class in their chosen field of study.

VE, I

Strategy 14
Reading Assessment

In order to judge which students are likely to need some form of remedial program (see Strategy 3), students can be given some kind of placement test before entering a specific program of study. For a truly integrated and effective workplace skills curriculum, the instructor needs to be advised of student scores to use in making assignments. If no such scores are available, the instructor can require students to read a case study and summarize it on the first day of class. For those students who have difficulty with this assignment, the instructor can require them to be placed in voluntary remediation programs while still enrolled in the class.

It is important not to let the student slip through. A student who is weak in basic skills and barely passes the class will have more difficult challenges to face later on in the job market. The instructor can help the student by developing a short, content-based remedial program (see Strategy 4) and/or by requiring students to participate in institutional remediation programs concurrently with the class.

VE, I

Strategy 15
Remedial Writing

This strategy is similar to Strategy 3. There may be instructional programs for providing remediation for writing. These programs can be used extensively but can also be supplemental. The instructor develops his or her own remedial program for writing to be given as extra credit opportunities for students who need some remediation in writing. A remedial system based on the area of study the student is interested in will provide the student with more of an incentive to work through the program.

In marketing, for example, if a student lacked writing skills, an instructor might develop the following remedial plan.

Remedial Writing Assignment

Write a two- to three-page essay (using correct spelling, grammar, and punctuation) on each of the following 16 topics:

- Why are there more elderly people in commercials lately?
- Advertising does not make people buy anything
- There is no such thing as ethics in marketing
- The most important part of the promotion mix is advertising
- Why I do/do not want to be a salesperson
- Transportation companies should pay more taxes for state highways
- Why the U.S. has a very small merchant fleet
- Why I do/do not think humor should be used in advertising
- Why psychographics are more important than demographics
- Why the objective/task method is superior in setting budgets
- Why every marketer should write a personal code of ethics
- Why retailers fail most often
- Why prices would not fall if we eliminated wholesalers
- Why companies should develop and use strategic marketing plans
- Why marketing helps promote competition within our economic system

Each of these essays should be written in correct essay format and would be given to a composition teacher who would grade the writing while the marketing teacher would grade for content. The final grade (as extra credit or participation) would be a combination of the composition grade and the marketing grade. A remedial program such as this is ambitious, but because these are essays of opinion (no research is required), it would not take students an inordinate amount of time to complete the project. The extra credit would provide an incentive to students to improve their performance in writing. This assignment would also provide students with the opportunity to delve more deeply into the subject matter.

VE, I

Strategy 16
Writing Assessment

Instructors need to be able to judge early in a course which students will need remedial writing (see Strategy 15). On the first day of class, students can be asked to write a one-page essay on a topic pertaining to the subject. Students who do not perform up to standards can be placed in remediation within the institution or can take part in voluntary remediation.

It is important to identify students who are likely to need remediation early in a course before they have an opportunity to fail. A student who is weak in basic skills and barely passes a class will face more difficult challenges later on in the workplace. The instructor can help the student by developing a short, content-based remedial program (see Strategy 15) and/or by requiring the student to participate in an institutional remediation program concurrent with the class.

VE, I

Strategy 17
Long-Term Writing Projects

Requiring students to complete long-term projects that require extensive research and writing encourages students to write and to use their critical thinking abilities. Instructors (even in technical areas) can develop projects that require extensive writing for their classes.

Some examples of projects that require extensive writing are:

- journals
- lab reports
- experiments
- feasibility studies
- term papers
- biographical sketches
- skits
- plans
- programs
- reports
- theses

The objective is to require projects that combine the content material of the class with writing skills that require students to integrate the material from the text, the class, and outside sources (a skill very valuable to entry-level employees who have to integrate knowledge from various sources).

VE, I, P

Strategy 18
Computer-Assisted Instruction in Writing

This strategy requires the instructor to develop a computer-aided instructional package for use in the school's remedial center, or by the student on his/her personal computer, or in the computer labs.

This program would be based on the discipline and would use examples of writing from the area of study. A marketing student, for example, would be given tasks of writing associated with marketing such as writing advertisements, sales presentations, and proposals. The package would not only help students upgrade their writing skills in general, but would do so in the context of the marketing profession so that students would be comfortable with the kind of writing required by marketers when they got jobs.

Instructors can get grants to help pay the costs of development required for creating computer-aided instruction packages. Even if a particular instructor does not know how to program, he/she can write content-oriented examples and coordinate with an instructor of computer programming to do the actual programming. Computer-aided training packages can provide students with discipline-oriented practice in writing that can help them perform better on the job.

VE, I

Strategy 19
Tutor Program for Writing

Students who lack basic skills may get discouraged and drop out of classes that require extensive writing. Unfortunately, it is those classes which, in the long run, are most likely to benefit them.

To keep students enrolled and improving, instructors can work together to set up tutoring programs for students who need assistance in writing.

Instructors can either pair students with students who are strong in writing or with professional tutors in writing. Instructors can offer extra credit for written work used in tutorial sessions if the work comes from the content of the course.

A key element in improving students' workplace skills is to use content-oriented (subject-related) material that will interest and encourage students to write and to use content-oriented concepts. If a tutorial program can be developed that uses subject matter effectively, the program is much more likely to have a long-term effect on the students' writing skills.

VE, I

Strategy 20
Grading Grammar

Writing correctly is not likely to be important to many students unless the instructor makes it important by giving a grade on grammar and punctuation. While instructors in business or technical fields are not writing teachers and probably don't want to get overly involved in grading grammar, spelling, and punctuation, they can at least mark off on those items that they notice are incorrect. If students know that 10% to 15% of their grade on a specific project depends on their writing correctly, they will pay more attention to their writing and strive to achieve better results.

Even if the instructor does not want to take off any points for grammar, he/she can at least mark items that are incorrect and recommend remediation (see Strategy 14) for students who continually turn in substandard work.

VE, I

Strategy 21
In-Class Essays

Students need practice writing, especially writing in the subject areas. One strategy that can be used with a great deal of flexibility is the essay. Students are required to write impromptu one-page essays (used like quizzes) concerning concepts from the subject area. The instructor requests that students take 10 to 15 minutes to develop a short essay on an important topic. The essays are graded for content as well as grammatical accuracy. The assignment can be repeated six to eight times during a semester. This strategy provides students with practice in writing. Over a period of time, they become more comfortable writing impromptu items from the discipline area.

VE, I

Strategy 22
Stylebook

Instructors in all areas can coordinate with teachers of composition and require their students to use a stylebook such as the *APA Stylebook,* or the *Chicago Manual of Style,* or the *Prentice Hall Handbook for Writers. The Gregg Reference Manual* can also be used in addition to the stylebook as a guide for making decisions on grammar and punctuation. No matter which stylebook is adopted, if instructors are consistent across disciplines in requiring students to use a stylebook, students' writing skills will be more transferable across disciplines.

Students in occupational and vocational programs are being prepared for the workplace. They need to learn how to write in a professionally acceptable manner even as they enter their new careers. What they learn should be consistently reinforced as they work through projects in every class.

VE, I, P

Strategy 23
Grading Template

The English departments of many community colleges and four-year institutions often use a grading template to grade composition more quickly and more objectively. This template can be used as an additional tool for grading any written project. If the writing of a particular project is part of the total grade, the template can be a valuable tool to help instructors (who are not English teachers) make decisions about the quality of the writing. The template also assists the instructor in giving valuable feedback to students to assist them in overall improvement of their writing. Templates are excellent tools for grading any subjective project for any type of discipline as well as for grading grammar.

VE, I

Strategy 24
Essay Journal

This strategy relies on the instructor to program into his/her course requirements an ongoing series of essays related to the topic. The essays can be collected and bound into a notebook at the end of the course, or the instructor can require that the essays be written in a journal.

The value of the assignment lies in requiring an essay for each class period to be turned in at the beginning of the class period. One method of using this strategy is to require a one-page essay on the reading assignment for the day, stressing, of course, that the student's ideas and opinions should outweigh material from the book.

Another method is to develop a list of topics relevant to the discipline and to require students to write an essay pertaining to an assigned topic for each day of class. The assignment reinforces the need to write in any discipline and helps students clarify their thoughts and integrate the material no matter what the subject area.

VE, I

Strategy 25
Mandatory Writing Assignments

The most important strategy for improving basic skills in writing is to require writing assignments in all classes (no matter what the course content). Students must have practice in writing, reading, and thinking in all courses in order to be adequately prepared for their future jobs. While this strategy may seem almost self-evident, many instructors do not require nearly enough writing assignments in their classes.

A rule of thumb is to require one large writing assignment per class (see Critical Thinking and Communication) as well as to require 30% of the other work to be developed using a written assignment. Take-home tests, journals, essays, projects, and lab reports can be used in almost every discipline. The emphasis must be on requiring more written work per course so that students get the practice they need to better communicate (and think!) on the job.

VE, I

Strategy 26
Letter to the Instructor

Students need practice in writing efficient, effective correspondence with a purpose. The instructor can require that students write brief letters or memos if they have questions or concerns about the course or need information. This strategy does not take too much time for students, but is an effective way to provide them with practice in constructing memos, notes, and letters that convey meaning and get results.

This strategy can also help the instructor because it provides requests on paper to jog his/her memory. The instructor does not have to require a very formal written format for the strategy to be effective. Just the requirement to put "things in writing" will provide practice for students.

VE, I

Strategy 27
Course Summary of Learning

The instructor can require a Course Summary of Learning at the end of the course, either as part of a final exam or as a capstone requirement. Students are asked to write a 10- to 15-page summary of what they have learned in the course. The assignment should be general so that students can choose the parts of the course most relevant to them.

This strategy is an excellent method for getting students to integrate the diverse parts of a course and to put the course in perspective. Students can use the assignment to relate the course work to their own goals and lives. The instructor can use the assignment as an informal measure of his/her ability to make certain parts of the course relevant and interesting.

Evaluation can be accomplished using a subjective measure such as one an instructor would use for an essay or composition paper. The instructor would not evaluate the opinions, but would evaluate whether the student used the terminology from the course correctly and seemed to have a good overall understanding of how the parts of the course related to each other.

VE, I

Strategy 28
Joint Writing Assignments

This strategy requires cooperation between different instructors. The instructor in a course such as biology, chemistry, or human relations cooperates with an instructor in English. Students complete an assignment, such as a research paper on marine animals. The student is given instructions pertaining to writing and grammar from the English teacher and is graded on these elements while the other instructor grades the student on knowledge and analysis of the subject.

The strategy is based on partnerships between disciplines. It can be used with team teachers (where both teachers are instructors in one class) or it can be used with guest speakers (and graders) from the English department. Strategies of this type are still controversial and may be difficult to implement depending on the institution, but they have great potential for integrating course work and providing students with interdisciplinary instruction to improve their job performance.

VE, I

Strategy 29
Computer-Aided Instruction in Computation

This strategy requires the instructor to develop a computer-aided instructional package for use in the institutional remedial center, or by the student on his/her personal computer, or in the computer labs.

This program would be based on the discipline and use examples of computation from the area of study. A marketing student, for example, would be given computation assignments associated with marketing such as forecasting sales figures, comparing media using rating figures, or developing an overall budget. The package would not only help students upgrade their computation skills in general, but would do so in the context of the marketing profession so that students would be comfortable with the computations required by marketers when they got jobs.

Instructors can get grants to help pay the costs of development required for creating computer-aided instruction packages. Even if a particular instructor does not know how to program, he/she can write content-oriented examples and coordinate with an instructor of computer programming to do the actual programming. Computer-aided training packages can provide students with the discipline-oriented practice in computation that can help them perform better on the job.

A, I

Strategy 30
Mandatory Computation Assignments

The most important strategy for improving basic skills in computation is to require assignments in all classes (no matter what the course content) that include a computation component. Students must have practice writing, reading, and thinking in all courses in order to be adequately prepared for their future jobs.

Many instructors do not integrate computation into their courses if they are mainly verbal courses such as social science and history. There are ways to include small computation exercises even in these courses. Students can predict population changes, for example, for a social studies course or can speculate about what would have happened if Napoleon's armies operated with 30% more troops. In some cases, the instructor may have to be highly creative to develop a computation component that is relevant to the course, but any such effort will aid students in practicing computation and getting over their fear of using numbers.

A rule of thumb is to require one computation component to an assignment (see Critical Thinking) per class if the class is a verbally centered course like history, sociology, or psychology, and to require 50% or more if the course is an analytically oriented course like electronics, calculus, or physics. Budgets, statistics, salary figures, historical statistics, word problems, and other computational challenges will help students get the practice they need to be able to compute and think on the job.

A, I

Strategy 31
Computation Questions

Similar to Strategy 30, this strategy places an importance on developing at least one computation question for each test given during the course. Even for verbally oriented courses, one question that deals with computation (even if it is just recognition of numbers and working with numbers) will reinforce the value of using computation for students and provide them with practice over time.

Of course, subjects such as electronics, mathematics, algebra, and physics have ample material for using computation questions. Instructors of English, history, social science, and psychology may have a more difficult time adding computation questions, but they can use numbers as statistics and ask for predictions, ratios, and other information. Business courses can use budgets and statistics. Language courses can use computation as a means to reinforce an understanding of numerical terms.

A, I

Strategy 32
Computation Using Newspaper Articles

This strategy requires students to review the newspaper and search for articles related to the subject they are studying that also use computation in some form. Business classes can use articles that discuss percentages of profits or layoffs, budget allocations, and market share. Mathematics and science classes can use reports citing experiments or mathematical theories. Social science classes can use statistics and demographics.

Almost any type of class can have a newspaper and computation tie-in. Students clip the articles and then explain how the computations were accomplished (or, in some cases, how the students assume the computations were accomplished), what the overall implications of the computations are, and how those computations affect the subject.

VE, A, I

Strategy 33
Grade for Computation

Computation may not be important to many students unless the instructor makes it important by giving a grade on computation. While instructors in business or technical fields are not math teachers and probably don't want to get overly involved in grading computation, they can at least mark off on those items that they notice are incorrect. In marketing, for example, students are often required to develop hypothetical budget figures.

If an instructor grades a marketing plan and notices that the student has incorrectly computed columns in the budget, it will help the student to take off for the error. It will reinforce to him/her the importance of correct computation in any format. If students know that a percentage of their grade on a specific project will be taken off if they do not compute correctly, they will pay more attention and achieve better results.

Even if the instructor does not want to take off any points for computation, he/she can at least mark items that are incorrect and recommend remediation (see Strategy 15) for students who continually turn in substandard work.

A, I

Strategy 34
Grade Process

One of the problems of teaching students to think and to develop their reasoning skills is the idea that the right answer is the most important goal. Too much emphasis is placed on getting the right answer and not nearly enough is placed on developing a process for getting the right answer. Plugging numbers into a formula may help the student get a correct mark on a test, but showing the student how to develop (and reason out) his/her own formula will help the student learn to get answers for many problems throughout his/her lifetime.

To encourage students to emphasize learning the process and developing formulas for themselves, the instructor should grade for process. If the course is a math course or electronics course, the instructor can give partial credit for correct process (even if the answer is wrong). If the process is correct, but there is a slight error in computation, the instructor should give more credit for the correct process than for the incorrect answer.

If the course is a course in social science, business, or psychology, the instructor can provide a percentage grade for "process"—how the student seems to have reasoned out the answer to the problem or question. The emphasis at all times should be on learning to use processes to solve problems and developing new processes.

A, I

Strategy 35
Search for Numbers

Search for Numbers is like a scavenger hunt for students. The assignment is for students to search through the text, journal articles, books, and newspaper articles to develop a list of examples of how computations (numbers) are used in conjunction with the subject.

Any use of numbers—tallies, votes, statistics, money, percentages—is clipped out (or written on an index card) and turned in. This can be accomplished with groups (see Teamwork), with each group turning in a compilation of its findings, or it can be an individual assignment with each student turning in a folder or notebook containing the findings.

The purpose of the assignment is to show students the relevance of computation to the course, to make them more comfortable seeing and using numbers in relation to the subject, and to provide them with the opportunity to work with numbers in conjunction with the subject.

A, G

Strategy 36
Decision Models Based on Computation

Many of the decision models discussed under Critical Thinking (Strategies 32, 33) and Leadership (Strategy 9) and Motivation to Learn (Strategy 24) can be adapted for use with a computation-based decision. Marketing case studies can be adapted to require students to make decisions based on how computations are affected by budget constraints. Social science case studies can show the effects of different decisions based on demographics. Electronics courses can develop scenarios of design based on computations with regard to resistance and power. Auto mechanics can use analysis techniques based on statistical data developed concerning materials and parts.

Most courses either already have case study materials or are highly adaptable to the development of case studies that require students to make decisions based on computations. For business and other industries, the ability to make decisions based on the numbers is an important responsibility associated with leadership and critical thinking. For many other academic and vocational areas as well, decisions are often made based on numbers. Students must be prepared to "crunch" the numbers, to analyze the meaning of the numbers, and to make decisions based on that analysis. This strategy can be used in conjunction with other decision model strategies to provide direction in the use and analysis of numbers.

A, I, G

Strategy 37
Statistical Summary

This assignment can often be used in conjunction with Strategies 32 and 36. It requires students to take an article, a piece of information from the text, or some other report that includes statistical data and to summarize the data in common, everyday terms so that students understand the meaning of the statistics being used in the reference.

Students can be given a handout with preselected statistical data related to the field and be required to review the simple calculations and then to analyze the meaning of the statistical data. The analysis is written up as a short statistical review or summary.

Students can also be given an assignment to research a secondary source for their own set of statistics to analyze. This assignment provides students with an opportunity to work with statistics and to use them even if the emphasis is not on calculations.

A, I

Strategy 38
Computation Handbook

The instructor can develop a handbook (or handout) outlining the different forms of computation common to the discipline including the processes used, methods for developing formulas, logic sequences, as well as uses for computation.

This may be a much more ambitious task for more analytical courses, requiring extensive research on the part of the instructor, but it can be invaluable to the student. For verbal courses, it can be an enlightening addition to the regular course material because it will show students the importance of computation (even in verbal courses) and give them an idea of how to enrich their learning by using computation.

Handbook on Computation for Marketing
Table of Contents

A, I

Strategy 39
Computer Software to Supplement Computation Assignments

This assignment requires the use of commercially available computer software and hardware. Many group and individual assignments can be supplemented with computational material by using popular computer software such as spreadsheet programs and forecasting programs. The instructor must first identify a common computational problem related to the industry and then either identify a predeveloped software package that can be used for it, or he or she can create his/her own software program.

The instructor develops a scenario for students to review the data and then requires them to input the various calculations into the computer and print out the results.

This approach can be used quite effectively with electronics, CAD, marketing, business, and many other areas. For a marketing course, students could be given certain budgetary figures and decision constraints and asked to develop budgets for a media campaign based on several different criteria.

If students have access to graphic software, they can generate pie charts that will graphically demonstrate to them the differences and implications caused by just varying the data. This kind of program can show students the broad reaching effects of making decisions based on various criteria.

Similarly, a science instructor could develop a program showing how size and strength percentages seem to affect the reproductive ability of animals. A nursing instructor could develop a program showing the effects of incremental increases in dosages of drugs per weight of the patient.

This approach requires students to use computational figures and to think through the process of their use, but not to actually "crunch" the numbers because the computer programs do the computations. If graphic software is used, the graphics will demonstrate how different computations (or computational error) can affect decision making. These assignments can be quite effective in presenting different outcomes to students based on different inputs and calculations.

A, I, VI

Strategy 40
Process Cards

As students complete the assignments given in a class, they are assigned the additional responsibility of constructing a "process card" for each problem they solve or set of computations they complete. At the end of the course, the cards are reviewed for accuracy by the instructor and then given back to the students to keep.

For example, a business instructor might require students to develop a business plan. As students complete any part of the work that requires problem solving or computation, the students would make out a 5×7 process card that would include the name of the problem and the steps included in solving the problem. The problem could be either a word problem with conceptual solutions or a computational problem with a formula. In the case of the business plan, students might have cards for:

• Decision on product (decision tree)
• Budget estimate (percentage formula)
• Sales forecast (percentage formula)
• Historical sales figures (computational formula)
• Decision on staff (decision tree)
• Decision on margin (pricing formula)
• Estimate of expenses (computational formula)

Students would leave the course with a permanent set of records to help them solve similar problems later. Yet, they will not simply have formulas; they will also have logical sequences of steps that reflect clear thinking so they can adapt these sequences to problems they encounter later on the job.

A, I

CHAPTER SIX

CLASSROOM STRATEGIES FOR COMMUNICATION

1. Role Play to Understand Power	21. Situational Analysis
2. Role Play to Understand Emotions	22. Abstracts of Articles
3. Role Play to Understand Communication Types	23. Book Review
4. Interactive Video	24. Survey Summary
5. Identifying Blocking Behavior	25. Feasibility Study
6. Information Relay	26. Essay
7. Question Groups	27. Speech
8. Pyramid Groups	28. Meeting Agendas
9. Crossover Groups	29. Research Note Cards
10. Seminars	30. Persuasive Summary
11. Tutorials	31. Writing a Sales Presentation
12. Syndicates	32. Letter
13. Role Reversal	33. Technical Documentation
14. Free Associative Discussion	34. Writing Instructions
15. Absent Friend	35. Case Study Analysis
16. Individual Presentations	36. Programs
17. Group Presentations	37. Developing Outlines
18. Proposals	38. Writing a Plan
19. Memos	39. Flow Charts
20. Reports	40. Writing Assignment Per Discipline

The ability to write well and to articulate ideas is crucial to the ability of employees to perform. No matter what the industry or field, a person must be able to understand concepts, to share ideas, and to learn through communication. Communication skills can be reinforced through any course (even mathematics and science courses). Stressing communication provides students with practice in developing clarity of thinking and expression. No matter how important the scientific discovery or the electronic or engineering solution, if it cannot be articulated and shared, it is meaningless.

Technical and mathematical courses may rely on short answers and multiple choice exams that stress the correct numerical answers but do not develop the students' abilities to share discoveries later in their careers. If the instructor can find opportunities to use essays, case studies, or lab reports in these classes, he/she can foster students' abilities to successfully complete the calculations and reasoning functions of the course as well as to communicate them. Similarly, writing and presentation skills can be stressed in social sciences, business, and occupational courses.

The strategies highlighted in this chapter stress a combination of oral and written communication skills likely to be required of an entry-level employee such as preparing memos, reports, presentations, agendas, speeches, and plans. Persuasion, negotiation, and selling of ideas are also required and can be developed through these strategies. (These are components of communication often neglected if the student is not a business major.)

Instructors will find that nearly any group activity, and most activities that involve speaking and/or writing, will enhance and reinforce communication skills.

Strategy 1
Role Play to Understand Power

Students should be made aware of the aspects of power in any relationship so they can analyze the situation and use it to achieve optimum communication. This strategy emphasizes the importance of identifying power relationships within an organization and learning to communicate within them. Some of the tell-tale signs of the power structure within an organization are:

- Who sits where
- Who takes initiatives
- Who has what skills

- The "pecking order"
- The communication structure

Although disciplines such as business, management, and marketing have innumerable possibilities for role playing these communications skills, almost every program can use a scenario for role playing such as this.

Some possibilities include:

- Doctor—patient
- Boss—employee (any discipline)
- Team—team leader
- Team—team members
- Customer—mechanic
- Customer—electrician

To use this strategy, the instructor would set up a scenario using real-life situations. A team of students would be asked to play out the roles (by reading parts as if they were reading parts in a play) and the rest of the students would be asked to identify who seems to have power in the situation. Does the power seem to shift? Or does it seem to stay primarily with one individual or group of individuals?

Identifying the source of the power such as referent, expert, or authoritative, and identifying how it affects the communication function is important also. Some discipline areas may find that sources of power change because the custom in that discipline is to share ideas and to communicate. In other disciplines, communication may become more of a downward process. The shop foreman or doctor, for example, continually relies on authoritative or expert power.

VE, G, SE, A

Strategy 2
Role Play to Understand Emotions

Understanding and communicating emotions is vital to the success of any student who plans to use his/her education to gain employment. As Luft concluded, emotions are part of life and as such students must be prepared to use emotions and communicate with emotions.

Even the physical science and engineering disciplines are beginning to understand that if we cut off the emotional part of communication it can lead to problems and to alienation. Behavior is determined as much by passions, anxieties, and convictions as it is by reason, the more so when we are not aware of the effects of our feelings [Luft].

To get students in touch with their emotions can be hazardous. The instructor can attempt to set up some exaggerated role plays that deal with emotions such as a dissatisfied customer, a grieving and anxious parent, an angry boss. These role plays need to be exaggerated though, so students see the emotions as "comic" and react to them in a light-hearted fashion. The instructor does not want to create a situation in which the class becomes a psychodrama or group therapy session (unless, of course, the instructor is a qualified psychologist/psychiatrist and can effectively handle the outcome).

Often written case studies can be used to create "emotional" situations the students can act out. The purpose of the role play is to allow students to practice identifying the emotions being communicated through the verbiage, behavior, and nonverbal cues.

A debriefing session is important for this type of role play so that students can begin to identify signals of emotionality. It is also important to identify techniques for handling certain kinds of emotional communication. An angry, irritated customer can often be calmed by a smile and a "let me help." A grieving anxious parent can be calmed by a touch on the shoulder.

Each discipline may have its own particular emotional problems (such as angry automobile customer) and certain "remedies" for emotional communication may need to be researched based on the discipline.

Some emotions that could be explored are:

• Anger	• Grief
• Confusion	• Jealousy
• Anxiety	• Happiness

VE, G, SE, A

Strategy 3
Role Play to Understand Communication Types

This role play uses four communication styles as the basis for communication interaction.

These styles, originally described by Carl Jung, have been developed by several research groups including David Merrill and Roger Reid and Anthony Alessandra, Phil Wexler, and Rick Barrera. Individual communicators are represented by the following types.

Expressive. An expressive person loves to talk, to express him/herself. An expressive will use gestures constantly. Expressives are often accused of "talking with their hands." An expressive is concerned with feelings and will use words connoting feelings frequently in a conversation. An expressive can be easily identified by noting his/her colorful office or clothing. An expressive has a high need for expression and a high need for sociability.

Analytical. An analytical person hates to talk and will go to great lengths to avoid talking or expressing his/her points of view. When an analytical does communicate, he or she will "stick to the facts"—letting the facts "speak for themselves." An analytical will use statistics frequently in conversation and will physically appear uncomfortable any time issues concerning feelings arise. The analytical often appears quiet and contemplative. His/her office is usually devoid of color displaying only the essentials for getting the job done. An analytical has a low need for expression combined with a low need for sociability.

Driver. A driver is an aggressive person who expresses him/herself in an overbearing and dominant fashion. This is the person who is "always right," who doesn't appear to listen to others' points of view, who tries to dominate discussions, and seems belligerent to onlookers. The aggressive is characterized by abrupt behavior as well as the tendency to talk over other people. An aggressive has a high need for expression combined with a low need for sociability. His/her office usually displays "trophies" depicting the aggressor as a "winner."

Amiable. The amiable is a person who wants to fit in with the crowd at all costs. This person wants to do and say what everyone else is doing or saying. A placater will often ask questions like "What does everyone else say?" "What is everyone else going to do?" A placater has a high need for sociability combined with a low need for expression. He/she does not want to "make waves," but to just go along with the crowd. The placater's office usually displays a larger than average quantity of photographs showing the placater with family and friends [Anderson, pp. 203-209].

Many individuals will not fall neatly into any of these categories and, some experts say, all of us tend to be one or the other of these communication types at some point in our lives.

Still, if an individual can be identified to have certain tendencies, this method of communication interaction can be successful. The idea is to match the communication style of the sender to the identified style of the receiver. If the receiver is expressive, for example, the sender would allow his/her message to contain elements of "feeling," using colorful and enthusiastic language. If the receiver is identified as an analytical, the sender would tone down any reference to feeling and would, instead, place emphasis on the facts and statistics associated with the exchange. If the receiver were a placater, the sender would construct the message to show the relevance of the exchange to the placater's social situation. If the receiver is identified as an aggressive, the receiver would have to tactfully allow the aggressor to "think it was his/her idea" and avoid conflict or debate at any cost. (With aggressives, it is best to let them always be right.)

For this role play, the instructor would develop a scenario relative to the discipline, and students would be selected to play various roles such as the boss, customer, programmer, computer user, or client. Each role, however, would be identified as to the communication style of the role. These styles, however, would be known only to individuals and the instructors so that the students looking on would have to identify the roles and the students involved in the role play and would have to identify the communication roles of all players.

Example: Two students are playing the roles of health professional and patient.

Health professional: Do you have a temperature? How long have you been sick? What prescription drugs have you taken? (Analytical)

Patient: I haven't felt well for days. My head feels hot. I don't like to feel this way. (Expressive)

Health professional: I think you'll feel better within the next day or so. The prescription I'm giving you will help you feel more relaxed. (Changing to expressive mode)

This kind of role play provides students with the opportunity to analyze communication styles and then to adjust their styles.

(Note: This method has been used by the author's students frequently on their jobs. Students say it has made a considerable difference in their ability to communicate.)

Debriefing, as in other role plays, is especially important for communication exercises because it will identify strengths and weaknesses associated with using these techniques.

VE, G, SE, A

Strategy 4
Interactive Video

Students (and instructors, too!) are often amazed at how they appear on a video screen. A video points out their flaws (especially) in a way that makes it almost impossible to deny the problem. In introducing aspects of communication to a class in any discipline, it can be a great asset to videotape a communication session, a discussion, a role play scenario or a debate (based on the content material). Students can benefit greatly from the nonjudgmental feedback of the video camera.

To be effective, the instructor can give each participant an evaluation/feedback sheet to fill out on him/herself as well as others (if the class agrees). This evaluation sheet would ask questions such as:

Individual

1. Do you appear to be confident?
2. Do you appear to be articulate?
3. Does your physical appearance on the video reflect the way you are feeling during this exchange?
4. Do you appear nervous?
5. Do you see any exchanges of conflict?
6. Are you happy with the way you handled it?
7. Are you satisfied with the assertion you displayed in having your ideas discussed? Why or why not?
8. Are you satisfied with your physical appearance as it relates to communication? Or do you think you showed too much or too little emotion?
9. What do you see as your communication strengths?
10. What do you see as your communication weaknesses?

Other Individuals

Name _____	Strengths _____	Weaknesses _____
Name _____	Strengths _____	Weaknesses _____
Name _____	Strengths _____	Weaknesses _____

VI, SE, G, A, SC

Strategy 5
Identifying Blocking Behavior

This strategy requires that the instructor develop a discussion segment pertaining to the discipline, preferably one that requires that students (in small groups or one large group) be required to come to a consensus. The instructor should let the discussion continue for 30 minutes while he/she uses interaction analysis techniques to map out blocking behaviors and identify any of them that appear.

Blocking behaviors are behaviors used by individuals (often in groups) to stop effective communication. A list of such behaviors follows [Jaques, p. 20]:

1. Aggressiveness
2. Stopping discussion
3. Seeking recognition
4. Pleading for special case (i.e, minority rights)
5. Withdrawing
6. Dominating

Once these behaviors have been diagrammed, the instructor introduces the concepts of blocking communication to the students and asks them to identify any blocking behaviors they recognized. The instructor can then point out (without mentioning names) any blocking behaviors the students failed to identify.

The issue of how to cope with blocking behaviors in a communication exchange is a major one. Critics and experts disagree on exactly what to do about blocking behaviors, but it is clear that it is important for students to be able to identify them. To overcome them, the participant can:

1. Repeat the message as many times as necessary.
2. Assert his/her point.
3. Recognize the blocker's need for recognition. Give it to him/her and then push the point again.
4. Pull withdrawing blockers back into the conversation.
5. Seek conflict with the domineering participant (not advisable).
6. Ask for reinforcement of a point from the group in hopes that a united front will stop the blocker from continuing.

The important lesson of this strategy is to be able to recognize blocking behavior as it occurs in a discussion so that the group (or individuals) can overcome that behavior and work toward a consensus.

A, G, VE, SE

Strategy 6
Information Relay

This exercise is familiar to most students and instructors. It is used frequently in elementary school. It is the familiar "rumor" game or "telephone" game with modifications. This version uses important terminology or case studies or events as the basis of the communication. The class is split into two relay teams and important concepts are relayed (without writing them down) from one person to another. The team that most accurately relays the information wins a review point and the team with the most review points gains some kind of reward such as a point or two extra credit on the next major exam.

This method is an excellent and fun method for reviewing information quickly. Concepts such as the following can be used:

- "The four P's of marketing are price, product, place, and promotion."
- "Emergency medical technicians should treat the inability to breath before stopping any bleeding."

Note: Once the class has used the relay method several times, students will begin to "listen" more carefully. Don't be surprised if the class begins to very quickly relay accurate messages every time. Once the class begins to relay the messages more accurately, students probably won't find the game challenging anymore. Even if they don't, the exercise still forces them to listen more carefully and that in itself may be reason to continue using it.

SE, VE, G

Strategy 7
Question Groups

Question groups are simply impromptu group communication sessions. The instructor assigns certain material to the class and requires that students be prepared to discuss the material. The instructor puts the students into groups of two to three people. Throughout the discussion, he/she asks open-ended questions and asks students to turn to their groups to discuss the answers. The student groups then prepare one answer to each question that satisfies them all.

In other versions of question groups, students are allowed to turn to discussion groups freely at any time during the open discussion in the classroom to clarify, speculate, and to pose additional questions.

VE, SE, G

Strategy 8
Pyramid Groups

This strategy uses pyramiding to provide further discussion and insight. The instructor requires students to be prepared to discuss a segment of the material. He/she then poses important questions to students concerning the material. First, the instructor puts the class into pairs. Each pair discusses the questions posed. After a 10- to 15-minute discussion, two pairs are added together thus putting the students in groups of four. The larger groups not only provide more viewpoints, but often bring new experience to the group that causes the initial pairs to rethink their answers. After 10 to 15 minutes in groups of four, the groups are again paired and the students continue discussions in groups of eight.

Groups of eight tend to bring out the key issues and the dynamics of large groups (as discussed in Teamwork) come into play. Finally, the groups of eight are brought back together into a whole classroom (unless the class is excessively large, in which case the instructor can pyramid on to 16).

An important aspect of this exercise is to debrief students to reveal how their opinions and answers changed as the groups got larger. What new information was revealed to them? Did a larger number of viewpoints affect their answers and in what way?

VE, SE, G

Strategy 9
Crossover Groups

Crossover groups can be used to blend different viewpoints. The instructor develops a segment to be covered by group discussion—something important or controversial within the discipline area. The instructor develops the discussion sequence so a two-tiered process can evolve:

TIER 1 (group)	1	2	3
	A	B	C
	A A	B B	C C
TIER 2 (group)	1	2	3
	A	A	A
	B C	B C	B C

This strategy (similar to Strategies 7 and 8) provides for diversity of viewpoints and opinions concerning the topic and ensures that each student has to mix with students who have differing viewpoints.

During Tier 2, each student should begin by reporting the information and findings discovered in Tier 1 by his/her initial group. Once each student has reported previous findings, the Tier 2 group can reassess available information and develop a new set of findings based in part on the interaction from Tier 1. The idea is to develop a better, more significant answer to questions through the examination and debate of differing points of view.

VE, SE, G, LC

Strategy 10
Seminars

The traditional "seminar" has been praised and maligned for decades. Yet, if a seminar is effectively supervised by the instructor, it can be an excellent tool to bring out the thinking and reasoning skills of students as well as their abilities to present material and answer questions.

To achieve success, the instructor should be careful to plan each seminar period thoroughly. The number of students in the class may greatly affect the outcome of the total agenda for the class. The instructor should allot approximately one-half hour per student.

During the first class period, each student is given a particular subject to research for his/her seminar date. It is more effective if the instructor provides a topic as well as a short bibliography of articles that will be covered.

All students can be assigned their topics and their seminar dates the first class session. The instructor should clearly stress to the students that a seminar is not a detailed report of what an article covers. The article should be used as a foundation for a discussion or a debate concerning the topic and its important issues.

A key element for a successful seminar is to provide students with training on how to lead discussions. Seminars in which students merely list off points covered in articles are boring to students. Likewise, seminars led by unprepared students who do not know enough about the topic are a waste of time for students and instructors. Students need to balance the content of the researched articles (or books) with the discussion and with input from other students.

To be successful, the instructor also must relinquish control of the seminar program but must also be prepared to take back control in situations where students are not being successful at leading the seminar. One or two ill-prepared students can cause this strategy to fail.

A variation of the seminar technique is to allow groups of students to lead seminar discussions. These students must still be trained in the art of facilitation to lead successful seminars, but this approach lessens the anxiety students may have about leading discussions.

I, VE, SE

Strategy 11
Tutorials

This strategy can be used in settings where 1) the class size is small; 2) the focus of the class is to develop and review projects such as a cooperative education; and 3) special projects classes focus on independent study.

A tutorial means one-to-one instruction. The instructor provides one-to-one attention to an individual student focusing on some product of his/her work. That work could be homework assignments, tests, reports, or individual projects.

The instructor keeps notes concerning the progress of the student, and each class session provides the instructor with the opportunity to reassess the progress of the student, to provide direction, to make recommendations, and generally act as a resource to the student.

Three main benefits result from the tutorial strategy according to David Jaques [p. 124]:

1. Checking student progress
2. Revealing misunderstandings from lecture material
3. Critiquing student work

I, SE, SC

Strategy 12
Syndicates

The instructor develops syndicates for learning by giving students assignments in small groups that require writing, reading, and discussion [Jaques, p. 104]. The syndicates serve as learning groups, where the group members reinforce the presentations of the instructor and serve to assist other students in understanding the material.

In some cases, all the syndicates in a class are given one assignment, the idea being that the results of the students' work can be contrasted and compared at the end of the project. This method works well for project work that is subjective and for which there may be many suitable solutions. Each syndicate develops a unique solution, based on the experience and skill levels of the individual syndicate members.

A variation of this approach is to assign each syndicate a different (but related) project. For this approach, the final projects can be shared and then students can be asked to relate the projects to each other.

All syndicate work should require a written and an oral presentation. This requirement ensures that students not only get practice thinking through discipline-based problems and developing creative solutions but also ensures that students get practice communicating solutions (both orally and in writing). The most important skill developed through a project (besides the successful solution) is the ability to communicate that solution. Without the ability to communicate, the solution itself becomes worthless. Syndicates provide an opportunity to learn about important content material from the subject discipline as well as the opportunity to hone communication skills.

VE, G, SE, LC

Strategy 13
Role Reversal

Role plays (as discussed in Strategies 1, 2 and 3) can often enhance both the perspective and the communication ability of students. Both, however, can be doubly enhanced if the instructor takes those role plays one step further to role reversal.

This technique is very simple. The role plays described in any of the previous strategies are conducted and then the roles are reversed. The students play the opposite roles from the roles they started out playing. This allows students to view the critical problem from all points of view, which can be a catalyst for understanding the communication and emotion associated with those differing viewpoints.

In the evaluation or debriefing component of the role play, the instructor should lead students to compare and contrast their viewpoints, feelings, and communication styles as they worked through each role. The conflicts or critical problems should be based on important conceptual information from the discipline, from the roles of actual people in history, from roles of scientists with differing hypotheses, from roles of doctor and patient, and from roles of members of different cultures. If the student can discover on his/her own how a difference in role affects his/her emotions and even his/her ability to communicate, the exercise will have been successful.

VE, G, SE

Strategy 14
Free Associative Discussion

This strategy relies on the power of the instructor to facilitate. The instructor opens the session by stating that for the next few minutes (20, 30, or more), the class will engage in free, open discussion. No one will be called on or called down. The following rules apply:

1. Never talk over anyone.
2. Do not monopolize the conversation.
3. Do bring any ideas into the discussion, no matter how trivial or off the wall.
4. Do participate fully.
5. When time is up, time is up.

The instructor begins the discussion with a statement derived from the subject matter of the discipline. (Ideally, students should be prepared to conduct a free and open discussion using facts and ideas from their text, from experience, or other readings.)

After making the initial statement, the instructor allows the discussion to flow freely—never interrupting the students—just observing and writing down important points (or inappropriate communication techniques to be debriefed).

At the prescribed time, the instructor closes the discussion and asks the participants to review key points. The key points can be written on the blackboard or on a flip chart and posted in the room. Once students have reviewed the important points, they can be debriefed concerning the strengths and weaknesses of their communication techniques.

G, SE, LC

Strategy 15
Absent Friend

This technique is discussed by David Jaques' *Learning in Groups* [p. 147]. The instructor develops a segment of the curriculum for open discussion in small groups. Once the basic structure of the discussion has been developed and communicated to the class, the instructor leaves the room for 10 or 15 minutes.

When the instructor returns, the class is likely to be engaged in a lively discussion, which may not have occurred had the instructor remained in the room. The instructor returns to the class quietly and unobtrusively and sits away from the groups where he/she can observe and note the communication process. The topics for discussion are taken from the content material relative to the discipline. The session should be debriefed so students can identify their strengths and weaknesses.

Strategy 16
Individual Presentations

Communication, both oral and written, can be vigorously reinforced by requiring a formal written paper at the end of all project work and by requiring an individual oral presentation.

These presentations can be as short as 10 minutes or as long as 40 minutes. The importance of the presentation is to require students to present their ideas for other students to listen to and critique.

Any discipline can provide the necessary foundation for individual presentations. Presentations should include the following components:

1. Introduction to subject premise
2. Body of evidence (Supporting the premise)
3. Persuasive conclusion (Advocating the premise)

One important element of the individual presentation, or any presentation, is the evaluation instrument. The presentation can be broken into categories to ease the burden of making subjective judgments. A guide can be developed to assist the instructor in evaluating the project work fairly.

Introduction (30 pts)

(5)—Speaker introduces broad topic
(5)—Speaker appears calm
(10)—Speaker sets up presentation for information to come
(10)—Speaker provides promise

Body (35 pts)

(5)—Speaker restates premise
(5)—Speaker provides evidence to support premise
(5)—Speaker is interesting
(5)—Speaker provides enough facts
(5)—Speaker uses quotes effectively
(5)—Speaker sets up the audience for the conclusion
(5)—Speaker uses audio visuals properly

Persuasive Conclusion

(5)—Speaker restates premise
(5)—Speaker restates 2 or 3 major evidence points
(5)—Speaker relates specific premise to general reality
(5)—Speaker is convincing
(5)—Speaker remains interesting
(5)—Speaker closes with anecdote or remarks

VE, I, SC, SE

Strategy 17
Group Presentations

Group presentations can be excellent tools for enhancing both group process and communication skills. The group of four to five individuals can be asked to prepare a cohesive written and oral presentation using audio visuals. Students will learn a great deal from working through such an assignment.

To be successful, the project should be broad enough to include several components yet related enough so that one cohesive presentation can be given. In most disciplines, it is acceptable to have the group split the work into individual parts and to organize those parts into a cohesive whole once the preliminary work has been accomplished. Each member of the group should have a speaking part in the final presentation as well as a behind-the-scenes role in the overall organization of the presentation and the development of audio visuals for his/her individual portions (material that goes together with other individual materials).

For evaluation purposes, a guide such as the one in Strategy 16 can be developed with an addition such as the following:

Group Achievement

- Did the presentation appear to be cohesive or did it appear to be several individual presentations stuck together?
- Did the group members provide smooth transitions between speakers?
- Did the presenters build on the ideas of previous presenters or were the parts so individualized that the project was disjointed?
- What was the overall impression of this group's work?

G, VE, SE, LC

Strategy 18
Proposals

Students who are planning careers in business and industry need a foundation of basic skills, but also need assignments that reflect the kinds of writing they will do in their jobs. Strategies in this book emphasize practical assignments that can be developed for any basic discipline.

Proposal writing is an important tool for many entry-level employees. Being able to develop a new idea or set of ideas and write a plan for accomplishment can be a tremendous asset to any employee. In fact, those employees who can articulate their ideas and establish proposed methods for making those ideas work are much more likely to be promoted than those who are unable to do so. For many employees, too, proposal writing to clients, as well as staff, may be crucial to obtaining and maintaining business in order to keep a job.

Short Proposals

Short proposals are often given to the boss, internal sources, clients, professors, or instructors. The short proposal usually consists of a one- to five-page letter or memo. This document contains the following items:

- Salutation—the audience the proposal is addressed to.
- Proposal idea—the main theme or new action idea to be presented.
- Body of evidence—the evidence supporting the main idea.
- Plan—the plan of action if the idea is adopted.
- Benefits and problems—the problems and benefits that may be encountered if the idea is adopted.
- Persuasive conclusion—the summary of the proposal in persuasive language.

In proposals, the main idea or theme should be presented directly following the salutation in direct, clear terms to make the reader understand clearly what is being proposed. The proposal idea should be followed by the reasons for adopting the proposal. (What has led up to needing the action? Why is it necessary now?) This should be followed by a brief outline of an action plan to bring the idea to fruition.

Once a plan of action has been articulated, a constructive list of possible benefits or problems that might occur with the adoption of the plan should be presented. It is important to list both problems and benefits because this will show the employer or the client that the implications of the idea have been thoroughly thought through, even to the extent of anticipating problems.

Finally, a persuasive summary should conclude the proposal that gives the main proposed idea, reasons for it, overview of the plan, and positive and negative outcomes. This conclusion should end with one persuasive sentence that seeks approval of the plan in strong terms.

In-depth Proposals

In-depth proposals are often given to clients, or professors, or instructors. An in-depth proposal is most often directed at a client and can range from

6 to 50 pages or more. A lengthy proposal is often sectioned into parts covering different aspects of the proposal. Often proposals are written in response to "requests for proposals" (RFPs), and the sections developed in the proposal correspond to sections requested in the RFP. The ability to write a lengthy proposal is an asset to any employee, especially an entry-level one. A lengthy proposal usually contains at least the following sections and may contain additional sections depending on the discipline:

- Executive summary—a one- to two-page brief summary of the whole proposal. This section is usually written *last*.
- Table of contents.
- Overview—a brief summary of what the proposal is about and what has led up to the need for the proposal.
- Problem/Opportunity—a restatement of the situation in brief, clear terms.
- Scope of work/solution—an outline of the proposed actions to be taken including proposed step-by-step procedures and schedules for completing work, etc.
- Expertise—a section that includes a brief history of the firm (if applicable) or of a particular department as well as resumes and backgrounds of individuals involved in executing the scope of work.
- Evidence—a section that might include projects achieved by the firm or individual, and the scope and basic achievements of each.
- Conclusion—a persuasive conclusion to sum up the main ideas of the proposal.

Using these general formats, instructors can develop real-life practical exercises by requiring their students to write proposals associated with their discipline. Evaluation of proposals, as with any report or plan, must be subjective. It can be effective to use a Likert Scale for each component of the project. In fact, many businesses develop such a Likert Scale System or a means for judging the quality of a proposal in order to give projects to vendors.

DE, SE, I, VE

Strategy 19
Memos

Students are often familiar with developing cover sheets as an overlaying document for their reports or projects. This is an acceptable method for their academic work, but with some changes, this task can give students valuable practice and work experience. It will be useful on the job if the instructor requires a memo to be developed instead of a cover sheet.

There are many styles of memos. In fact, each company invariably develops its own style and format. Any style that pleases the instructor can be effective. A simple style memo and one used frequently in the workplace is as follows:

Date:
From: (Student's name)
To: (Instructor's name)
Subject: (Name of project)
Body paragraph

Simple, yet effective, a memo will help students to see their project work as a product of their labor.

I, VE, EE

Strategy 20
Reports

Students are often very familiar with reports, at least the kind often assigned in school science classes and English classes. The kind of reports often used by employers is of a different sort. Work reports are often succint, clear, and contain formal references. The purpose of the work report is to communicate.

Students in any occupational/vocational discipline can be assigned basic reports on aspects of the subject matter. The emphasis of a work report should be to state the facts and their implications directly and clearly.

Some ideas for reports are:

• Top five ad agencies in the city
• Hospital procedures for cardiac arrest
• Basic workings of a camera
• History of modern dress design
• Types of silk screen processes

The topics that could be covered by a report are infinite. Lengths of reports vary, but a good rule of thumb is to ask for approximately ten pages (typed double-spaced) with a bibliography. Students should direct their efforts toward communicating, and instructors should evaluate the report for its of level of writing, clarity, content, thoroughness, and not for mechanical elements of grammar. It's useful for students to receive feedback about their abilities in basic skills, English composition, and grammar, but for this strategy more emphasis should be placed on communicating concepts and ideas.

Students should be encouraged to use quotations and to use statistical data where applicable. Footnotes are acceptable but should play a small role in the overall evaluation.

VE, SE, I

Strategy 21
Situational Analysis

A situational analysis is a useful tool for a student to develop, especially if the student is going to be working in business, medical or technological fields. A situational analysis is a prerequisite to solving common sense problems or developing a scope of work or solution for a request or proposal (See Strategy 18).

A situational analysis is a research product in which the student chooses some aspect of a discipline and researches to find out the current state of the art within that discipline. It differs from a simple report in that a report simply restates the facts with some implications while a situational analysis requires extensive critical thinking.

In a situational analysis, the student must restate the facts and then interpret those facts. He/she must "read between the lines" to distill what is occurring and what trends this analysis indicates. A situational analysis can be used in conjunction with several different project strategies—reports, plans, and case studies. Examples of situational analysis could be:

- Research on the current nurse shortage
- Market analysis for marketing disposable diapers
- Market situation for freelance underwater photographers

A situational analysis requires more than a restatement of facts. It requires that the student review those facts—like pieces in a puzzle—to come up with overall trends that the pieces when taken together reflect.

A situational analysis covers the following:

1. Facts about the topic
2. Assumptions about the topic

3. Predicted trends concerning the topic
4. Inferences regarding 1-3 (above) in combination

VE, A, DE, D, I

Strategy 22
Abstracts of Articles

A technique often used in graduate school, writing abstracts of articles within a discipline helps force the student to research and review current journals and literature associated with a discipline. The assignment can be as easy as asking each student to write a one-page summary of an article based on research in the trade journals, or it can be a much more in-depth exercise requiring students to research, locate several articles pertaining to the same subject, write a one-page abstract, and then write a piece comparing and contrasting different viewpoints in the article.

Requiring abstracts can be a preliminary assignment before asking students to provide a report in situational analysis. It's often useful to have each student briefly discuss his/her abstracts before turning them in. The instructor should require every student to follow a distinct format and insist that the abstract be one page, double-spaced, and typed. This forces students to read, interpret, and summarize information as well as to learn to communicate briefly and clearly.

The articles themselves may be either assigned as in the case of a master list of 20 to 50 articles from which students choose, or the instructor may give some loose guidelines and leave it to the students to decide what constitutes a "journal" and other acceptable articles. Either way, the abstract is an excellent way to foster a sense of research and curiosity for the students.

VE, EE, I, SC

Abstract
Name Date Author's last name, author's first name, title of the article, publication, volume, date, pages.   Two Paragraphs: one paragraph restates or summarizes the main idea of the article, and the other paragraph discusses the strengths and weaknesses of the article.

Strategy 23
Book Review

Similar to Strategy 22, the book review forces students to begin reading and researching within their discipline. A book review (that is, a book report) requires students to read a current book associated with the field and then provide a written and/or oral report on the value of the book. A key element here is to report on the value of the book to the field, not just to give a step-by-step overview of the details of the book.

A format for a book review is as follows.

Book review
Date Name Book: author's last name, author's first name, title, address, publisher, date.   Two paragraphs describe the book and offer a summary of important sections and overall information. One paragraph discusses the strengths and weaknesses of the book. The other paragraph asserts the value of the book to the field (i.e., compares it with similar books, etc).

The instructor should provide strict formatting considerations for book reviews, keeping them to one or two typed, double-spaced pages with full bibliographical data and a value analysis and a comparison of the strengths and weaknesses. Without these elements, a book review simply becomes a rehashing of the book and provides little or no opportunity for critical thinking and clear communication.

I, VE, SE

Strategy 24
Survey Summary

This strategy requires some research skills on the part of the student. It can be adapted for any discipline. The student chooses a topic crucial to the discipline that he or she has a great interest in and develops a questionnaire or survey pertaining to the topic. The survey can consist of 10 to 20 questions. Although it is not necessary to use a Likert Scale or any scale, it may be easier for students to tabulate the results if such a scale is used. An example of a typical survey follows.

The student then conducts the survey attempting to get 30 respondents. A short survey such as this can be very valuable in helping the student to understand aspects of a topic as well as the fundamentals of the process. Once the student tabulates the results, he/she converts the tabulations to percentages.

When the surveys have been converted to percentages, the student can look for trends, aspects of the topic revealed by either very high percentages or very low percentages, authors' findings that reflect "common sense" and findings that do not.

The most important aspect of the survey is to analyze the results and then effectively summarize the results, analysis, and implications of the survey. Even if the discipline seems to be one in which surveys are seldom used, like air conditioning repair or auto mechanics, the experience of developing a survey will help sharpen both analytical and communication skills.

Example survey

	Strongly agree	Agree	Neutral	Disagree	Strongly disagree
1. Computers are used extensively in your place of work.					
2. Your organization relies heavily on computers for word processing.					
3. Your organization relies heavily on computers for accounting.					
4. Your organization relies heavily on computers for statistical analysis.					
5. Your organization provides 3 to 5 days of training on computer systems.					
6. Your organization provides more than 5 days of training on computer systems.					
7. Your organization uses IBM-compatible systems.					
8. Your organization uses Macintosh systems.					
9. Your organization uses computerized graphics.					
10. Your organization uses computer-aided drafting.					

Sample percentages

	Strongly agree	Agree	Neutral	Disagree	Strongly disagree
1. Computers are used extensively in your place of work.	40%	20%	10%	10%	10%

A, VE, D, DE, SE

Strategy 25
Feasibility Study

This strategy can be used to enhance the critical thinking and communication skills of students who may need to assess the probability and feasibility of occurrences within their discipline. The purpose of a feasibility study is to determine the likelihood of an event occurring. For example, a medical student might want to assess the likelihood of contracting measles from a patient contact, a data processing major might want to assess the probability of downtime on a mainframe computer, and a marketing student might want to assess the profitability of introducing a new product in the marketplace.

The first step in developing a feasibility analysis is to write a summary of the feasibility requirement, for example, "The purpose of this study is to determine the feasibility of using a program to detect a software virus."

The next step is to research the factors involved (whether by primary or secondary data) to determine the (subjective) pros and cons of each course of possible action as well as the likelihood of its occurrence.

Once the pros and cons of likely events have been outlined, the student makes decisions based on an analysis (both objective and subjective) of the data. This means the student would be required to assess the impact of various probabilities to make judgments as to appropriate courses of action. This analysis should be developed in the body of the report. It should include a scope of the study (what areas are to be covered in the study) and limitations relating to the data to be collected. Any assumptions made about the data or events relative to the data should be clearly stated in this section.

The next step is to develop a section in which recommendations are made based on the findings of the report.

The final step is to summarize briefly each of the sections described above in a one-page executive summary that would appear at the front.

The feasibility study would be organized as follows:

Executive summary
Overview
Scope
Limitations
Assumptions
Body (Analysis)
Recommendations

The value of the assignment is to 1) provide a forum for analysis within the discipline; and 2) provide students with practice in writing an analytical report. The evaluation of the assignment should not be determined necessarily by what the instructor sees as feasibility but by the thought process the student used to determine the scope, limitations, assumptions, pros and cons, and recommendations as well as how well the student was able to communicate those ideas.

A, VE, DE, D, I

Strategy 26
Essay

Students are usually familiar with essays as a form of communication because essays are used so frequently in first- and second-year English composition courses. Essays can be effective learning tools in other disciplines as well because essays require students to express their own thoughts about pertinent subject matter. The instructor can ask for a 300- to 500-word essay on a discipline-related topic and then compare the kinds of issues and ideas that are developed as each individual student expresses his/her opinion.

Some topics that could be developed are:

• Use of self blood storage services to prevent AIDS contamination
• Development of a personal marketing code of ethics
• Development of a system approach to data base management
• Client responsibility in commercial art

Another variation of the essay assignment is to provide a list of possible topics and have each student choose one. The essays can then be presented throughout the semester as textual material is presented that is relevant to the topic.

Whatever the discipline, an essay assignment can enhance the course by providing a forum for individual expression.

I, VE, SE

Strategy 27
Speech

Although there are many disciplines for which the development of a speech may seem unnecessary, students who can write and deliver a speech that is relevant to the topic can gain valuable written and oral communication skills. The strategy is similar to Strategy 26 in that there is a wide range of possible topics that can be developed. Each student would be given a topic to research and then asked to write a 10-minute speech related to that topic. This differs from ordinary "presentations" in that the speech should be carefully written to gain the most impact from the words, make transitions easily from one point to another, and make liberal use of statistics, quotations, and anecdotes. The speech should end with some "call to action" and concluding comments.

Topics for a speech could include:

- Use of photography in layout
- Use of tutorials for new software
- Importance of following directions
- Why fashion cycles back
- Importance of research in marketing

To evaluate a speech assignment, the instructor can place more emphasis on mastery of the content material than on the mechanics of giving a speech. The assignment will assist students to learn to write well-organized succinct oral communication that will provide them the skills they need on the job.

I, SE, VE

Strategy 28
Meeting Agendas

Students can role play meetings based on topics developed to bring together the research of several people for the purpose of making a decision or solving a problem. For this assignment, students are discreetly given topics to research in advance of the "meeting." The purpose of the meeting is to share information and come to a consensus.

The project is established in phases.

1. General sessions. Students are given general topics and told they will be involved in a "meeting."
2. Research. Students research their topic.
3. Agenda. Students submit three points to be included in an overall agenda for the meeting.
4. Students meet and are given the overall agenda which contains their individual agenda items. Students discuss their topics per the agenda and come to a consensus.

Students learn their content material by using the experience of the meeting to achieve consensus. This exercise is valuable in providing true-to-life experience in communication.

I, VE, G, SE

Strategy 29
Research Note Cards

Instructors can encourage students to think through reading material and to learn to communicate and relate concepts by encouraging them to use effective research methods as they read the text and conduct in-depth literature searches for various assignments. One of the keys to effective communications is the efficient use of data management, that is, research note cards. Students should develop some kind of system for ongoing note taking throughout their college career. One such system relies on 3×5 or 5×7 cards and can be used easily. This system uses a bibliography card (usually a colored card). This bibliography card is used to record bits of information.

The student fills out this type of card when beginning his/her review of a specific book or piece of literature. The *code* is a three-letter code referring to the book and is usually taken from the first three letters of the author's name or the author's initials.

The student then takes notes by putting only one idea on each card. The student puts a three letter code, such as "LSK," and the page number from the source at the top of the card. It is advisable for the student to rephrase or paraphrase material into his/her own words. Any time the exact words of the author are being used (or even key words) these words should be written within quotation marks. This system tells the student the source the note comes from, the page, and whether or not the note is a direct quotation. If the note cards are dropped or otherwise separated, they can simply be put back in order of the pages from which the notes were taken. The code system allows students to refer back easily to the author and book.

Note cards can be taken in major categories:

- Conceptional information—unquoted
- Conceptional information—quoted
- Ideas—original to the student

These categories allow the student to manipulate most types of data. A note card using this system would have a keyword printed on top of the card and underlined. This key word would allow students to pull out key ideas from different sources, put them in order, and then use the cards as a basis for an outline.

Another method for using this system is to use a second color for ideas original to the student. As ideas are developed, the student jots the ideas down on a special colored index card and can refer back to his/her own ideas easily.

Quoted Info   PET 22
"Creativity should be pursued to the limit of one's time and energy resources."

IDEA

Develop a systematic approach for tapping into creativity

Bibliography Card

Petersen, Carol, *Awakening Creativity,* New York, NY: Appleton Publishing, 1987

Code: PET

Students should be encouraged to keep their notes in note boxes or some other container. If students have been especially interested in certain subjects, they will accumulate data and ideas from many sources over time. Often, notes taken for one class can help the research process in other classes.

A research journal is also an excellent tool for planning and conducting research. A research journal is simply a spiral notebook used as a place to write down plans for research, books that may be appropriate for reviewing, and overall thoughts and impressions of written sources as well as human source material. A research journal allows the student to keep his/her thoughts on the process in one place, helping to shape and refine the overall inquiry process.

Finally, a three-ring binder is useful for keeping photocopied information that is easier to store in hardcopy form than on index cards. Students should still make a bibliography card for each article in the binder however. (It is helpful to make journal bibliographic cards a different color than book cards). The student *takes notes* on articles *just as if they were books,* referring to the copies only in the case of charts, graphs, tables, etc., that are easier to store or referring to quotations outlined or highlighted that need not be written over again on a card if a photocopy has been stored permanently. Students can cross reference the note cards with the photocopies.

I, SE, VE

Strategy 30
Persuasive Summary

This strategy requires the student to write a summary to be placed either at the beginning or at the end of a given piece of analytical or written work. This summary would provide an analytical overview of the assignment as well as the reasons the assignment was accomplished in the specific manner. The purpose of such a summary is two-fold:

1. It forces the student to consider what evidence or actions make a piece of work a *strong* success.
2. It forces the student to then communicate using persuasive/negotiative language to "sell" his/her ideas.

This summary can be one or two pages. The use of a summary as a adjunct to a project assignment helps the student to synthesize the assignment— to tie it all together into a meaningful piece of learning.

SE, VE, I

Strategy 31
Writing a Sales Presentation

Whether or not a student is likely to find him/herself in a job that requires "selling," the requirement of a sales presentation can be helpful in teaching students how to sell their own ideas. For this assignment the instructor identifies 15 to 30 "sellable" ideas, services, or other functions of a discipline and requires students to write a 10- to 15-minute script for a sales presentation. This script would include:

1. Introduction to the goods, service, or idea.
2. Positive benefits of the goods, service, or idea.
3. Possible objections to the goods, service, and idea.
4. Answers to possible objections.
5. Persuasive summary (see Strategy 30).

Whatever the discipline, there are ideas that may need to be "sold" to management, to peers, to the public, to subordinates. This assignment forces the student to think of persuasion as achievable. Students use sales techniques to identify positive and negative aspects of a specific object or idea and then overcome the negative aspects by using persuasive communication.

The assignment is much stronger if students are required to both write the script and give an oral sales presentation. All students will need to learn how to persuade—how to persuade a boss to accept an idea, persuade a potential employer to hire them, and persuade other people to adopt their ideas. This assignment provides practice in negotiation and persuasion.

I, VE, G, SE

Strategy 32
Letter

Many students who have not taken a formal technical communication course do not learn how to write a simple business letter. Whether the student is to be employed in health care, technology, business, or any other occupation, the ability to compose a simple letter is extremely important.

This strategy involves assigning two or three business letters to be written and sent by each student. Usually, the student can benefit from an assignment requiring the student to write to organizations requesting information on a topic that the student will use in a research report or other project.

The students are asked to identify two or three sources of information such as business organizations or other institutions. The student composes a draft of a letter requesting information on a topic. The instructor evaluates the draft, offering recommendations for improvements and correcting grammar. A grade is given for the draft.

The student uses the input from the instructor, revises his/her letters, and then turns in a final version of the letters. If the letters are acceptable, they are sent. If they are not acceptable, the student revises them until they are acceptable. The student is given a grade for the final letter and is asked to share any responses from the organization with the class.

Formats for business letters can be found in many sources. One standard format is to use a block left format without indentations and with an extra space between each paragraph.

More important than the format, however, is the content of the letter. The first paragraph should quickly and clearly state the reason for the letter and present the evidence substantiating the reason for the letter. Each body paragraph should further substantiate the reason for the letter and/or offer information and solutions to the problem or area of concern and should make a smooth transition to the next paragraph. The closing paragraph should summarize the evidence and the premise of the letter and end with a call to action—a request for action on the part of the recipient.

Students need practice in writing letters for future jobs. Letters and memos are the most common forms of organizational communication, and students must know how to communicate through this medium.

I, SE, VE

Strategy 33
Technical Documentation

For students in technical fields (and even those who are not), an assignment requiring them to document technical information can help assist them in understanding the importance of communicating detailed, complex information. Employers in technical, medical, and other fields are often called on to write manuals containing technical information, instruction sheets, and technical specifications. This assignment can fit in well with lab work and scientific literature review.

The instructor would identify a process specific to the discipline and ask students to outline the steps involved and then to document each step in a clean, accurate, concise, and logical manner. Students would then trade papers and each student would follow the documentation to see if the writing is clear.

Another variation of the assignment is to require students to explain some complex technical idea or concept instead of a process. This would be tested in a similar manner, with fellow students reading the work out loud and commenting on the clarity of the documentation. This assignment requires students to clarify their thinking in technical data and processes and requires them to communicate that thinking in writing. Students in technical fields especially need to learn how to accurately communicate technical information.

Some ideas for topics are:

• Findings of electronics experiment
• Findings of lab results
• Working a software program
• Using a fashion pattern

SE, A, VE, G, I, DE

Strategy 34
Writing Instructions

This strategy involves using opportunities provided by the discipline for students to write instructions for some special procedure or topic. This strategy has often been used by instructors who ask students to write instructions for something generic like tying shoes. The instructor can also use a discipline-specific task or procedure for the general focus of the assignment and this will help students to learn the material as well as improve their communication skills.

As in Strategy 33, students can test their writing by asking other students to follow the written instructions.

Examples for topics are:

• Logging onto a computer file
• Laying out an ad
• Giving a vaccination
• Cleaning a camera lens

VE, I, SE

Strategy 35
Case Study Analysis

This strategy can be used with prepackaged case study materials that accompany many texts. It involves assigning students a case study to read and then, instead of simply answering the questions posed at the end of the case study, requiring students to write a formal brief of the case study that includes:

I. Summary of case
II. Problem statement
III. Situation analysis
    A. Information important to case
    B. Analysis of information
    C. Trends
    D. Assumptions
    E. Implications
IV. Recommendations
V. Persuasive conclusion

This differs from a simple case study in that it requires a formal, written brief of the case including the recommendations in a specific format. Position papers are often used in industry to outline specific problems and possible solutions. Instructors who require such written briefs of cases will be preparing students for the kind of analysis they will be required to accomplish on their jobs. Case study analyses must be evaluated subjectively (like most of the strategies in this series). The instructor might assign different weights to each section, developing two or three criteria points for each section.

I. Summary 5%. Is the summary accurate? Clear?
II. Problem statement—10%. Did the student accurately pinpoint the problem?
III. Situation analysis—10%. Are important elements developed?
IV. Recommendation—10%.
V. Persuasive conclusion—5%.

Students should be encouraged to systematically dissect the case to accurately identify the problem(s) and to think through the facts given in the case to see how they affect the recommendations of the case. If students can identify important information, trends, assumptions, and implications, they can develop a fairly accurate overview of the case. This ability to analyze case information and communicate that information is a skill that is highly transferable to the workplace.

VE, A, DE, D, SE, I

Strategy 36
Programs

This strategy is taken from the practice common in architecture of developing "programs" to analyze situations. (It does NOT involve computer programs.) The architectural method uses five categories of information for in-depth analysis of problems. The five steps involved in programming are:

1. Establish goals
2. Collect and analyze facts
3. Uncover and test concepts
4. Determine needs
5. State the problem

These steps as outlined in *Problem Seeking* by William Peña [p. 12] are excellent steps for identifying problems and analyzing situations. This programming phase is used before the creativity stage or brainstorming stage of problem solving.

For this assignment, students are given a written case study or information from a true "client" or other scenario involving creative work and accountability for that work and are asked to brainstorm the ideas that go under each heading. A card is placed on a wall in each step and topics that fall under that category are tacked under the heading so that ideas are easily identifiable and can be quickly organized.

The most important part of the program is to take those facts, concepts, and ideas and write a document summarizing the situation. Often called a situational analysis, a program is a written analysis that uses each of these steps to help organize and make sense of a situation.

Programming can be used in conjunction with case studies, feasibility studies, and reports.

VI, VE, G, DE, SE, P, A

Strategy 37
Developing Outlines

Although many students have been introduced to outlining at some point in their academic careers, many have stopped using outlining as a viable communication technique. Industry employers often require employees to outline situations or information so that it can be quickly and clearly communicated.

In this strategy in instructor requires students to turn in a formal outline with any long-term written project. By requiring students to turn in a formal outline, the instructor forces students to better organize their thoughts. For business and non-technical classes, a regular outline can be used.

I.
  A.
  B.
    1.
    2.
II.
  A.
  B.
    1.
    2.

For technical courses, a technical or scientific outline can be used.

1.
  1.1
  1.2
  1.3
2.
  2.1
  2.1.1
  2.1.2

The evaluation of the outline can be a small percentage (10%) of the total evaluation of the project.

I, SC, VE

Strategy 38
Writing a Plan

For courses in business, photography, fashion design, and merchandising, the inclusion of an original written plan can be a major asset to the course. This strategy combines the research techniques of the research paper and the analytical techniques of programming and case study methods with the creative skills of creative thinking and written communication skills. Some examples of written plans include:

- Plan for marketing a product
- Plan for opening a photo studio
- Plan for designing a line of formal wear
- Plan for developing a new service

A written plan requires extensive thinking and communication skills on the part of the student as well as the ability to combine knowledge and skills in several different areas into one cohesive plan.

A typical plan might include:

- Executive Summary (1 page)
- Program or situational analysis (including 5 pages of research)
- Strategies (5 pages)
- Projection/operation (5 pages)
- Persuasive conclusion

Evaluation for a written plan is subjective but can include a percentage for each category:

- Executive summary   5%
- Program   30%
- Strategies   30%
- Operation   30%
- Persuasive conclusion   5%

The instructor would then develop criteria based on the specific discipline for each section required in order to more accurately assess the plan. Although students often get the opportunity to write reports that simply restate or retrieve data, they rarely get the opportunity to plan real projects. Providing them with the experience of actually developing and writing a plan can greatly enhance their self-esteem and communication skills.

VE, I, P, A, SE

Strategy 39
Flow Charts

This strategy can be used in conjunction with feasibility studies, case studies, presentations, programs, situational analyses, and other long-term writing projects. It requires students to use the formal scientific flow chart method to chart various processes involved with a discipline. Students might be asked to chart information such as:

- Flow of electricity through a resistor
- Flow of blood through arteries
- Computer program
- Process of developing black and white prints
- Flow of steps involved in designing a suit
- Flow of chemicals through sewer system
- Process of marketing a new product

The basic criterion is to use flow chart symbols to represent different decision points, options, flow of action, and/or information.

Flow charts, just as outlines (see Strategy 37), can be required in the appendix of a major project. The development of flow charts will enhance the students' abilities to communicate models and processes and help clarify their thinking as they complete the major project.

VI, A

Strategy 40
Writing Assignments Per Discipline

In every discipline, there may be opportunities for writing assignments specific to that discipline. In marketing for example, the instructor can require a variety of writing assignments such as:

- Writing an informative ad
- Writing a persuasive ad

- Writing an emotional ad
- Writing a marketing plan
- Writing a consumer survey analysis
- Writing an international marketing plan
- Writing a group sales presentation
- Writing an individual sales presentation
- Developing a total ad campaign
- Writing a press release
- Planning an event

For every discipline, there will be ample opportunity to require students to write. The important consideration is to make the writing assignment something students will be asked to write on the job and to make it challenging and fun.

VE, I, A, G

CLASSROOM STRATEGIES FOR CRITICAL THINKING

1. Research Techniques	21. Seeking and Analyzing Information
2. Socratic Method	22. Open-ended Essay Exams
3. Peer Coaching	23. Exams With Reasons
4. Group Projects	24. Performance Testing
5. Group Tests	25. Multiple Answers Tests
6. Role Playing Case Studies	26. Thinking Journal
7. Approaches to Thinking	27. Thinking Maps
8. Testing for Thinking	28. Thinking Skills Related to the Discipline
9. Training Approach	29. Research in Learning
10. Teaching for Process	30. Facilitation Instead of Teaching
11. Daily Controversies	31. Decision-Making Skills
12. Model Thinking	32. Identifying Fallacies in Thinking
13. Teaching for Transfer	33. Practice Analysis
14. Distinguishing Fact, Inference, Judgment	34. Separating Problems from Issues
15. Developing Arguments	35. Causal Theory
16. Uncovering Evidence	36. Case Studies
17. Deductive/Inductive Reasoning	37. Identifying Points of View
18. Observation Techniques	38. Letters to Editor
19. Generalization Techniques	39. Defining Problem Scope
20. Models for Reliability of Sources	40. Organizing Data

The most important skill students must develop for their future work is critical thinking. Critical thinking involves more than problem solving, although problem solving, is an important aspect. Critical thinking includes problem solving, reasoning, objective judgment, the ability to weigh beliefs (including one's own), the ability to argue and persuade using evidence, the ability to make decisions based on rationality, and the ability to think through situations. This kind of thinking—the kind that is required from employees—is simply not being taught at most secondary and post secondary institutions. This important facet of human learning is either ignored or, a rudimentary attempt to cover it is made through the teaching of mathematics.

Unfortunately, the kinds of thinking skills required in a democratic society are not usually developed through the study of mathematics. The skills in theoretical mathematics do not transfer as easily to common place situations as educators would like. Most mathematics courses, for example, provide formulas and teach students to use those formulas. The problems of everyday life have few, if any, formulas. Teaching students to solve these types of problems, to develop "nonprogrammed" solutions to problems and challenges of life, can provide students with lifelong survival skills for the modern world.

This is not to say that mathematics is not important. It certainly is, especially as a subject and precise methodology for calculating uncommon problems of engineering, mechanics, or science. The majority of the work force will not need to solve these kinds of problems though. The problems of life involve more effective rational thought, such as the ability to identify logic that is not conclusive or information that is incorrect, unethical, or blatantly misleading. The problems of daily life require the ability to develop special, tailored solutions (nonprogrammed solutions) to one-in-a-life-time situations.

Factors that contribute to the ability to think critically are the ability to develop objective viewpoints, to weigh consequences, to identify faulty logic and incorrect analogies, to develop a case for one point of view over another, to create new thoughts and ideas, to form individual beliefs, to challenge the status quo and develop new systems, to question the bases (or premises) for other people's conclusions and claims, and to synthesize facts and opinions for making decisions, while keeping opinion separate from fact.

To teach critical thinking, an instructor must first delve into his/her own thought processes using metacognition. An instructor must develop his/her own total commitment to the critical thinking process and allow and encourage his/her students to think for themselves, to question, to challenge even the instructor's (and certainly the text's) authority. The instructor needs to foster an atmosphere that encourages freedom—freedom to challenge, to argue, to contribute, and to create.

The strategies presented in this chapter will challenge not only students, but the instructor as well. Even what may seem to be an easy, simple tool such as the Socratic method (Critical Thinking, Strategy 2) requires exceptional planning and practice. Some of the strategies involve adopting an attitude toward teaching that places the teacher in the role of facilitator and requires students to explain their thinking. The instructor will teach more to impart processes for life rather than content material, create and encourage controversies, encourage students to challenge assumptions, and create tests to teach instead of tests for grading.

Other strategies emphasize the importance of sharing the elements of critical thinking with students by making them aware of their own thinking processes. They also emphasize explaining common flaws of thinking, teaching how to recognize flaws of thinking, providing students with methods for solving nonprogrammable problems, and providing tools for analysis and synthesis of information. The Critical Thinking Strategies emphasize either theories of learning, such as the strategies for metacognition, the Socratic method, and Bloom's taxonomy; the critical thinking process, such as teaching for process, model thinking, and teaching for transfer; or they provide specific tools for students to improve their own thinking, such as approaches to thinking, reliability of sources, exams with reasons, practice analysis, and hypothesis development.

Strategy 1
Research Techniques

Critical thinking skills are important to all types of employment, especially those involving any type of research. The most common research assignment is the research paper. For many students, a research paper is a haphazard collection of unrelated facts, written at top speed the night before the due date. Often these papers are written with no thought or plan to bring the research together into a cohesive piece of work. A research paper can be a disjointed recounting of information found in articles or in books with little or no original thinking on the part of the student.

The reason for this may be that students wait until the last minute but, more than likely, it is because they do not know that a research paper is supposed to spur their thinking—to give them an opportunity to go beyond the content information and formulate new ideas. The instructor can safeguard against the "unoriginal" paper by clearly defining the type of research paper expected—not just delineating topics. He/she should give clear instructions about the type of information gathered and the type of inferences students should make based on that information.

A part of the grade can be given for the critical thinking students demonstrated with the assignment. Students should be instructed to 1) define carefully any terms they include in the research; 2) determine whether they want to develop an expository research paper (or one that merely provides information about a subject); or 3) decide whether they want to develop an argumentative research paper that argues pro or con for a certain position with regard to a topic.

In her book *Thinking for Yourself,* Marlys Mayfield provides several points that help students to use the research paper as a forum for critical thinking. She says that just one paragraph must define what kind of study is being undertaken. She points to lack of precision in communication between the instructor and students as a primary cause of confusion. Next, she emphasizes that effective research papers must move from a subject area to a topic. "A college research paper is not a scrapbook or a random collage of encyclopedia and magazine articles. It is an essay that thoroughly explains, argues, or proves a single main idea of the writer: from the topic, one must develop a thesis and from this an outline is developed" [p. 268].

In addition to researching articles and books, students should develop the skills necessary to identify individuals who might be able to add insight to the facts already gathered as well as to identify events or places that could be observed to provide first hand information about the topic.

Other Types of Research

In addition to the formalized research paper, many of the projects and learning requirements developed in a workplace skills course require a research foundation to complete the project. This type of research is often more applicable to the kind of research often required on the job. This type of research is fundamentally different from research involved with a formal research paper. Often, one must continue to gather information until one has "enough" information to make a decision or a set of decisions. Then the information is used to write a summary outlining the facts that led to the decision. One must constantly decide whether the information he/she is collecting can and will have implications for the decision(s) at hand. The pros and cons and the reasonable implications should be developed. This kind of research is often open-ended, without the kind of definition one finds when developing research for an essay. For this reason, it is often more difficult, and students or employees may be overwhelmed trying to decide whether particular information is relevant. Sometimes only exploratory research can be achieved.

Instructors can suggest students consult "experts" to help them with their research. Students should be encouraged to call on or write to knowledgeable people in the field they are researching. Experts can quickly point out avenues that need exploration.

The success of a research project as a decision-making exercise is that students are asked to analyze and interpret the data they discover. This can be accomplished by asking them to look for trends and implications that might create different versions of the project based on different decisions. Asking students to explain the trends and implications as well as the pros and cons of any controversial items can help them define the problem to be addressed.

A, P, I, D, DE, SE

Strategy 2
Socratic Method

Instructors can use what Arthur Costa calls "mediative strategies" in his book *Developing Minds* [p. 151]. One important technique is often referred to as the Socratic method because it is based on the instructor taking the role of the mediator or facilitator—raising questions and leading students to develop and criticize their own discoveries, theories, hypothesis, or explanations. The instructor takes the role of catalyst to stimulate ideas from students and then helps them evaluate their own ideas.

"Students are motivated by the curiosity inherent in the cognitive task: explaining phenomena, finding patterns, designing systems for generating needed improvements, explaining causality, inducing concepts (such as metamorphosis), establishing proof, considering alternative points of view, constructing real problems to solve and hypothesizing" [p. 151].

According to Paul and Binker in *Critical Thinking,* the Socratic method "allows students to develop and evaluate their thinking by making it explicit" [p. 269]. By slowing students' thinking down with careful questioning, students have a chance to evaluate their ideas. They can then redesign ideas and develop a more coherent view of a particular problem.

The instructor asks "probing questions" about their thinking, motivating students to be curious, to see more clearly, to understand more comprehensively. The instructor helps students generate ideas, delineate between concepts, and think through evidence. The discussion is designed to help students think through the logical implications of questions until he or she has thoroughly examined premises and convictions. According to Paul and Binker, three types of Socratic discussion can be used in the classroom.

Spontaneous

Discussions that arise spontaneously in a classroom can be a primary forum to Socratic questions. The instructor can use the Socratic technique to explore the ideas of students as they come up concurrently with the topic. The spontaneity precludes advance planning for specific issues, but the instructor can train to use Socratic questioning techniques.

Exploratory

Exploratory questioning explores broad interrelated issues. It has loose structure and does not require excessive preplanning. Instructors should have some general questions prepared and should try to prepare for likely student responses.

Issue-specific

Issue-specific questioning provides students with focused discussions that proceed from one plateau of logic to another until students can view the logic associated with an issue. Instructors are required to do extensive preplanning to assess each line on the progressive logic chain in order to lead students through the logic by questioning.

VE, A, LC

Strategy 3
Peer Coaching

Students as well as instructors can benefit from an objective view of the critical skills they are demonstrating. Student thinking can be enhanced if students are paired while solving a problem or case study and then advised to observe and comment on the critical thinking of their partners. Students essentially take on a role of coach—giving ideas, criticizing, and reviewing carefully the thinking skills of another student while trying to help the student by bringing out ideas their partners may have overlooked in identifying faulty thinking.

An excellent approach is to pair students in such a way that the relationships between them are not preapproved, allowing one partner to be "easy" on the other. If the partners are changed each time a problem is given until all participants have been coached, no preapproval relationships can be established.

It's helpful to set ground rules before proceeding into the exercise:

1. Coaches will strive to identify weaknesses and strengths in their peer's thinking.
2. Students in the roles of mentors and helpers should strive to improve their partners' ability.
3. The participant should not be criticized but coached.
4. Both the coach and the participant need to take turns listening and talking.

VE, G, A, SE

Strategy 4
Group Projects

Critical thinking skills can be greatly enhanced by using group projects that have been carefully planned to elicit thinking from the individual members of the group as well as the group as a whole. Case studies can be used that relate to the discipline but that ask specific questions such as "What caused . . .?", "What evidence is there to show . . .?", " Can you agree with . . .?", "What would you do, say, act, and why?", "Compare and contrast . . ."

Group projects provide students with thinking opportunities that allow them to interact with other group members. Students can learn how to approach problems by observing how other students approach those same problems. Students will often learn from each other by modeling behaviors of their peers. The group project strategy is also similar to the teamwork usually required by companies for major company projects. For group projects to enhance critical thinking, the instructor must structure the assignment so that:

1. Each individual plays an important decision-making role in the project and is held accountable for that section of the project.
2. Groups have designated structure in that certain team members are responsible for spearheading the project while other team members support the coordination of the project.
3. The project involves a written analysis of decisions made, evidence considered, conclusions drawn, and research conducted.
4. The accountability scale includes partial credit for a final group effort, but a larger proportion of the scale gives credit for individual effort to assure that students continue to achieve.
5. Projects have interim check points, and some in-class structure and time are used to keep the project moving forward.
6. The instructor periodically reviews progress with the group and uses review sessions to bring up important issues and discussion topics.
7. The instructor requires rationale for all important points so students not only complete projects but must have bona fide reasons for each step they are accomplishing.

G, A, VE, DE, SE

Strategy 5
Group Tests

Group tests can be administered as easily as individual tests and can be used primarily to spark student discussions over content materials related to a specific discipline. The structure of group examinations can vary, but the group test idea can work if instructions are clear and precise.

The group test procedure is as follows:

1. Inform students that the test will be a group test.
2. Tell them whether it will be an open-book or a memory test.
3. Divide class into groups of four or five students the day of the test.
4. Hand out the test (which can be essay or objective).

5. Advise students that while they are allowed to discuss and debate answers, each student makes his/her final decision about the answers and will be accountable (in terms of grades) for final output.
6. Advise students to pace themselves as they go through the exam so that they do not expend too much time in discussion and not finish the exam.
7. Advise students to "think for themselves" and weigh the comments and input of others with their own judgment.

The group test approach forces students to use their critical thinking abilities to weigh their own ideas and judgments with those of their peers to come to final decisions.

Tests can be structured so that they cover enough material to be both thought-provoking and challenging for students. Students will probably need to study intensely for this type of test because they will have to be so well versed in the material they will be able to recognize false assumptions by peers as well as provide evidence for their own point of view. (This idea is adapted from a group test developed by Jeff Petry.)

DE, SE, G, P, VE

Strategy 6
Role Playing Case Studies

A major approach to teaching thinking as well as to training individuals to excel in a certain job is to provide students or trainees with opportunities for role playing in situations similar to those they would encounter on a job. Written case studies can be easily adjusted to provide scenarios for students to practice. Case studies that describe individual decision makers can be rewritten so that students can play the roles identified in the case study.

These role playing case studies provide the interaction factor—the factor that helps the student understand dynamic forces involved in decision making, in planning, in strategizing. In the working world, most decisions are not made by a single person with no knowledge of political, social, or economic forces. Role playing case studies provide information for individual members as well as circumstances to support their ideas. Request individuals to write down their thinking processes on specific points in order to share them with the class. Comment on students' thinking processes especially with regard to their reactive thought processes and final decisions.

A, G, P, VE, DE, D

Strategy 7
Approaches to Thinking

Instructors can develop a module at the beginning of a course or can highlight specific thinking approaches throughout a course in a specific discipline. By separating thinking skills and promoting them as necessary and marketable skills, instructors can assist students in using these approaches for improving the quality of their thinking.

The following is a list of thinking approaches students can be encouraged to use:

1. Separate relevant from irrelevant facts.
2. Identify faulty reasoning.
3. Identify issues you agree with.
4. Identify issues you disagree with.
5. Identify your beliefs.
6. Scrupulously examine the meanings of all important words.
7. Distinguish creditable from noncreditable sources.
8. Analyze all arguments.
9. List new facts needed for clarification.
10. Identify beliefs of others.
11. Compare your beliefs with others.
12. Contrast your beliefs with others.
13. Evaluate your own and others' prospectives.
14. Identify new sources.
15. Summarize final conclusions.

VE, A

Strategy 8
Testing for Thinking

It is important for instructors to not only test for content, but also to test for thinking. Within each discipline, the instructor can use a panel or focus group of employers to identify tasks assigned, planning requirements, special considerations, and other thinking requirements for the discipline. Once these have been identified, a diagram can be developed for each requirement that shows the direction and extent of the thinking processes required for entry-level jobs in that discipline. Several types of tests can be developed to enhance thinking. Tests (over content material) can be developed based on criteria specific to a discipline. This will allow students to be tested based on the context of the discipline. These tests can be used to help tailor the program to students' capabilities.

The instructor should emphasize the thinking component of learning in all testing situations. Essay tests, short answer tests, group tests, and performance tests can be used. Tests should require students to not only get the right answer, but also to arrive at the right answer through excellent thinking.

If multiple choice tests must be used, adding a line asking students to formalize their answer and explain their thinking can improve their thinking skills. Not only will students be required to think about their thinking and to think critically, they will also develop the attitude that just having the right answers isn't necessarily as important as knowing how to reason to arrive at that answer.

A, VE, DE

Strategy 9
Training Approach

Instructors can take the role of trainer instead of educator in constructing their assignments and developing their curriculum. There is a clean-cut line between knowing what to do and knowing how to do something. For most employers, being able to do a task proves that a person knows what to do. Unfortunately, most programs used in institutions today emphasize the ability of students to "say they know how to do"; that is, to repeat or list items. To memorize the steps involved in printing a photograph does not assure that an employee can print photographs.

An instructor who wants to develop critical thinking abilities in his/her students can assume the role of trainer. A trainer revises content material to emphasize content required to do a specific job. The detailed information that is "nice to know" but not crucial to the task at hand is covered. This material is emphasized differently just as it would be in a entry job. If it's not essential, it can be reviewed later.

The trainer does not stress memorization of content merely for knowledge sake as academic disciplines do. Instead, a trainer emphasizes memory of crucial points and practice of the skills. Other information such as handouts can be used as reference material. The main emphasis is on doing. With less content to cover, the trainer can provide more practice for the trainee in actual accomplishment of tasks.

Some might argue that learning the details of content material by memory cannot be totally incorrect as all persons can benefit from knowledge. However, others might argue that the human brain has only a finite capacity for details; therefore, we should teach the essential details pertaining to the job and leave the rest of the brain's capacity for general education such as history and philosophy. For most employers, if an employee can do a job well, it doesn't matter if that employee looks up the details of the task or researches the situation.

A, VE

Strategy 10
Teaching for Process

Instructors who emphasize the process for development of solutions instead of merely citing appropriate solutions provide students with incentives to use critical thinking skills throughout a course. If students understand that having a correct answer does not equate to formulating a correct answer, they will begin to use more care in solving problems and case studies and will be more aware of their own problem-solving skills. The following strategies can be used to emphasize problem-solving ability versus correct answers:

1. Develop essay exams that specifically ask students to trace the thought processes they have used to arrive at an answer or, if using multiple choice exams, have students write down their reasoning for particular answers.
2. When testing, spread the points so that the method for finding an answer is worth more points than a correct answer.
3. When discussing answers and processes in class, have students explain their methods to the class. Allow other students to question their methods.
4. Compare student thinking processes especially in cases in which two or more students in a class arrive at the same answer by using different thinking methods.
5. After using Strategy 7, continue to use the terms for thinking approaches and require students to use those terms.
6. Whenever possible, bring examples to the classroom from the work place so that students can see how employees on the job use these problem-solving skills.

VE, A

Strategy 11
Daily Controversies

In most disciplines, there is a myriad of topics for discussion that are controversial. These topics are excellent vehicles for the development of reasoning skills.

An easy method for using these topics is to play "take a stand." This is a game in which four sections of the room are marked off by cards labeled **strongly agree, agree, disagree, strongly disagree.** The controversial issue is read to the class in the form of a question and the students must choose to stand under one of the four cards. They must choose the cards they feel most comfortable with. When all students have chosen their card, the instructor facilitates a discussion going from one extreme view to the other, giving several students under each card the opportunity to speak.

Whether this method or simple class discussion is used, students should be encouraged and rewarded for seeking out controversial issues related to the discipline for discussion and debate. Students can sign up for a particular class date so that each day there will be at least one issue to debate.

It is helpful in cases where the issue comes from an important event in industry for students and/or instructor to also research the popular "solution" to the debate. For example, if the issue involves a question of ethics on the part of a company or industry, the class might want to debate how they think the legislature, or the press, or the public will deal with the issue.

Understanding that debatable issues may be resolved to an extent through the legislature and other social conventions is important for students. It demonstrates to them how advocates of an issue can push for resolutions in their favor.

VE, A

Strategy 12
Model Thinking

In Critical Thinking, Paul and Binker state that "by wondering aloud, teachers simultaneously convey interest in and respect for student thought and model analytical moves for students" [p. 269]. No other strategy for motivating students to appreciate the importance of individual thought and critical thinking can have as much impact as an instructor who models critical thinking for students in the front of his or her classroom. A teacher who demonstrates aloud his/her thinking provides a role model for thinking that students will emulate and remember long after the content material of the text has faded.

To become a model for critical thinking, instructors will need to become conscious of their own critical thinking process and practice step-by-step reasoning by writing down their reasoning processes for some of the problems or issues. It will be far easier to articulate these processes if the instructor has carefully thought through the common reasoning patterns prior to discussing them out loud with a class.

The important point is to develop a systematic method of writing down steps of reasoning involved in major problems and working through those steps for the benefits of the students. Asking their input and help throughout the thinking process will help them learn to use their own thinking capacities far better than simply stating steps from memory.

VE, VI

Strategy 13
Teaching for Transfer

When adopting a set curriculum to a workplace basics program, the instructor should develop the curriculum to provide for optimum transferability across courses. Examples and exercises can be used that highlight not only the importance of a particular thinking skill to a discipline but relate that thinking skill to other disciplines as well. Analysis methods used by entry-level market researchers may be used, for example, by auto mechanics who might find these methods useful in assessing customer needs to improve customer service. Or, creative thinking approaches discussed in a commercial photography class might be useful to a student taking a computer programming class.

If instruction is developed to give students consistent examples that can be adopted into other course work as well as on the job, students will benefit far more from their classroom instruction. For this strategy to be successful, the instructor should mention those specific disciplines that might benefit from a transfer of knowledge.

Some ways to teach for transfer are:

1. Always provide at least one example of application outside the discipline.
2. In developing curriculum for a particular program, take care to use elements of critical thinking strategies that require the same skills and use the same terminology across the curriculum.

3. Develop a handout to students that highlights transfer strategies for the students themselves.

4. Stress skills that can easily transfer from lesson to lesson.

5. After teaching a particular content section using a skill, brainstorm with your students to identify work-related tasks that the skill will help to achieve.

SC, LC, G, I, VE, VI, A

Strategy 14
Distinguishing Fact, Inference, Judgment

An important aspect of learning to think for oneself is being able to distinguish between pure fact, inference of fact, and opinion. Students often have never been shown how to make such distinctions or the importance of being able to make such distinctions. The instructor can use these skills as the basis for assignments in the discipline.

An example to help students make that distinction could be:

Fact: Sales are low this quarter as compared to last quarter.

Inference: Sales are low because the advertising campaign is not working.

Judgment: The advertising agency is doing a poor job.

[Chaffee, pp. 341, 352, 366]

Assignments can be developed using already prepared case studies for material based on the discipline. Students can analyze the "facts" presented in the case study to determine which of the ideas are facts, inference, and judgment. Students can use this determination to argue for or against a particular solution.

Once students are provided with a framework for this kind of reasoning, it becomes easier for them to analyze written cases more objectively and to analyze information they may read or hear as part of their everyday life.

The following are definitions provided by John Chaffee in *Thinking Critically:*

- *Reporting factual information*—describing the world in ways that can be verified through investigation.
- *Inferring*—describing the world in ways that are based on factual information yet beyond the information to make statements about what is not currently known.

• *Judging*—describing the world in ways that express our evaluation based on criteria.

A

Strategy 15
Developing Arguments

John Chaffee [pp. 384–385] also offers these definitions:

• *Argument*—a form of thinking in which certain statements (reasons) are offered in support of another statement (a conclusion).

• *Reasons*—statements that support another statement (known as a conclusion) justify it or make it more probable.

• *Conclusion*—a statement that explains, asserts, or predicts on the basis of statements (known as reasons).

Students must understand these definitions in order for them to distinguish sound reasoning from incorrect reasoning. In order for a conclusion to be correct, one must accept the reasons supporting that conclusion. If a student can identify faulty reasoning—a conclusion that doesn't logically follow from a particular set of reasons—the student can identify faulty logic. Identifying faulty logic may be an essential skill, not only in life, but on the job. Arguments often are composed of inference, not facts. By identifying certain reasons as incorrect, students can learn to make more sound decisions.

Again, the instructor can use prepared case studies and require students to debate the case study outcome, paying special attention to arguments both pro and con, and to identify faulty logic as well as conclusions based on inference, not fact.

A

Strategy 16
Uncovering Evidence

Richard Paul's book *Critical Thinking* defines evidence as "the data on which a judgment or conclusion might be based or by which proof or probability might be established" [p. 549].

Being able to seek out and identify evidence is as important to students in occupational fields as it is for students working on degrees in academic areas or employees being retrained within companies. Students need to develop a sense of obligation to discover evidence and to identify evidence to strengthen or weaken arguments for taking certain actions or adopting certain solutions, and as Paul points out, critical thinkers learn to distinguish evidence or fact from inference and are able to draw more accurate conclusions on which to base decisions.

Persons who have not learned to uncover new data or evidence often make costly decisions. Many students need to develop the ability to assess: 1) what new evidence is needed either to strengthen or refine an argument; 2) what type of evidence should be discovered; 3) where to find such evidence; and 4) how to recognize the evidence once it's found.

Case study analysis can provide opportunities for curriculum development in this area if students are required to delve beyond the case study evidence provided in a case. Group assignments can require the group to research the events pertaining to the companies or persons highlighted in the case. Groups can provide the class with an updated review of the case, including actual discussions, outcomes, and evidence developed since the case was written.

Many cases are written using only a fraction of the evidence available for review. Students can be assigned to research additional information that might affect the outcome of the case. A specific number of articles and/or other sources of supplementary material can be required in the course.

Students can be provided with resource guides to "uncovering evidence" that identify specific sources for researching various discipline-related topics. These guides can provide models for step-by-step investigation of a topic (see MOTIVATION TO LEARN, Strategy 25).

Providing updated information after students have developed their own hypotheses with evidence and arguments helps students assess their own thinking.

A, VE

Strategy 17
Using Deductive and Inductive Reasoning

Arguments can take two forms—deductive and inductive arguments. A deductive argument is "an argument form in which one reasons from premises that are known or assumed to be true to a conclusion that follows logically from these premises." Syllogisms are deductive arguments that have two supporting premises (or reasons) and a conclusion [Chaffee, p. 395]. If one accepts that the premises are true, one must accept the conclusion.

A disjunctive syllogism is one that provides an "either/or" choice to the reasons. "Either I parked my car in the back or it has been stolen. It is not in the back; it must have been stolen" [Chaffee, p. 395].

An inductive argument is an "argument form in which one reasons from premises that are known or assumed to be true to a conclusion that is supported by the premises but does not follow logically" [Chaffee, p. 412]. The premises make it "more or less probable" that the conclusion is true but the reason cannot assure that the conclusion is true.

Generalizations often reflect this kind of reasoning. A general statement is made about an entire group on the basis of an observation made on a sample of a group. It is assumed that the sample represents all of the group, which may or may not be true.

For any particular discipline, case studies can be used as the foundation for leading students through inductive/deductive reasoning with regard to controversial issues or trends. Once students hear the differences between inductive/deductive reasoning and observe the differences, they can use case study material about a particular problem or trend in a discipline using (and defining) their own reasoning approach.

A

Strategy 18
Observation Techniques

In his book *The Zen of Seeing,* Frederich Franck makes the point, "We do a lot of looking: we look through leaves, telescopes, television tubes. . . . looking is perfected everyday—but we see less and less" [p. 3]. Instructors often make assignments for adult learners to observe experiments, video cassette tapes, role playing exercises, behavior, natural phenomenon, documentaries, for example, but instructors often do not include important directions specifying what students should be looking for in their observations. Students simply have not been trained to observe. Instructors can develop a handout specific to their course that explains how to observe for a specific assignment and what kinds of observations will enhance student understanding of content material.

A marketing instructor can provide an assignment requiring students to view the top 20 advertisements produced in a given year. He or she might ask the students to look for:

- Design elements such as color, graphics, type style
- Verbal communication cues
- Nonverbal communications cues
- Type of appeal
- Suspected target market
- Use of humor
- Information provided about the product
- Casting—use of actors to present a certain type of appeal to customers

An instructor in photography might show a film to his/her students and ask them to look for:

- Framing
- Lighting direction
- Composition
- Texture

An instructor in history might show a film and ask his/her students to analyze:

- Cause and effect of events
- Tone and viewpoint of scriptwriter
- Use of effects to strengthen viewpoint

An instructor of sociology might show a film and ask his/her students to observe:

- How customs of the people in the film differ from ours
- Viewpoint and tone of scriptwriter
- Apparent status of individuals shown in film

VI, A

Strategy 19
Generalization Techniques

Many basic fundamental courses prepare students for more in-depth specialized courses to be taken later. These courses often are composed primarily of vocabulary terms, content material, and process information. An important emphasis should be placed on teaching students to generalize from large amounts of data and to make inferences from the data.

- *Generalization*—"a rule, principle, or a formula that governs or explains any number of related situations" [Costa, p. 310].
- *Inference*—"to arrive at a conclusion that evidence, facts, or admissions point toward but do not absolutely establish or draw tentative conclusions from incomplete data. Inferring is the result of making an evaluation or judgment in the absence of one or more relevant facts and requires supposition" [Costa, p. 311].

Students who have participated in a course in which the instructor used strategies to link information across disciplines should be able to apply specific knowledge to job tasks as well as specific processes to a variety of similar circumstances.

Possible Assignments

An instructor in a computer class could provide students with a number of software features and ask the students to infer which software will most appropriately satisfy the needs of the user.

An advertising instructor could provide students with a scenario pertaining to the state of the market for a certain product type and then expect students to infer what type of advertising and advertising appeal should be used.

VE, A

Strategy 20
Models to Determine Reliability of Sources

In elementary and high school, students are taught not to question the authority of the text, of their parents, or their teachers. For students to evolve into critical thinkers, they need to be given permission not only to question authority, but also to constantly judge the reliability of the sources of the information they receive, whether that information is a text, a video, newspaper, magazine article, or speaker.

To judge the reliability of the source, students should ask [Chaffee]:

- Is this person/source objective?
- What point of view does the author or source take?
- What is or was happening at the time this information was developed?
- What are the main contentions the author is trying to convey?
- What evidence supports these contentions? Do you agree with the evidence? Why or why not?
- Do you think anything in the evidence is misrepresented or false?
- Based on your assessment of the evidence, do you agree with the contention? Why or why not?

VI, VE, A

Strategy 21
Seeking and Analyzing Information

When a student encounters what appears to be a false assumption or a piece of information based on an assumption that is not complete, he or she should learn to identify the information as an assumption and analyze additional information that can either verify the assumption, refute the assumption, or at least provide additional input that can be used in making judgments concerning the assumption.

Instructors can encourage students to screen out assumptions in several ways:

- Ask students to write out their reasons for accepting or rejecting a conclusion.
- Provide students with extra credit when they screen out and analyze additional information as evidenced by filling out a form created by the instructor that highlights evidence discovered, analyses undertaken, and conclusions drawn.
- Provide extra credit for students who seek out, analyze, and either prove or disprove assertions in the text.
- Provide an assignment to students in which they choose an assertion in the text and then provide two articles that reflect and support the assertion. The important consideration is to have two opposing viewpoints.

VE, A

Strategy 22
Open-Ended Essay Exams

Students in community colleges and universities are being trained to go into the workforce to hold entry-level, semi-skilled, and skilled jobs.

To prepare them for the kind of thinking and problem solving that will be required on the job, instructors should develop open-ended essay exams for the particular discipline instead of traditional multiple choice exams.

Open-ended questions require more thinking from the student because they force the student to make the following decisions:

- What content material have I learned that is relevant to this situation/problem?
- Which facts and ideas are most important?
- What is the best method of organizing this material?
- What elements should I begin and end with?
- How do I build my arguments to be convincing?

Every open-ended essay question forces students to think because essay answers require them to provide ideas that must be carefully thought through. Constructing essay questions should go beyond mere recognition and require students to compare and contrast, evaluate, authenticate, assess, agree or disagree, and make predictions about the future.

VE, A

Strategy 23
Exams with Reasons

For many instructors, it may still seem easier to develop objective exams (at least from the standpoint of scoring). Objective exams can become tools for learning if instructors go beyond the usual multiple choice response by requiring students to explain their response by giving reasons why each alphanumeric answer was chosen over others.

The instructor inserts a blank comment line after each answer and requires students to write in the thought processes they used to choose a particular answer. This kind of exam requires much more grading time because the answer may often be incorrect but the student's explanation gives merit to the answer and deserves to be scored as correct. On the other hand, students may have correct answers, but have no identifiable justification for their choice or have an incorrect explanation.

These tests can become excellent learning tools, however, because they force students to think and to articulate their thinking processes. They show the instructor the reasoning processes the students used to arrive at their answers. In some cases, this method of testing may even identify questions that are ambiguous and poorly written. Asking students to identify reasons will also eliminate guessing.

VE, A

Strategy 24
Performance Testing

When appropriate to the discipline, instructors can develop a system of performance testing to assure not only basic knowledge and understanding of key concepts, but also the ability to actually perform skills to the extent that entry-level employers would be satisfied with the students' performance.

To develop such a performance test system, the instructor must take exceptional care to choose skills that are representative of the kinds of skills most often required on the job. For some disciplines such as emergency medical technology or auto mechanics, skills can be easily defined. For others such as commercial art, desktop publishing, marketing or management, the skills required are much more difficult to identify. The instructor may need to develop some type of research instrument such as a questionnaire to pinpoint the top 10 to 15 skills required by the majority of individual entry-level jobs.

Specific curricula can be rewritten so that the content material is clustered around certain job skills. The culmination of the learning is not a paper and pencil exam but a performance of those job skills.

For example, the following skills might be identified as important skills for an entry-level marketing employee in a typical job in advertising:

1. Ability to write reports.
2. Ability to compare media by cost per thousand.
3. Ability to communicate verbally to clients and other employees.
4. Ability to select media and appeal pertaining to client's situation.
5. Ability to analyze client's situations.
6. Ability to research information pertaining to client's situation.

7. Ability to develop and write a proposed plan to assist client with advertising.

8. Ability to use sales skills to convince client to adopt proposal.

9. Ability to schedule activities in order to meet deadlines.

Many more skills may be defined. Once these skills have been identified, the instructor can rearrange the textual material to support the practice of each skill. For example, to test skills 2 through 8, the information pertaining to selection of media in the text as well as popular studies and literature such as *Ogilvy On Advertising* can be used to support a culmination of the process—a written plan by the student pertaining to a real client such as a important not-for-profit group.

To test skills 1, 3, 4, and 10, students can be required to write a report on the progress made with their clients, to work as teams, and record their team efforts daily, and to write the appropriate letters and proposals to their real clients as necessary.

To test skill 9, students can be required to provide a sales presentation to their client in front of the instructor and other students. The students will have the unique experience of presenting a real presentation, answering a real client's questions, persuading people in a real-life situation, making necessary adjustments, revising their work, and then presenting it again.

The important point is that reading the content material from an advertising text will not prepare students for performing higher level thinking skills and performance skills. Their instructors must revise curricula to provide for learning experiences and then performance tests. No multiple choice or even short answer essay test can prove to a student (or an employer) that the student has ability. Only a performance test (or learning activity) can do that.

VE, A, DE, SE

Strategy 25
Multiple Answers Tests

In many work situations, as well as life situations, there may be many possible solutions to a given problem. One of the fallacies of our educational system is the continual emphasis placed on having right (vs. wrong) answers.

On the job, most employers are not faced with problems that can be easily identified as having right answers. Most, in fact, are faced with problems for which there are many right solutions and the trick is to develop the solution that is most appropriate, given the time limitations, resources of the company, and skills of the people involved.

Therefore, for many disciplines, students may benefit from the development of tests that provide students the opportunity to create and analyze multiple solutions, give pros and cons for each, and then select the one most appropriate for the situation.

As with open-ended essay exams, these tests can often be developed from already available case study material provided by publishers. To be effective, instructors should require students to develop a certain preset number of multiple solutions, such as three or five. This gives students practice in creative thinking as well as critical thinking.

For example, a photography instructor might provide students with a case study problem involving a room that has available light and ask students to generate solutions as to how a particular photograph might be taken without a flash.

Possible answers are:

1. Slow the shutter speed
2. Open other windows/drapes for more light
3. Use faster film
4. Use different aperture
5. Move subject outdoors

The student would then be asked to provide pros and cons for each solution and to choose the most appropriate solution based on those pros and cons.

Even a subject like biology or sociology can use this method. The sciences can ask for different approaches to *expressing* the relationships. In biology, an instructor might ask a student to graphically express how the photosynthesis process works. There may be several ways to represent the process. The student will have to know the content material (facts about photosynthesis) to complete this, but will also have to think through several ways of expressing what he/she does know.

For a sociology class, the instructor can set up examples of human behavior such as the caste system in India and ask students to develop at least three theories about how this system developed through society. These various theories can be discussed and evaluated in light of what the social scientists believe caused the caste system.

This testing method, like others that require a great deal of student thought, is subjective in terms of grading. The judgment of the instructor will play a major role in the grading; however, the advantage to the student far outweighs that disadvantage.

A

Strategy 26
Thinking Journal

In order to improve thinking, students need to become aware of their own thinking processes and their approaches to problem solving, decision making, and creative thinking. The metacognitive aspects can be taught as items to be understood, but new methods can be more effective when the instructor asks students to think about their own thinking process by writing a journal tracing their thought processes for specific assigned case studies, problems, and issues. Students can begin to see patterns in their thinking approaches that can help them analyze their strengths and weaknesses in thinking.

For a 16-week course, a 15-entry journal can be required as an assignment. The instructor may ask for journal entries in six to eight assignments in class, and two to nine outside assignments, as well as three thinking activities required by instructors of classes in other disciplines or on the job.

The instructor should provide a sample entry to the students at the beginning of the assignment so that students can be made aware of the methods for recording thinking processes, the kinds of information required, and the specific activities the instructor would like recorded.

Two example journal entries follow.

Example 1

8 Feb. 1991. Media Planning Assignment. I was asked to develop a media plan for a cigarette company that sells low tar cigarettes. Because I was given no information other than the company is targeting hispanic males, my first step was to research media and advertising in the cigarette market. I found out that cigarette companies can only advertise in print publications and outdoor billboards. Once I found out this information, I decided to use Spanish language publications directed at males as well as a high percentage of outdoor billboards located in hispanic communities.

Example 2

8 Feb. 1991. Resume Writing Assignment. I was asked to write my own resume and then to use computer graphics to do a professional layout for printing. My first step was to locate an example of a resume I liked and which my source *Resume Writing* (author's note: fictitious source) deemed an effective resume for obtaining employment. My choice was a chronological resume because I think (from experience) that more employers take an interviewer seriously with a chronological resume. In fact, I have heard that a functional resume may automatically mean that a person will not get an interview. Anyway, after I located an example, I looked up the exact dates I started and ended each of my jobs and then I wrote short descriptions of my responsibilities. I used a format example given to me by my instructor. It included such things as hobbies, achievements, and organizations. I included them and then looked up the awards I couldn't remember. Once I had a draft, I typed the whole resume in the computer. I did not take time to choose fonts and type styles as I wanted to see what it looked like in type. Once it was inputted, I edited it for grammar and style, and then I went back and chose Geneva type and used different type styles, such as bold, and type sizes to organize it so it was easy to read. I had to edit it further in order to keep it to one page (which the author of *Resume Writing* said was a must). I printed it out on the laser printer and reproofed it because I often see mistakes on the printed page which I don't see on the computer screen and corrected two items and reprinted it. I turned it in on Tuesday.

The journal entries above might be reviewed in class. The student would be asked to highlight statements where he/she make assumptions and then decide if he/she put enough thought into adopting those assumptions. A thinking journal can be a wonderful self-motivating and learning tool for students if it becomes a welcome and enjoyable part of their assignments for a class. By scrutinizing their own thought processes over time, students can learn to adjust their approaches to certain thinking problems and develop more successful solutions.

VE, A

Strategy 27
Thinking Maps

Throughout much of the 1900s, the main organizational tool for thinking has been the outline. The use of Roman numerals and Arabic numericals in a certain sequence was practically the only way to organize detailed content information or ideas for the development of a piece of written work. As our society becomes more and more influenced by technology and communications, educators are realizing that many adults are visual learners.

The organization of material in such systematic methods as outlining makes the task of learning more difficult for visual learners because it requires extensive preorganization and because it does not inherently connect ideas, it merely places them in a conformed sequence.

In *Thinking Critically,* John Chaffee outlines a process for developing "Thinking Maps" [pp. 251–252]. A thinking map requires the student to identify main ideas and then to determine the relationship of these ideas to other ideas. Information that supports these main ideas is shown as "Side Streets" connected to, but smaller than, main ideas.

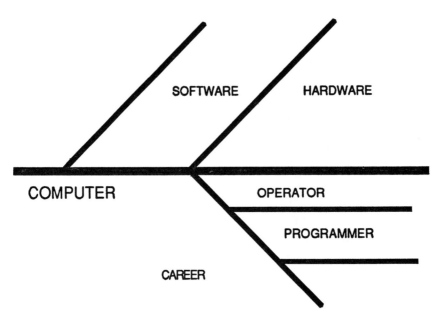

An example of a Thinking Map.

The implications are that this kind of mind mapping allows visual students to relate concepts visually and therefore to ease recall. It provides a step that the outlining method does not. It makes students see more clearly how ideas or even sections of ideas are related. It's an easy approach to teach and can be very beneficial for students in composition and other highly creative disciplines as well as disciplines like science and computer programming.

VI, A

Strategy 28
Thinking Skills Related to the Discipline

Each separate discipline may require a vastly different set of thinking skills. To develop activities appropriate for skills required within a particular discipline, the instructor should conduct preliminary research to determine *exactly* the skills that need to be practiced. This research can take the form of a questionnaire to local businesses. The questionnaire should try to identify specific job types for the discipline as well as the skills required for those job types. Ideally a questionnaire should be collected from at least 300 representatives to be truly indicative of how the majority of entry-level employees will be challenged on a job and the thinking skills most useful to them.

VE, A

Strategy 29
Research in Learning

From grade school to high school, students are told to be inquisitive in reading and listening. "If you don't know the meaning of a word, look it up." But, students often do not look up the words. They infer the meaning from the context. When students do not take care in being precise with language, they do not truly understand what they are reading and do not comprehend the precise meanings of important terms. To encourage students to be precise in their written communication as well as thinking skills, instructors can use the Socratic method and call on students to provide definitions from assignments and materials. In addition, students can be encouraged to write and organize their own glossary of new terms in the back of their thinking journal (see Strategy 26).

In any case, requiring students to research and precisely define unknown terms can encourage students to think more effectively throughout their collegiate careers and on the job.

VE, A

Strategy 30
Facilitation Instead of Teaching

In the past, many instructors enjoyed having and keeping control of the classroom by choosing assignments to be given, choosing grading systems, and controlling discussions. Today, however, research indicates that adult learners are much more likely to learn if the instructor takes the role of facilitator instead of traditional teacher.

To be a facilitator, the instructor would allow student to have more choices over the material covered, over the method of presentation, and the weights of specific assignments. The method used for students to learn a specific kind of material can be left open for student input.

The instructor would devise a series of learning experiences that students would accomplish either individually or in groups. The emphasis would be on students accomplishing these experiences (some of which they will have chosen). Instead of the teacher taking the most active role; that is, as lecturer, students would begin to take on a more active role and the teacher would act as coach/advisor. The instructor would provide materials, assignments, and questions to "prompt" thinking and accelerate learning of the skills necessary to do the job in a particular discipline.

Examples of the teacher acting as facilitator are:

1. The instructor assigns the material and has each group present it.

2. The instructor develops group projects and the groups report results.

3. The instructor uses panel discussion.

4. The instructor uses Socratic method and asks individual students to take the role of facilitator and lead discussion.

VE, A

Strategy 31
Decision-Making Skills

Entry-level jobs require a high degree of decision-making skills on the part of the entry-level employee. The instructor should look for opportunities to infuse decision-making skills training into the curriculum. Decision-making skills should be taught in the context of the disciplines involved (marketing, history, sociology, etc.) because the risks involved in making incorrect decisions in certain disciplines, such as emergency medical technology, are much greater than in other disciplines.

While many different formal approaches may be taught to make specific decisions, most follow a format such as:

1. What is the problem? Or what is the decision to be made?
2. What is the situation that has created this problem or the need for this decision?
   - What are the facts, issues, implications, constraints?
   - What do we know about the situation?
3. Based on the situation (#2) what are the options or solutions?
   - What are the pros and cons of each?
   - What are the future implications of each?
4. Based on our analysis of what is possible do we
   - have enough information to make a decision?
   - or do we need more information to make a decision?
5. What would the best solution be?
6. What actions should be taken?
7. What results might be expected based on actions in #6?
8. What future trends or implications can we predict if we take the course of action in #5?

For any particular discipline, the instructor can develop a decision-making format that outlines possible decision-making approaches to the course.

Math

1. What is the instructor asking you to find?
2. What information have you already been given that you can use to find the answer?
3. Which facts are important and/or usable?

4. Which facts are not really important in finding the answer?
5. Do you know any formulas or algorithms that will help you find the answer?
6. How can you derive what you need from the information you have to get the answer?

Management

1. What is the decision you are being asked to make?
2. Why are you being asked to make it?
3. What factors of production (human resources, capital, information) will be needed to implement any solution?
4. What are several possible solutions?
5. How will they be influenced by factors of production?
6. How will factors of production influence operations?
7. Which solution is best, based on efficient and effective use of factors of production?

VE, A

Strategy 32
Identifying Fallacies in Thinking

Students need to be able to identify when conclusions are being made based on faulty or incorrect premises. Courses of formal logic teach students to identify the grounds involved in making an argument, along with the warrant (assumption without which there is no argument) that provides the foundation for that argument. Warrants for arguments must be solidly backed with proof based in fact, or the warrant is false; therefore, the argument is false. These courses also teach students to identify syllogisms that set up an "if a, then b" scenario. A syllogism starts with a major premise that is developed as it relates to a minor premise and the relationship of the two creates a generalization that is compelled (or must be) because of the two premises.

An example of a correct syllogism is:

If all faculty must schedule two office hours in the building and I am a faculty member, then I must schedule two office hours in the building.

An example of an incorrect syllogism is:

If Jane is blonde and Jane is a good secretary, then secretaries need to be blonde to be good secretaries.

Syllogisms must be painstakingly analyzed to assure that their logic is correct.

Other fallacies of thinking include [Mayfield, pp. 252–257]:

- **Generalizing too quickly**—coming to a conclusion without studying the facts.
- **Assuming an either/or posture**—assuming there are two and only two choices.
- **Unprovable statistics**—using statistics as an authority when they are not proven, are assumed, or when the methods of developing those statistics are unknown.
- **Contradictions**—failing to identify and rectify contradictions in an argument.
- **Loaded questions**—using questions that are worded with a negative persuasive element that make a person want to adopt the point of view or reject it.
- **False analogies**—using analogies that are so loosely constructed they do not really represent the relationships the arguer claims they do.
- **False cause**—assuming two events are connected though they cannot be connected reasonably.
- **Domino theory**—assuming if one accepts one premise, one must accept another; if one event occurs another event must follow.
- **No exception generalization**—assuming a generalization is true and that it can have no exceptions.
- **Misapplication of wise sayings**—using a wise saying in a context that is unrelated to support personal opinion.
- **Assertion of conclusion**—reasserting a conclusion as if it were an explanation.
- **Ambiguity**—using arguments that contain words that are unclear.
- **Euphemisms**—using inoffensive words that distort truth and meaning.
- **Equivocation**—drawing an unwarranted conclusion because the wording of the premises has shifted the meaning of the premise subtly.
- **Slanted language**—using highly emotional words to persuade.
- **Appeal to authority**—using appeals to authority to make the opponent lose confidence in his/her own judgment by deferring to someone else's.
- **Appeal to popularity**—arguing that something is right because it is popular.

- **Halo effect**—arguing for or against something by crediting or discrediting the total viewpoints of a source.
- **Red herring**—throwing someone off the point of logic by diverting them.
- **Pointing to another wrong**—assuming "two wrongs make a right."

Students can be asked to identify conclusions that other students, instructors, or writers have made and then to "mindmap" the premises or evidence that support those conclusions. While students may not have completed a course in formal logic, exercises within the discipline will help them practice identifying faulty assumptions and conclusions in their reading, writing, and testing.

VE, A

Strategy 33
Practice Analysis

Some disciplines may place more emphasis on analysis of case studies and problems than others. For example, the analysis of problems is so crucial to architecture that schools of architecture generally offer courses specifically devoted to analysis techniques in problem solving. In marketing, management, and other disciplines, the ability to take a situation or circumstance and break it into parts (and see how those parts relate to a whole) is increasingly important in being able to do the job.

An excellent source in developing exercises to provide practice in breaking situations into different parts (analysis) is the use of written case studies or real-client case studies. The written case study provides instructors and students with a limited amount of data for the student to dissect and classify. The benefit of using a written case study provided by publishers of textual materials is that this is an agreed on "solution" or model of the analysis provided by the scholars of the text. This solution may make the instructor feel more comfortable in introductory material and may provide students with satisfaction for having approximated the solution.

More advantageous to the learning process of analysis is the use of the real-client case study in which a real organization works in partnership with the institution and "allows" students to analyze its situations and develop a situational analysis. No matter what discipline is involved—commercial art, photography, marketing, or agriculture, the real-client approach provides students with practical perspectives and information to analyze in a real-world setting. Having to dig through facts involved in real situations is much more difficult than analyzing a neatly composed and organized written case study. This provides students with the experience they need for entry-level positions.

A

Strategy 34
Separating Problems from Issues

When confronted with a "problem," which can come in the form of a situation to be analyzed, a case study, or some other formal problem, students need to be able to recognize the differences between the problem itself and issues related to that problem. Newspapers and magazines (including trade publications) can be effective tools for teaching students how to differentiate problems from the issues related to those problems. Articles that identify situations in a discipline and discuss those situations can be excellent material. The instructor provides students with reprints of the articles and then asks students to identify the underlying or major problem as well as the issues related to it.

Students can develop this skill in group activity format or individual format. Mindmapping (see Strategy 27) can be used to graphically express the relationships between the issues and the problem. The exercise can be taken one step further by asking students to identify how the issues relate to the problem and how different scenarios based on issues would improve the situation or worsen it.

A

Strategy 35
Causal Theory

This strategy is similar to Strategy 34 in that the instructor can use a variety of media (text, case studies, articles, videotapes) to present methods for identifying and analyzing possible causes for problems, events, or situations. For many work environments, the ability to analyze information and to develop theories about the possible causes is a highly valued element. Many industries have entire departments for "troubleshooting" or "debugging."

For this strategy, the instructor uses a problem defined in a case study, article, or other medium, and asks students to 1) identify all possible causes for the situation, using terminology and issues related to the discipline; 2) analyze the situation to come up with a judgment on which possible cause is the most likely cause; and 3) develop hypothetical solutions to alleviate the problem.

Although this strategy is similar to Strategy 36, the skill being developed is more transferable—defining and analyzing possible causes. This strategy seeks to provide practice in recognizing causes and strengthening students' abilities to generate multiple ideas for causes and to identify causal relationships.

In *Thinking for Yourself* [pp. 242–244], Maryls Mayfield identifies several flaws of thinking associated with the identification of causes:

- **False cause**—identifying a causal relationship between two events which cannot be related. "Everyone who has cancer has eaten pickles; therefore, pickles cause cancer."
- **Domino cause**—assuming that one event must always cause another event to occur. "If democracy comes to the Soviet Union, Red China must follow."

VE, A

Strategy 36
Case Studies

Many two-year and four-year colleges are beginning to use case study methods more extensively to teach practical applications in areas such as business administration, premedicine, and law. Case studies can be used quite effectively, if the instructor takes time to develop a guide for the students in how to develop a case study analysis. Cases can be taken from written cases developed into the text (usually with several questions for students) or through stand alone written cases or computer cases. The instructor can also develop his/her own case study materials, gleaned from articles and information about the subject.

Using case study materials with predeveloped questions may be easier for the instructor, but may not provide real experience in analysis for students because the questions are already developed for them. An important workplace skill is to be able to *identify the important questions and issues of a case.* The case study method may actually be more effective if students are given only the case material (in whatever form—text, video, article) and then are asked to generate a list (individually or in a group) of the questions that should come to mind as well as the issues involved. When students have to generate their own lists of questions, they will begin to understand how difficult it is to analyze a problem from outside an academic area. (Often, the predeveloped questions are so transparent they do the major abstract thinking for the students by giving away too much information that students should learn to identify.)

Guide for Analyzing Case Studies

1. Identify what appears to be the main problem.
2. Identify other problems that influence the main problem.
3. Identify issues that relate to all problems.
4. Identify possible causes for problems (see Strategy 35).
5. Identify evidence or facts from the case that relate to possible causes.
6. Develop hypotheses about causes of problems.
7. Test hypothesis using evidence and theories.
8. Make a judgment on most likely causes.
9. Develop possible solutions for each problem based on theoretical cause and also possible solutions.
10. Study each possible solution and forecast effects of solution on future situation.
11. Develop solution scenario for resolving the problem.
12. Develop detailed solution.
13. Document your thinking process.
14. Write final case study analysis with recommended solution(s).

This guide can be used to give students direction for identifying problems and issues on their own and then they can use the case study information to think through possible causes and solutions and their effects. It provides for decision making as well because the student makes decisions on issues, causes, and solutions. It provides the student with more real world practice in solving problems.

VE, A

Strategy 37
Identifying Points of View

This strategy uses media such as articles in trade publications, newspapers, consumer publications, videotapes, and audiotapes to help students learn to identify points of view and to think through the perspectives of sources with specific points of view. Students need to think through which point of view an author seems to take on an issue and then to identify reasons for that point of view, possible actions the author wants the reader to take, possible attitudes the author wants the reader to adopt, as well as how the point of view adopted by the author might cloud the information presented. Even the authors of texts write from certain points of view and their materials are presented differently based on those points of view.

For this strategy, the instructor would identify a source of information related to the discipline and then ask students to answer questions such as the following:

1. What is a one-paragraph summary of the article, video, etc.?
2. What is the major point the author seems to be making?
3. From the language used and the syntax, can you identify a specific point of view the author is taking?
4. Why would the author take this point of view?
5. Does the author appear to want you to believe something specific about this information?
6. Does the author appear to want you to do something specific with this information?
7. Can you identify any motives for the author to want you to believe or do a specific thing?
8. Do you think an author with this point of view is reliable?
9. Is this author objective? Does he/she make reference to points of view that are opposite his/hers?
10. Based on his/her point of view and objectivity in providing information, do you accept the information?

The answers to these questions will help students judge whether certain types of sources can be considered a reliable base for decisions.

Another way to use this strategy is to provide materials that offer two opposing viewpoints and have students answer the set of questions about each source. Students then have to decide which of the opposing viewpoints they deem more reliable and why.

Identifying points of view is important in developing overall critical thinking skills because so much of what students are exposed to as citizens, as students, and as employees is subtly biased information and is not reliable information on which to base decisions.

VE, A

Strategy 38
Letters to the Editor

This strategy involves having students think through issues involved in the discipline and then asking them to express their opinions on those issues. Students are required not only to analyze the situation in terms of issues, but also to decide their own opinions and to express those opinions.

The instructor identifies several journals that relate to the field and asks students to read them, looking for issues. Students are required to bring an article to class and to analyze (see Strategy 37). Once the articles are analyzed, the instructor requires students to write to the editors of the publications involved and express either a positive or negative opinion of the article (or issue) discussed.

The instructor would evaluate the thinking process apparent in the letter and require students to actually mail the letters. Any letters to the editor that are published could be highlighted during the semester.

This strategy forces students to begin to analyze and develop opinions and to express those opinions. Students who do not take journalistic writing or formal essay writing may never be asked to form and communicate an original opinion in their entire scholastic careers.

VE, I, LC, SC

Strategy 39
Defining Problem Scope

For case studies as well as individual and group projects, an activity to define the scope of a problem can be very valuable. Defining the scope of the problem requires analysis of causes of the problem as well as a definition of the extent of the problem. Case study texts can often be used for foundation material, as well as interviews with mentors from companies in the industry.

The instructor would require a written report or brief similar to that of a regular case study, but would also require a special section to be written that would highlight the "scope of the problem." This section would be a brief analysis of the size of the problem, far-reaching effects of the problem, and extent of the solution necessary to solve the problem. An exercise such as this can be valuable in helping students to think through problems and solutions. In disciplines such as marketing, architecture, engineering, creative writing, photography, electronics, CAD, commercial art, and even archeology, the ability to analyze the situation and develop a problem definition can be a great asset. Much of the work of engineers, architects, lawyers (and many others) is based on how these professionals define problems.

VE, A

Strategy 40
Organizing Data

An important part of thinking critically is developing the ability to take a wealth of evidence and to organize the data so that relationships between the data can be discovered. There are many methods for organizing such as mindmapping, making formal outlines, and using idea cards that can be rearranged. An overabundance of data (that relates to a specific decision) can be overwhelming to a fledging decision maker and critical thinker. Giving students mental tools for putting highly diverse data into some kind of order will help them learn to make decisions based on evidence rather than intuition (which is often the case when students give up on using information because there is just so much they cannot organize it into meaningful input).

This exercise is much like a puzzle. The instructor uses a formal case study (such as one that would come with a text) but takes each segment of information (or each distinguishable piece) and puts it on a separate card. When finished, there should be approximately 200 pieces of information. Students are divided into groups and then are required to reorganize the information so that it is meaningful. Each group is required to organize the information so it makes sense, analyze the case, and then write up a brief on the case. This organization can be done in outline form or mindmap. The key point is that students have to organize data so that, placed together, different pieces of information mean something to the case.

A, I, LC, SC, SE

CHAPTER EIGHT

CLASSROOM STRATEGIES FOR CAREER DEVELOPMENT

1. Resume
2. Portfolio
3. Mentor Program
4. Code of Work Ethics
5. Research State of Industry
6. Interview with Personnel Director
7. Interview with Person in Industry
8. Research Project to Predict Trends
9. Job Description
10. Five- and Ten-Year Career Plans
11. One-Year Career Plan
12. Cover Letter
13. Analysis of Job Ads
14. Day at Work
15. Job Interview
16. Role Play for a Job Interview
17. Confidence Builder Essay
18. Successful Image Video
19. Internship
20. Cooperative Education
21. Mini Report of Top Ten Career Choices
22. Panel Discussion
23. Mini Report on Government Jobs
24. Employment Agency Presentation
25. Career Strengths and Weaknesses
26. Interest Essay
27. Video Profile of a Profession
28. Career Game
29. Research of Top Three Professionals
30. Visualization of Success
31. Bibliography of Career Titles
32. Abstracts of Career Articles
33. Job Evaluation Form
34. Career Survey
35. Self-Esteem Tape
36. Definition of Success
37. Success Notebook
38. Reference Sheet
39. Project Sheets
40. Guest Speaker

The importance of learning to develop and manage one's career cannot be overemphasized. The academic and training community may train individuals to have knowledge and concepts, to accomplish a certain task, to be able to do a series of tasks that make up a job, but if the individual does not understand the dynamics of the employment marketplace and the importance of self direction for a long-term career, he or she may not be successful in his or her career. The majority of key issues involved in managing a career are not being taught at all in secondary and post secondary institutions except in business curricula. Counselors or placement professionals train students in techniques for getting and keeping jobs, but because students usually spend very little time with counselors, they do not usually get a broad enough background in this area.

Important issues such as how to get a job, how to write a resume, how to dress for an interview, how to find out what is available in the field, how to plan one's career, and how to motivate oneself need to be addressed in the classroom. These skills will help students learn to plan and to direct their own futures.

The strategies outlined in this chapter may be more difficult to integrate into a content-oriented course (which is not a business course), but the benefits to the student of doing so far outweigh the effort. Most of the strategies involve developing self-directed planning skills (such as the five-year plan, one-year plan, ten-year plan); increasing self-esteem (such as the success notebook, definition of success, and confidence builder); or the mechanics of getting and keeping a job (such as resume writing, interviewing techniques, techniques for dressing appropriately for the discipline, and analysis of job ads.)

These strategies are crucial to the success of future employees. While it may seem that an instructor has to stretch his/her time allotment to fit these strategies into a course (unlike Communication, Teamwork, and Leadership strategies that fall easily into a course), it is imperative that students begin to have this kind of experiential training before they leave the classroom. Even one strategy per course will better prepare students for the tough task of obtaining and maintaining a job. If the instructor is hesitant to take up class time on assignments not related specifically to the discipline, he/she can make these homework assignments or assignments out of class for a certain number of participation points. Even using a quarter of one class period to discuss career development (and key issues of career development for a specific discipline) will benefit the student. No matter what the instructor is teaching—mathematics, chemistry, psychology, history, auto mechanics, marketing, or computer-aided drafting—the instructor is preparing the student for future employment at some point.

Strategy 1
Resume

Students can learn to write and use resumes even if they never attend a formal class in how to manage their careers. Students in any occupational/vocational program can be asked to develop a one-page resume that should cover the following areas in a similar format.

	Name **Street** **City, State, Zip** **Home Phone** **Other Phone**
Employment	

(last first—only go back 10 years)	
From–To	Company name, Job title (brief description of duties and responsibilities)
From–To	Company name, Job title (brief description of duties and responsibilities)
From–To	Company name, Job title (brief description of duties and responsibilities)
Education	Degree (latest)
	Degree (first)
	High school
	Technical schools
	Military schools
Special	
Accomplishments	Name and dates of awards (up to 10 years old)
Memberships	Professional groups
	Civic groups
	Other groups
References	Available on request

This assignment can be invaluable to students who have never been required to develop a resume. They will have a current resume to share with mentors, potential employers, and others as well as a format to use later in their job searches.

I, SE

Strategy 2
Portfolio

The use of a portfolio to showcase their work and abilities is familiar to many students in the commercial art, fashion design, and photography fields. The portfolio approach can also work well for many other situations: data processing, management, marketing, electronics, geophysics, fashion design, merchandising, and business careers.

This assignment can be given as a major project for a semester course. Students can use the following guidelines to develop a suitable portfolio.

Guidelines for developing a portfolio

Step 1. Look through your projects in all of your classes. Identify those projects you are particularly proud of even if you did not get an "A." Identify any special letters of appraisal or recommendation you are proud of. Identify any piece of work that you think is exceptional, thorough, analytical, creative, or original.

Step 2. Retype any projects as necessary to remove any comments or other marks that might be distracting to a potential employer.

Step 3. Keep letters intact and in original form. Ask instructors, mentors, and others to write letters of recommendation for you.

Step 4. Mount any loose items on colored paper or some sort of protector.

Step 5. Put all projects (not letters) in order starting with the most impressive piece of work first. Put other items together in categories.

Step 6. Put letters in order starting with most impressive first.

Step 7. Put award certificates, etc., in order starting with most impressive first.

Step 8. Design a cover page with your name, address, phone, and the title "portfolio." (It is impressive to have this cover page produced using desktop publishing.)

Step   9. Purchase a small or medium portfolio case from the local art or business supply store.

Step 10. Insert items in order. (You may have to rethink choices depending on the capacity of your portfolio. You can purchase refills. Also, large portfolios are cumbersome and tend to make potential applicants appear clumsy).

The instructor can require such a portfolio as an adjunct project for a class in almost any discipline. This strategy will benefit students in several ways. It will provide them with the opportunity to research their backgrounds to discover those projects they accomplished particularly well (which they may have forgotten about). This should be self-esteem enhancing in any case. In addition, the assignment will be an excellent catalyst for them to use in getting formal letters of recommendation from mentors, professors, and others. The project will also provide them with a reason to review awards, letters of appreciation, and other accomplishments, and will give them a reason to organize all of these accomplishments for someone to review.

Evaluation of such a project must be subjective. The instructor should keep evaluation criteria limited to such requirements as:

• Organization
• Clarity
• Pleasing appearance

This means that the instructor should not make evaluative comments about the content of the portfolio unless the comment is to indicate exceptionally impressive referrals. No evaluation of the materials should be conducted. Students may have had varying opportunities for producing materials to include in a portfolio.

I, SE

Strategy 3
Mentor Program

This strategy is similar to the mentor program discussed under Leadership. In this case, however, the instructor would identify a group of mentors from the industry and assign from three or four students to work with each mentor. (If there are plenty of willing mentors, a one-to-one ratio is fine).

The mentor's role would be to assist students by answering questions such as:

1. How does one go about getting a job in the field?
2. What skills are most important?
3. What experience will employers of entry-level personnel likely require?
4. How does one find out about openings? Are they advertised or is it basically word of mouth?
5. What are the most important personal attributes one should have to excel in the field?
6. What is the mentor's opinion of the student's resume? Recommendations?
7. What is the mentor's opinion of the student's portfolio? Recommendations?
8. What is a typical work schedule?
9. What kind of salary can be expected at entry level? Year 1? Year 5? Year 10? Year 20?
10. What is a typical career pattern for someone in the field?
11. What are the top ten companies?
12. Does the mentor know if any companies are hiring?
13. Is recruitment from college recruiters unlikely?
14. What is typical dress?
15. What is the one most important piece of advice the mentor would share with the student?

This strategy assists students by providing their first networking contact within their field. The advice they get from a mentor can help shape their whole future. Not only can they receive highly practical, knowledgeable advice from someone who has a job similar to the type of job they're looking for, but they also have a personal contact to help them make connections with others in the field.

This strategy requires the instructor to seek out and develop contacts in a specific industry and to screen those contacts carefully to be sure that people are identified who truly want to be mentors. (A poor experience with a mentor could shatter a student's self-esteem).

I, SE

Strategy 4
Code of Work Ethics

For this strategy, students are required to write a two-page personal code of work ethics covering issues such as:

- Personal attitudes toward work
- Importance of reputation
- Integrity
- Attitude toward tardiness
- Attitude toward ethics
- Attitude toward on-the-job crime (larceny, perquisites, expense account abuse, bribery)
- Being a conscientious worker
- Loyalty to organization
- Substance abuse
- Morality

This assignment requires students to explore ethics and develop the rules they want to work by, that is, to develop their own work standards by which to live. The papers should be shared with the class as a whole so that students can get a sense of the differing points of view. The various points of view may actually serve as a catalyst for the revision of the ethics codes. The ethics codes can be added to the portfolio (see Strategy 2) and given for review to the mentor (see Strategy 3).

I, SE

Strategy 5
Research Project on the Current State of Industry

This research report involves assigning students the task of developing a full-length (10- to 20-page) report on the industry in which they want to be employed using secondary and primary data. The purpose of the report is to provide students information about their future area of employment. Some of the key areas for which students should obtain information are:

1. Amount of annual business in terms of dollars
2. Major industrial/organizational mission

3. Major competitors
4. Major competitors' market share
5. Major competitors' operational sites
6. Types of persons employed
7. Major processes involved
8. Current salaries of employees
9. Annual report data
10. Long-range forecast for employment

This project gives students an understanding of the state of the industry they want to be employed in. It can be evaluated similarly to any other research project (see Communication).

A, SE, P, I

Strategy 6
Interview with Personnel Director

For this strategy, students are required to identify a personnel director or manager with a firm that could possibly hire them and to interview that director about hiring procedures and practices in their industry.

It is important that the student use this as a general interview. Students are much more likely to get good information from the personnel director if he/she knows the information is general in nature and will be used in a class (and does not believe the student is trying to get hired from the interview).

Students can ask questions such as:

1. How many applicants are there per entry-level job?
2. What is a personnel reviewer looking for on the resume of a potential entry-level employee?
3. What kind of resume does the manager prefer in terms of format?
4. If someone has applied for a job, what does the manager see as appropriate behavior for following up?
5. What key positive and negative behaviors do the interviewers look for?
6. What key positive and negative nonverbal indicators do interviewers look for?
7. What is the manager's advice on the problem of having no experience? What can make up for a lack of experience?

8. What does the manager think are the most important skills necessary for the kind of work the student wants to do? Why?
9. What kind of salaries can be expected at the entry level? Year 1? Year 5? Year 10?
10. What is the best piece of advice the manager would give to anyone in the field?

This strategy (like Strategy 3) provides the student with a networking contact in the field. It provides a different perspective, though. The "gatekeepers" of jobs in most companies are in personnel. The personnel staff people often have differing views about how people are hired. They know the statistics involved in hiring and often look very objectively at resumes to decide who gets an interview and who does not. Obtaining information from a personnel director's or manager's viewpoint can be useful in teaching students how to progress past the gatekeepers in personnel. This can show students what items to include (and leave out) of a resume, how to dress for an interview, how to use verbal and nonverbal communication to make a good impression, as well as other important factors involved in finding a career position.

I, SE, VE, P

Strategy 7
Interview with Person in Industry

Similar to Strategy 3 and Strategy 6, this strategy requires students to identify a person from the industry he/she wants to work in and to interview that person about the industry. This strategy is similar to Strategy 3 but the interviewee in this case has not been identified by the instructor. The student must seek out his/her own interviewee. In addition to the questions listed in Strategy 3, the student may also ask the following.

1. How do you like being in this industry?
2. What has your career path been?
3. What are some negatives about the industry?
4. What are some positives about the industry?
5. What kind of education is really necessary for this type of career?

SE, VE, I

Strategy 8
Research Project to Predict Trends in Industry

This project is similar to Strategy 5, but it requires students to research more than just the current state of the industry in which they want to work. It requires them to identify predictions about future trends in their industry.

This project can have three separate components:

Part 1. State of the industry. This includes the history, billings, etc., of major companies or organizations (see Strategy 5).

Part 2. Trends. This includes predictions from reliable sources such as reports, briefs, publications, and interviews.

Part 3. Student's predictions. This requires original, creative, analytical thinking from the student to develop his/her own predictions about the industry based on parts 1 and 2.

This strategy helps students to assess the potential future of the industry in which they want to work. If they are studying to work in an area that is declining, this assignment will help them identify that problem. If their area of choice has potential for expansion and high earnings, they can identify this too.

P, VE, SE, I, A

Strategy 9
Job Description

Students are asked to find a company that could potentially hire them and obtain a copy of an actual job description for review. After obtaining the job description, students should analyze it for the following:

1. Skills involved
2. Personality characteristics implied by skills
3. Actual tasks involved
4. Cooperation involved
5. Coordination involved
6. Any other important data that can be derived from the job description

This assignment will provide students with a point of contact in the industry for networking, practice in critical thinking and analysis, practice in communication, and an objective look at what industry requires for employees on a certain job. By completing this assignment, students should "discover for themselves" what skills and characteristics are important for an entry-level job in their field.

VE, I, SE, A, P

Strategy 10
Five-Year and Ten-Year Career Plans

This approach can be used in conjunction with Strategies 5, 6, and 8. Students are required to research their industry and develop a year-by-year plan reflecting where they want to be in their careers in five and in ten years. Students should use the plan to set their goals for education, career, training, salary, professional reading, and professional associations. Without a set of goals, students are much less likely to achieve success.

> Goal setting is a process whereby we can translate wishes into reality. It enables us to get our act together by providing us with a methodology to identify what we need or want, and then helps us establish a plan for reaching that goal. Goal setting helps reduce procrastination, increases personal organization, and brings about a commitment to action on our part and the part of others who are involved [Morrisey].

A format similar to the one that follows can be used (See p. 190).

This goal sheet can be filled out for each year starting with the fifth or the tenth year and working backwards. It is best to set between 1 and 5 goals in each area. Once the goals for each year have been written, an action plan can be developed for each goal.

The overall goal sheet and action plans can be kept easily in a three-ring binder for easy reference later. Goals will, of course, change frequently over time but the use of a systemized goal setting approach will provide students with benchmarks showing progress. Such a system also enhances self-esteem because students can actually mark off their achievements and know they are reaching their goals. For a five-year or ten-year plan, each year's goals should lead up to the next year's. It is helpful to put all five or ten years' worth of goal sheets together when setting goals. It is also helpful to fill out draft goal sheets in pencil and then type them or write them in ink. Writing in pencil allows for flexibility in setting the goals, while making entries in ink assures that the goals are permanent benchmarks. Even though goals will change, they won't be too changeable.

Year-by-Year Career Plan
YEAR 1

Career Goals
1.
2.
3.
4.
5.

Training Goals
1.
2.
3.
4.
5.

Educational Goals
1.
2.
3.
4.
5.

Salary Goals
1.
2.
3.
4.
5.

Professional Reading Goals
1.
2.
3.
4.
5.

Professional Associations
1.
2.
3.
4.
5.

Action Plan

Career Goal 1: _____
Deadline: _____

Steps	Date Accomplished
1.	
2.	
3.	
4.	
5.	
6.	

Students are given the assignment as a class project. Instructors would evaluate the project on the basis of organization, completeness, clarity, and logic.

I, SE, VE

Strategy 11
One-Year Career Plan

Strategy 10 is an excellent tool for someone who has a job already or even for someone who does not have a job but knows that he/she wants to work in a specific job area. For many students who do not have a job yet, it would be difficult to write a five-year or ten-year plan because their field of study varies and so do their job options (as in the case of management or marketing students). For these students, a better option is to write a one-year plan to map out what they need to achieve to get that first job. Or, if the student has just started a job, the one-year career plan can help the student concentrate on meeting his/her goals during the first year.

This one-year plan uses the same goal sheet and action plan format as Strategy 10. It should be much more detailed however, even to the point of actually setting days of the month as due dates.

The action plans can be much more detailed in this case, because the detail of required actions should be clearer if the student is only looking ahead one year. The student may also want to set more than five goals in any particular area.

Goals will change, but using a systematic approach gives students direction as well as the ability to begin accomplishing their personal goals.

VE, SE, I, P

Strategy 12
Cover Letter

Students should know how to prepare a cover letter to send with their resume (see Strategy 1). This strategy requires students to prepare a general cover letter that can be used with any resume, making it easy for students to respond to requests for resumes.

Students would be required to draft a generic cover letter in a format similar to the one that follows. The instructor (and mentor if there is one) would review the cover letter and provide input and guidance for improving it (see Strategy 3). The student would then revise the cover letter and send it and a resume to a company that might consider hiring the student. This part should be completed even if the student is not currently seeking

---

Sample cover letter

Date
Mr/Ms. First, Last name
Title
Company
Street
City, St, Zip

Dear Ms./Mr./Mrs.:

I am currently seeking employment in the (insert subject discipline) area. I have heard that your company is a major employer of (insert job title). I have recently completed (a degree in, course work in) and I am looking for a career position as a (job title).

I am sending you my current resume. I would appreciate it if you would send me more information about your company, a listing of any openings in my field, and an application form.

I will call you in two weeks to follow up. I appreciate your help and look forward to talking with you.

Sincerely,

Your name

Your address

Your phone

---

employment. The reaction of the company to the cover letter and the resume can indicate whether the letter and resume are effective.

SE, I

Strategy 13
Analysis of Job Ads

Students can gain a great deal of knowledge about jobs and salaries and opportunities in different areas by studying job ads from the classified section of a newspaper.

For this assignment, students must be given at least one to two months. They are required to scan the paper each Sunday and cut out all display ads that pertain to the job they want to obtain after college. Each ad should be marked with the publication and the date.

After a period of about a month, the student can analyze the ads to assess the following:

1. What are common job titles for this kind of work?
2. Which are the major companies hiring individuals in this field?
3. Are salaries mentioned? If so, what seems to be the salary range?
4. What job skills are specifically mentioned?
5. What personal characteristics are specifically mentioned?
6. What is mentioned about career opportunities for later in a person's career?

This information can be summarized in a general analysis of the type of jobs available. This assignment will give students a "snapshot" of the current job market in their field of study.

The instructor would evaluate the project in terms of completeness, clarity, analysis, logic, and critical thinking (see Critical Thinking.)

I, P, SE, VE, A

Strategy 14
Day at Work

This strategy should be used in conjunction with Strategy 3. Once a mentor had been identified (or another person in the field if no mentor can be identified), the student would "spend a day at work" with someone in the field who holds a job similar to the one the student wishes to get.

This field trip is an experiential learning activity. Students can get to know and to understand what it feels like to be on a certain kind of job by spending a day on the job with someone. Nothing can take the place of living through a learning experience. No amount of comments and quotes in books or articles can ever give a student a sense of "being there" as can a day spent working.

This strategy can be developed in several ways. First, the instructor can arrange the field trip so that the student is assigned to a particular mentor for a day. Second, the instructor can require the student to find someone in the field who will allow him or her to spend a day. The first approach is the best from the standpoint of coordination. It's much easier to get cooperation from companies if they are approached by the instructor or someone else from the institution.

The second approach, although more difficult for everyone, actually does provide the student with an even richer experience. In this case, the student has to "pound the pavement" to locate a sponsor for a day and then has to sell that sponsor on the program. This salesmanship is exactly what many students need to get over their fear of talking to professionals. The assignment forces students to be assertive, resourceful, and to make contacts in the field. Students would be asked to write a one- to two-page report on what they saw, did, who they talked to, what they found out about the company, what they found out about the mentor or sponsor, what they observed about the tasks themselves, what they found out about the "corporate culture," and the results of any interviews. The students should be instructed to obtain printed information such as annual reports and other materials. The evaluation can be made with regard to the content of the student-generated report.

DE, SE, D, I, P

Strategy 15
Job Interview

Students may need practice interviewing for the career positions they want. One way to assist them is to require (as part of the overall class work) that they go out in the job marketplace and find a potential employer to interview them for a position. (Whether they accept the job, or even want it, is irrelevant.) The leads can come from the classified ads in the paper and from networking (see Strategies 3, 6, and 7). The job does not have to be one for which the student is seriously interested, although the experience may be of more value if it is.

The objective of this strategy is to provide a vehicle for students to practice job interview skills. The student would obtain the interview and then fill out an evaluation form like the one that follows.

This job interview form can be copied and used for each interview to keep a record of the interview for future reference. The section on "surprising questions" is important because as students are asked questions they had not anticipated, they can practice formulating acceptable answers to those questions. This will help prepare them for other interviews later.

The section on follow up is very important, also. Students would note here any additional things they have promised the interviewer they would do by a specific deadline. The form should be filled out immediately after the job

---

**Job interview
evaluation**

JOB TITLE _____

COMPANY _____

ADDRESS _____

_____

PHONE _____

CONTACT _____

TIME _____   DATE _____

DESCRIPTION
OF OFFICE

_____

_____

_____

IMPLICATIONS _____

ATTITUDE
OF INTERVIEWER _____

IMPLICATIONS _____

_____

```
SURPRISING
QUESTIONS
1. _____
   _____
IMPLICATIONS _____
2. _____
   _____
IMPLICATIONS _____
3. _____
   _____
IMPLICATIONS _____
4. _____
   _____
COMMENTS _____
   _____
   _____
   _____
   _____

FOLLOW UP REQUIRED                      DEADLINE

_____    _____
_____    _____
_____    _____
_____    _____
_____    _____
_____    _____
CALL BACK DATE  _____
```

interview. The form and the one-page report on the job interview are turned in for evaluation by the instructor.

I, A, SE

Strategy 16
Role Play for a Job Interview

Students need practice with job interview skills. The class can be divided into student pairs for this strategy. The students have a week or so to prepare a resume (see Strategy 1) and cover letter as well as a set of questions they would want to ask a potential employee.

On interview day, the students take "the hot seat." Two chairs are set up in front of the class. One student plays the role of the interviewer, while one plays the part of the interviewee. Students should be coached to ask tough questions (if they are the interviewer) and coached to remain serious and diplomatic (if they are the interviewee).

After each group has gone through one session, the roles are reversed so that every student gets to play the role of both interviewer and interviewee. This exercise gives students the opportunity to experience how an interview will "feel," how to think "on his/her feet," and how to remain composed under stressful circumstances. It also provides them with some insight into the feelings and attitudes of job interviewers. (It is interesting to note the difference in attitudes adopted by the students as they reverse roles.)

The instructor should make evaluative comments regarding the students' confidence, knowledge, tactfulness, friendliness, and communication skills.

VE, SE, G

Strategy 17
Confidence Builder Essay

Most students have many past experiences that helped boost their confidence and self-esteem. This strategy requires students to research their past and to write an essay discussing their own confidence and self-esteem using examples of past successes as reasons for enhanced self-esteem.

The essay should be one to two pages in length. It would provide students with the opportunity to explore their feelings about themselves and to look at their past to identify accomplishments that could be impressive to employers (see Strategy 2).

The essay would be evaluated in terms of content, logic, and style.

VE, SE, I

Strategy 18
Successful Image Video

Many students have not dealt with the issue of dressing to obtain and keep a job. Clothes and appearance are quite important, both in getting and in keeping a job. Students need to be coached about planning wardrobes that will fit well into their career choices. It is not enough to purchase one suit for interviewing. If a student is called back for a second or third interview, the interviewers will know the student does not have an appropriate wardrobe for work if they see the student in the same suit during each interview. Students need to begin to assess their wardrobes and develop their own clothing styles for work before entering the job market.

This strategy can be combined with Strategy 16. Students can be required to do a presentation on a topic related to the subject area or an interview in the clothes they would wear to an interview. The class session could be videotaped and then the video played back for the students. The instructor can provide a self assessment for the students to fill out containing the following information:

1. Did you like the way you appeared?
2. What nonverbal communication did you exhibit?
3. What mannerisms did you see that you would eliminate?
4. Did you appear confident?
5. Did you like the way you were dressed?
6. What improvements would you make in your appearance prior to an interview?

(Be sure to notice haircuts, hands, fingernails, makeup, shoes, and teeth.)

This exercise is best if instructors do not evaluate student appearance. Students should evaluate themselves on what they see with a little "gentle" input from the instructor.

VE, SE, DE, P

Strategy 19
Internship

Students should be encouraged to seek job experience wherever possible. Unpaid, voluntary internships can provide excellent experience and can be easily arranged by the instructor with groups such as the United Way, UNICEF, Red Cross, and others.

Even students in technical fields can often find unpaid internships in science and research foundations. Some areas may require the student to "volunteer" to work for a profit organization such as an engineering firm or a firm in another area where there are few nonprofit opportunities.

Internships can vary in length from two or three weeks to two semesters, whatever is acceptable to the student and the organization. Students will gain more insight and experience from an internship if they are required to provide a report at the end of their internship highlighting the major ideas they learned, the processes they learned, and other information. The report should be approximately one page for each week of internship. Students should be given a role in identifying and developing contacts for the internship.

DE, VE, SE, I

Strategy 20
Cooperative Education

Cooperative education (COOP) requires that the student work at least 20 hours per week (in Texas, anyway) and that the student be paid in some way. The student is required to set three objectives that the supervisor/sponsor agrees to help the student achieve by providing resources, answering questions, giving direction, and providing advice.

The COOP class itself is usually a one-hour lecture class per week. Students can be encouraged to attend a cooperative education class that is relevant to the content area. If no cooperative education programs are available, instructors can develop them to go along with the in-class strategies.

To accomplish this strategy a separate course must be set up. In many cases, however, a special COOP class can be developed to provide students with specific skills related to a specific course. A course in advertising, for example, can be supplemented by a COOP class that places students in a company that needs them to develop an advertising campaign.

VE, SE, P

Strategy 21
Mini Report of Top Ten Career Choices

Many journals and magazines such as *Working Woman, Self, Fortune,* and others publish annual summaries of career choices, indicating to their readers which career choices seem to have higher salaries, more flexibility, more travel, more long-term benefits, and greater potential for promotion. Students can be given an assignment to research one or more of these articles and to provide a written mini report on the most recent list of top ten career choices.

The assignment can be used to reflect several disciplines such as:

- The top ten science career choices
- The top ten business career choices
- The top ten social science career choices
- The top ten career choices for writing

This assignment can enhance a course by making the career choices the course is preparing students for more specific. Students will be able to match a career choice with salary, specific tasks, and responsibilities. Students will also see the value of continuing their work toward their career goals.

I, SE

Strategy 22
Panel Discussion

The instructor would invite three to six professionals to be a part of a panel discussion on career opportunities within their fields. The instructor should be careful to include different levels of experience and expertise on the panel so that students could get a sense of the difference between an entry-level job in the field and a managerial job in the field. The panel would be given a variety of questions to prepare for.

- What interested him/her in the field?
- How did he/she break into the field?
- What is good and bad about the job?
- What salary range is represented?
- What actual tasks are accomplished on the job?
- How are employees evaluated?
- What advice does he/she have for students?

Students would listen to the opening of the discussion and save their questions until the end. Students would be required to write a reaction paper to the panel discussion to highlight their impressions of the job market as reflected by the panel.

VE, SE, G

Strategy 23
Mini Report on Government Jobs

For this report, students would be required to research current government jobs available within their discipline. Usually, the state employment agency has copies of the job listings for federal, state, and local government.

Government-related jobs may not be available for every discipline. However, the purpose of this assignment is to provide students with the practical experience of uncovering job bank lists and of seeing which types of jobs are related to their major area of study. Even if a student has no intention of working for the government, just knowing how to look up the government positions may be of use to him/her later as his/her goals change.

A key to the success of the assignment is to require students to research and list those jobs that are relevant to the course of study. For many students, this exercise will point out opportunities that the students were unaware existed.

VE, SE, I

Strategy 24
Employment Agency Presentation

Employment agencies can be a unique source of discipline-oriented information for both students and instructors. Representatives of employment agencies usually will agree to come to speak to a group of students about their agency, specific fields of inquiry, and other topics related to job search because the agency gets free publicity from the experience and also an opportunity to become better known in the community. These agencies place hundreds of people a year. They have the kind of practical knowledge to help students obtain employment.

It is most helpful to have an agency that specializes in the kind of jobs associated with the discipline. There are agencies that specialize in marketing, management, engineering, and science. There may be many other types of agencies as well. When contacting an agency, be sure to stress (in writing) that there will be no compensation for the discussion and that the agency may not solicit the students unless the students themselves inquire about placement services.

VE

Strategy 25
Career Strengths and Weaknesses

Students are asked to set up a "Ben Franklin Decision" form. For an in-class exercise, students are required to fold a piece of paper in half. On one half they write "Strengths" and on the other "Weaknesses." They list what they perceive to be their strengths and weaknesses in terms of getting and keeping a job. After the class has taken 15 minutes to complete the lists, students share what they perceive their strengths to be.

Once everyone has shared their strengths, individuals are given an additional ten minutes to write out three action items to help them correct their weaknesses. Each student shares with the class his/her weaknesses as well as their three-step plan of action.

A, I, VE

Strategy 26
Interest Essay

This strategy is a good opener for the first day of class. It requires students to write an impromptu essay of one to two pages discussing their interest in the subject and how the subject relates to their desired careers. It is important to tell students not to write "I'm taking this course because I have to. It's on my degree plan." Even if that is the case, students should be able to relate the worth of the course to their futures in the workplace.

Each individual would discuss his/her paper. The culmination of this discussion can work well as a transition for a discussion on the importance of the topic in general. As with several of the other strategies that require written essays, the assignment can be evaluated with reference to ideas as well as grammar, punctuation, and usage. Even though most instructors are not English grammar instructors, they can assist students by pointing out problems with grammar and with writing. If students begin to see the value of using correct grammar and punctuation (and teachers across the discipline areas require it), their performance will improve.

VE, SE, I

Strategy 27
Video Profile of a Profession

This strategy requires group work. (See strategies under Teamwork). Students are divided into teams of four to six students and given an assignment to videotape some aspect of a profession related to the class. If it is a science class, some of the groups might arrange to videotape astronauts or medical researchers. A marketing or management class might videotape the creation of an ad campaign at an ad agency or a manager's typical day. A class of emergency medical technicians might videotape a night on an ambulance run. A social science class might videotape social scientists working in the city to alleviate poverty and other social disorders.

The assignment should be to produce a 10- to 15-minute profile (on video) of some aspect of a profession that is associated with the course. The results will vary widely. The instructor will not evaluate, of course, the ability of the group to use the camera or edit. Instead, the instructor will look for the various aspects of the profession the students identified and evaluate the means the students used to relate those aspects. The point of the assignment is for students to get a feel for the profession, to view it, and to be able to distill its importance into a 10- to 15-minute summary. The videos can be viewed as separate products and shown to the class or to the mentors. Or, if all groups are asked to videotape the same profession (via different sources), the work of all the groups can be edited together to provide a composite of the profession.

This exercise will provide students with a glimpse into a specific profession. If the instructor can arrange for students to videotape meaningful situations, students will get more insight into the day-to-day activities of the profession than they would by simply interviewing professionals.

G, VI, SE, G

Strategy 28
Career Game

The instructor develops a game that represents major aspects of the professions associated with the course. In marketing, for example, an individual might choose to be a copywriter, a market researcher, a salesperson, a marketing coordinator, or a public affairs director. In the health care area, a student might choose to be a nurse, a paramedic, or a dental assistant. In science, a student might choose to be a researcher, a chemist, or an engineer.

The instructor identifies as many potential jobs as possible. Each job title is written on the blank side of an index card with a one- or two-paragraph job description on the other side. Underneath the job description, the instructor indicates the skills required to do the job and any important information necessary to obtain employment in the field.

The instructor uses the game at the beginning or end of the course or wherever the theme of careers seems to fit in best with the curriculum. He or she passes the cards out to the students who review their cards. Students sit in a large circle and as the play advances around the room, they assume the role of a person in the job their card indicates. They read the job description and the other members of the class guess what kind of job is represented. Students read the requirements of the job to the class once the job has been identified.

Although designed to be enjoyable, this strategy provides overviews of possible career choices and reviews requirements in a nonthreatening environment.

VE, G

Strategy 29
Research of the Top Three Professionals in the Field

This strategy requires students to research the field and to choose the three professionals they feel are the top professionals of all time. Students may have to research quite a few professionals in order to identify which ones they think are the best. Of course, in some professions, it is easy to find articles that identify the "best" professionals of a certain field, or those professionals who make the most money, or those who are the most popular. Students must decide what their own criteria are for being "the best."

Each of the professionals is then given a profile. This would include:

- Birth date
- Birth place
- Brief history of rise to top
- Major accomplishments
- Salary
- Why the individual is important in the student's view

As a final commentary, the instructor can ask students to reveal which of the three professionals they identify with the most, which one they identify with the least, and why. What does the student think it takes (in terms of character) to rise to the top of the field? Is he/she willing to pay the price for success?

VE, A, I, SE

Strategy 30
Essay on the Visualization of Success

This strategy uses an impromptu essay such as the one described in Strategy 26. The instructor asks students to pause to visualize themselves in ten years. He or she asks them to describe to themselves what it would feel like if they were successful in their careers. How much money would they be making? What contributions would they make to society? What would their life achievements be in ten years?

Students then write a vivid description of their visualization to refer back to when they need motivation and encouragement. Each student shares his/her visualization with the class and describes why the type of success visualized is important to him/her.

I, VE, SE

Strategy 31
Bibliography of Career Titles

This strategy can be used as an extra credit assignment or an adjunct to a report on careers and career choices. The instructor requires students to develop a list of 20 to 30 titles of books on careers in the discipline area. The list should include at least a one-paragraph description of the book as well as the pertinent bibliographical information.

The information could be used as a basis for reports (such as Strategies 8, 23, and 29) or it could be used as a stand-alone assignment to familiarize students with resources available concerning jobs and careers in the field. The instructors should emphasize that students should begin collecting this information to review before they begin searching for an entry-level position.

VE, P

Strategy 32
Abstracts of Career Articles

In addition to a bibliography on career topics (see Strategy 31), the instructor could require students to turn in at least three abstracts per course of articles related to careers in the field. The abstracts should be written in proper format (see Communication) and should be thorough, including all bibliographical information as well as a one- or two-page synopsis of the article.

This assignment requires a more detailed review of the articles than does Strategy 31, but it provides students with the opportunity to delve into the resources to find information on careers. Students may find useful information on careers in trade journals and other publications not necessarily considered academic journals. Students could use the information they develop for assignments such as Strategies 8, 23, and 29.

VE, A, I

Strategy 33
Job Evaluation Form

This strategy can be used in conjunction with strategies 3, 9, and 15. It requires students to obtain a copy of a job evaluation form from a representative of a company in the field and to analyze the evaluation form. Students should analyze each question on the form and respond to it with ideas about the kinds of skills and behaviors that are being evaluated as well as the kinds of behaviors that might be acceptable indicators of excellent performance.

This exercise shows students what is expected from an employee. It gives them a concrete model of performance and details those skills that will be necessary to be successful on the job. It gives them a practical description of the kind of work they will need to do to be successful in a particular field.

I, A, VE

Strategy 34
Career Survey

This strategy is similar to the strategies in Critical Thinking and Communication. Students are required to develop a list of 20 questions that are pertinent to the career field they have chosen. They give a draft of these questions for the instructor to review. After the instructor makes his/her comments, they rewrite the questions and develop a questionnaire that can be duplicated.

Students are then required to call on as many companies as possible (perhaps 10 to 15) to find a representative to answer their questions about the career. Once the students have the responses, they analyze the results, develop a summary of the "study," and describe what the study revealed to them about the career field. This strategy is an excellent tool to develop analytical and communication skills as well as for career enhancement.

The instructor should evaluate it on the amount of pertinent data the student developed and on the student's new insights into the career field.

A, P, I, VE, SE

Strategy 35
Self-Esteem Tape

Students are asked to write as many positive statements about themselves as possible. This part of the assignment is completed during a 10- to 15-minute period of class time. Students are required to write at least 20 items. (Few will have trouble writing at least 20).

Once the students have completed their lists, they review them with the instructor who offers advice, help, and suggestions for students who may be stuck or need an objective viewpoint. Students are then assigned the task of recording these statements on a videotape. They can play this tape on their way to job interviews. Over time, their new tape can replace some of the old negative subconscious "tapes" that erode their confidence.

I, VE, SE

Strategy 36
Definition of Success

Students are asked to develop a two-paragraph definition of what success means to them without using the dictionary. This definition may include items such as contribution, admiration of peers, salary, authority, creativity, or any other criterion for success they may deem important.

Once students have finalized their definitions, they could share the definitions with the class orally or by developing a success poster. Each definition could be put into a permanent booklet representing each class the instructor taught and the definitions could be compared with previous classes.

The emphasis of the strategy is to get students to think through what real success means to them and to provide them with more of a framework for judging their achievements than an amorphous, veiled concept of success.

SE, I, VE

Strategy 37
Success Notebook

This strategy can be used in conjunction with Strategy 36. The student develops a notebook containing a least 25 items that somehow symbolize success. The definition from Strategy 36 can be used as well as other items like photos, award certificates, check stubs, or whatever the student feels reflects his/her success.

The results are shared with the class. Each student presents his/her notebook and discusses the items briefly. The important aspect of this, like Strategy 36, is to show the student his/her previous successes, help him/her re-celebrate those successes, and make a firmer commitment to success in the future, based on his/her own personal definition.

This can also be used as an extra credit project to spark those students who may need reminding of their own abilities.

VI, VE, I, SE, P

Strategy 38
Reference Sheet

Many employers will ask for references when an applicant provides a resume or portfolio. Students can begin now to develop a comprehensive list of references starting with their instructors. To begin, the student should get a three-ring binder and put the names of everyone the student can think of as a reference on the top of the pages (one per page). The student should obtain a complete address including a zip code and a work phone number from each reference. The student should also **ask each possible reference to write a letter of recommendation for the student.**

Even if the student does not like the letter of recommendation or does not want to use that many letters, the letter itself acts as an "insurance policy." If the student uses that person as a reference six to eight months down the road, the person will remember writing a letter of recommendation and will be less likely to give any negative information. (The references will not want to contradict themselves. If they wrote a glowing letter of recommendation, they certainly will not come back with a negative reference later.)

The student can then alphabetize these references and type a single sheet of references to give to potential employers on request. The top two or three letters of reference can be given along with the resume. The additional letters can be saved to be used at a later time and as insurance. It is imperative, however, that the student review the reference sheet each and every time he/she gives it out. If there is someone on the list who may not be as appreciative of the student's qualities as he/she was the previous year (for whatever reason), that person's name should be taken off the list.

VE, SE, I

Strategy 39
Project Sheets

Students and other applicants are often asked about previous work experience. Employers want to know what projects the applicants have been involved with and what they have accomplished, either in previous jobs or at college. One method of keeping track of accomplishments is to develop a notebook of project sheets.

This strategy is taken from the common practice among professionals (such as architects, engineers, and designers) of documenting each project activity in a consistent form.

A form such as the one that follows can be used.

Project Sheet

Name of Project _____

Duration of Project _____

Client or Employer _____

Responsibilities on Project _____

_____

_____

Description of Project _____

_____

_____

_____

_____

_____

Project Outcomes _____

_____

_____

The client would be the instructor if the project was accomplished for a class. The outcome of the project would be the product of the project in some cases ("We prepared an ad campaign for a nonprofit agency") or it may be what the student has learned ("I learned how to conduct a research study from this project and gained a knowledge of cultural differences"). The project write-ups can be kept in a binder and if the student keeps up with them, he/she will have a wealth of information to share with a potential employer. Some of these projects may be represented also in the portfolio (see Strategy 2), but many intellectual projects that don't have much visual impact can have a dynamic impact using the project write-up forms.

SE, VE, I

Strategy 40
Guest Speaker

Guest speakers from industry and business often add a unique dimension to a semester course and can provide a valuable overview of the world of work for the students. One or two guest speakers per course can provide students with a contact person in their chosen field as well as someone to answer questions.

Keys to Success with Guest Speakers

1. Coach the speaker. Give the guest a specific time limit and require him/her to stay within that time limit. Tell the speaker to remain positive. Even if it is tough to get a job in a particular field, it's not impossible or the guest speaker would not have a job in that field. Students need encouragement and need to improve their self-esteem. If the job outlook in an area is so bleak that the speaker feels obligated to discuss it, tell him/her to provide action-oriented suggestions on how to overcome adversity.
2. Provide specifics. Ask the speaker to cover at least the following items:
   • industry history
   • industry outlook
   • company strengths
   • competitors' strengths
   • usual process for obtaining a job
   • speaker's background
   • important interview components
   • important resume components
   • common day-to-day tasks and activities
   • questions from the students
3. Coach students. Ask students to prepare questions ahead of time so that important questions are answered for the whole group.
4. Evaluate students. Ask questions on exams pertaining to the guest speaker's presentation. This forces students to attend the guest speaker's session and to listen more carefully.
5. Evaluate guest speaker. Develop a short questionnaire such as the following one to assess the credibility of the guest speaker. Even though guest speakers may be highly recommended and willing to speak to students, they may not be as credible as the instructor would like. Developing an ongoing method for evaluating the presentations of guest speakers can help the instructor to better plan for guest speaker presentations in the future. (A file can be kept of evaluations that can be used when asking guest speakers to return for another course or semester and for recommending guest speakers to other instructors.)

Guest Speaker Evaluation

1. Did the guest speaker seem to have adequate knowledge of the industry?
2. Did the speaker seem to have adequate knowledge of the job potentials within the industry?
3. Did the speaker appear to be prepared?
4. Did the speaker relate well to the students?
5. Did the speaker adequately respond to questions from the students?
6. Was the speaker interesting to listen to?
7. Did the speaker seem willing to help students by providing information to them individually in the future?
8. Would you recommend the guest speaker to another instructor?

VE

CLASSROOM STRATEGIES FOR TEAMWORK

1. Class Group Project	21. Collegial Model
2. Series of Group Projects	22. Facilitation Techniques
3. Complementary Individual Projects	23. Team Score for Evaluation
4. Group Projects with Competition	24. Debate Teams
5. Group Projects with Coaches	25. Group Investigations
6. Team Problem Solving	26. Team Experimentation
7. Cooperative Learning	27. Conceptual Model Building
8. Team Decisions	28. Concrete Model Building
9. Understanding Roles	29. Multiability Tasks
10. Conflict Resolution	30. Team Roles
11. Coordination	31. Team Evaluation
12. Meeting Role Play	32. Building Identity
13. Team Scheduling Exercise	33. Interdisciplinary Curriculum Units
14. Goal Setting	34. Group Contract
15. Learning Centers	35. Team Board Games
16. Group Tests	36. Team Simulations
17. Observer Scoring Sheet	37. Critical Panels
18. Team Guidelines	38. Cooperative Games
19. Multimedia Tasks	39. Group Diaries
20. Short-Term Discussion Groups	40. Group Essay

Teamwork is important to success in employment, even if the employee has a position that seems to be highly individualized. No matter what the job, working with or coordinating with other people is necessary. Teamwork is taught randomly throughout the educational system. It is covered, in some measure, through sporting activities, but these activities are not open to all students and the concepts of teaming emphasized in sports are quite different from those emphasized for working teams. In sports, much of the direction and authority for the team comes from outside the team, usually from the coaching staff. For work group teams, straight line authority is not necessarily given to anyone. The team itself may have to develop its own leadership structure and internal authority and set its own direction.

Breaking down barriers to effective teaming is difficult for work teams. The workplace requires individual employees to look out for themselves, to be competitive with other employees, and to perform so that management recognizes their individual achievements. On the other hand, the organization itself benefits from the achievements of employees in groups, project teams, work group units, and other particular parts of the company structure. This behavior is ingrained in the work process but it may be difficult for employees to suspend competitive barriers long enough to complete team-oriented projects. This leads to conflict, dissension, and ineffectiveness for the work group.

Students need to be put into situations require teaming so they can develop attitudes and skills to allow them to dissolve their own barriers and to contribute to group work. In an academic environment, instructors who do provide for teaming do not closely relate it to the kinds of teaming required in the workplace. Instructors set up activities that require group work but for which evaluations (grades) are individually set and based on individual achievement. This may be easier and less risky for the instructor, but it creates a situation in which a different set of abilities and skills is developed in students. Students learn to complete individual tasks and to combine them loosely together, but the emphasis is on developing an individual portion of a piece of work so that it stands out from the rest, gains more attention, and gets a better grade. Students in this situation can choose whether they want to work with other students. If they do, the total project may have more cohesiveness, but working with others does not bring them any specific reward. Similarly, if they choose not to work with the other students, they miss the opportunity to learn to work on a team and yet they experience no negative consequences individually, although the total project suffers.

If instructors base at least a portion of the evaluation on the ability of the group to develop a project (for example, a report, case study, or presentation), students could be required to work together as a unit. If the students do not, they would all suffer the consequences through the evaluation. More coordination, more communication, more organization, and more overall teamwork would occur, and these would begin to develop the students abilities to work as a team, to coordinate, and negotiate.

Similarly, instructors often set up teams without leaders, assuming (as is the academic way) that each student should have an equal chance to contribute to the team. While work teams may not have direct written lines of authority, there may be an unwritten line of responsibility. On a work team, the roles of individuals may be to develop information, ideas, and other essentials to provide to the team leader. The team leader may be the one individual who gets "credit" for the team's work, with other team members playing subordinate roles. Learning to contribute when credit is given to some other team member is a difficult concept for many students who are individually oriented.

Instructors rarely set up team activities that support this experience, but developing more realistic team activities in which individuals have different responsibilities and different opportunities for recognition and success may more truly reflect the kinds of situations students will have on future jobs. This chapter develops a series of group activities that emphasize realistic teaming. Many of the strategies outline general types of group activities, such as group projects with competition, group projects with coaches, team problem solving, debate teams, model building, and simulations.

Other strategies emphasize developing and improving the teaming process itself, such as understanding roles, conflict resolution, observer scoring sheets, individual and group worksheets, and team guidelines. Still others treat teamwork as a subject area to be briefly introduced to students and outline methods for using teamwork content material, such as cooperative learning, setting team roles, and orientation to group process.

The majority of the Teamwork Strategies can be effectively paired with strategies from the Leadership section. (Where there is a team there is an official or unofficial leader.) A few strategies relate to methods of evaluation of teaming activities, such as group tests, team evaluation, and team score for evaluation.

Strategy 1
Class Group Project

Students who are training to enter the workplace should be taught group interaction processes that involve working toward a common goal or set of common goals through a team effort. Instructors will inevitably face the problem of students who believe that their evaluation and grades should be limited to those activities they can accomplish individually. It is important to develop tasks that can challenge students at various learning levels as well as provide them with learning exercises that allow them to experience the responsibilities, pressures, and satisfactions of working on a team.

One excellent method for providing group work in a team setting is to involve the entire class in a community-related project. The project should involve problem solving, communication, collaboration, and the development of some type of specific product.

The first step in such a project is to involve the entire class in research and situational analysis pertinent to the project. The instructor divides the class into groups, and each group is responsible for researching a specific related topic area. Next, the instructor asks the small groups to come together to present information to the class. With this information, the class develops key points pertinent to the project; that is, situational analysis.

From situational analysis, the students develop a list of key tasks (roles) that are required to accomplish the overall project. Each class member is given a specific role to play during the course of the project. The role of each member is defined explicitly through class discussion and feedback from community representatives as well as the instructor. In fact, an actual job description should be written for each role so that the class and the individuals involved are aware of the specific requirements of the role.

The next step is to have the class, either as a whole or through facilitation by the instructor, choose a leader and an assistant leader, as well as students to head up individual task groupings. In effect, this step establishes a chain of responsibility that is agreed on by everyone on the team.

The elected leaders have the ultimate responsibility for achieving each task in their areas of responsibility. They are responsible for developing a deadline and schedule of tasks to be accomplished. These schedules should include integration points for getting students together to relate and collaborate on their tasks in order to integrate the work of several students into a finished product. The leader of the group assumes the role of integrator, editing, discussing, and approving the work accomplished by others.

Once the tasks are scheduled, the plan is developed by the class. Inevitably, some of the individuals will either have trouble with their tasks or will not finish their tasks on time. While the students in the project might grumble at the low performance of certain individuals, the experience of dealing with team members who are and who are not responsible and committed is an excellent learning experience for those who will ultimately be required to work as a team on their jobs. Students who wish to excel, in many cases, either will have to coach the nonperformers or take over their responsibilities. This is an excellent learning situation because in the workplace, team efforts often include "pitching in" when others are unable to or refuse to fulfill their responsibilities.

The instructor should stress that deadlines for community projects are firm. That way, the class gets a sense of the management skills necessary and the team effort required to meet a deadline in the business world. Once the project is completed, the community representative should be involved in critiquing the value and professionalism of the final product.

Ideas for Class Projects

- Research and write articles on local landmarks (history)
- Develop a position paper on political issue of local relevance (social science)
- Research and provide solutions to environmental problem (social science, science)
- Research and provide articles on relevance of mathematics/chemistry, etc., to everyday life (mathematics, science)
- Develop marketing materials for favorite charity (marketing)
- Develop photography/commercial art materials for favorite charity (fine arts)
- Develop free auto repair service to elderly (auto mechanics)
- Host a fashion show with proceeds going to charity (fashion design)
- Develop a one-volume anthology of creative student writing (english)

For almost any subject, a project can be developed that would use the skills of the class in a total class, community-oriented project.

A key component to the development of a class group project is that the instructor must delegate to the class the authority and responsibility for getting a project completed. The deadline must be firm with no adjustments allowed. The class leaders must be responsible for reporting to the community representative. The instructor essentially takes on the role of a "coach," sitting on the sidelines, providing ideas and resources, and helping with the project, but *not* necessarily giving orders or telling the students how to accomplish the work.

VE, SE, G, P

Strategy 2
Series of Group Projects

This strategy is based on using a series of group projects that are similar and related to each other and work together to provide an experiential base for students in a specific area. The instructor divides the class into groups of three or four students. These groups work together throughout the semester on each project, culminating in an overall integrated project that helps pull the experiences of the series together and speeds transference of skills across previous projects.

To be successful, the series of projects must be carefully planned in order to build upon the successful completion of each component. For a series strategy, each project should be similar in approach so that students can easily develop group norms and standards and quickly get on with each project.

For planning, the instructor starts with a list of primary objectives separated by text chapters or by topic, and then designs a workable project for the first topic. Once a "prototype" project is developed, the other topics and objectives can be adopted to the format.

For example, in a computer programming class, the first project could involve problem solving—finding a group solution to a programming situation. Each succeeding topic objective could be handled using the same group problem solving—programming. Ideally, the level of difficulty of the programming would increase throughout the course during each subsequent project.

Once each major topic of the class had been treated using a group project technique, one overall project would integrate ideas developed throughout the course. In the case of the computer programming example, each group might be responsible for developing a major program that would include components of the others and would be responsible for presenting both the final program as well as an explanation of how each project helped build the final project.

The series of projects must be planned carefully in sequence in order to make results cumulative. Clear directions as well as an overview of the entire series at the beginning of the course are imperative for success.

G, VE, DE, SE, LC

Strategy 3
Complementary Individual Projects

This strategy involves the division of labor of a major project into separate, but complementary, individual components. This strategy is similar to the class group project in Strategy 1, but involves providing components that are accomplished individually. When each component is finalized, the class members integrate what they have into an overview of everyone's projects, analyzing and then synthesizing to create a hypothesis that individually none of their projects would necessarily present.

To develop a complementary project, some controversial (or at least unusual) topic should be chosen within the discipline area that would allow for investigatory learning and would also point to a specific hypothesis when each separate part had been investigated. For example, for emergency medical technician training, individuals could be assigned to research the anatomy/physiology of a certain part of the human body. Each student would thoroughly investigate his/her topic, develop an overhead or visual, and prepare a written report and presentation. During the final overview, a lengthy discussion could be facilitated in which the whole class would develop a theory of how all the body parts work together, using the information learned from their research.

As another example, in a marketing class, individual members could be assigned a company to research within a product category. After the individual presentations, the groups could be asked to summarize a situational analysis of that product industry based on their individual findings.

VE, SE, G, P, A

Strategy 4
Group Projects with Competition

For this strategy, the classroom is divided into three to five groups. Each group is given a project to complete in a specified amount of time with specified resources. The groups are essentially in competition with each other in completing the task. The groups are given the same basic set of information and instructions. Each group is required to come to a consensus in both solution of the problem and process.

There is competition between groups because an outside source of evaluation such as the instructor or a mentor/observer from industry actually reviews the final products of the task and then ranks the projects based on predetermined criteria. For example, a fundamental course in business might include a group project in which each group would be required to develop a business plan for a new business. At the end of the project, the groups would present their plans to an actual banker who would assist the instructor in critiquing the overall project and who would choose the one project he/she would be most likely to fund in an actual situation.

For a commercial art course, the class could be divided into groups, each group representing a different design team. An actual client, such as the director of a nonprofit organization, could be brought in to provide an overview of some design problem, such as a new logo, brochure, or poster, and the teams could develop designs to solve the problem. The client would then critique the work and, if possible, choose the work of one of the design teams for actual use and production.

This strategy provides for several real life learning experiences.

1. Students must work together to have a product.

2. Students must compete with other teams as they would in a job situation.

3. Students are critiqued by a professional in the field. This may be uncomfortable for them but is a valuable learning experience provided the professional is both tactful and honest about their work.

4. Students' work, if used, can be a valuable contribution to their portfolio or resume.

P, VE, G, SE, DE, LC

Strategy 5
Group Projects with Coaches

This strategy is similar to Strategy 4 in that the class is divided into groups and each group is required to develop a solution to a specific problem or case study scenario. The teams compete to develop the best possible solution and the solutions are critiqued by outside reviewers.

For this group work, however, each team is "coached" by a different mentor or volunteer from industry and as such receives different advice and coaching based on the mentor's experience. At the end of the project, each team presents its work to a panel that critiques the work, while the mentors also discuss the advice and coaching they provided the team so that all teams then benefit from the variety of experience.

VE, SE, G, P, DE

Strategy 6
Team Problem Solving

For courses in which students are required to solve logical problems, such as electronics or computer programming, this method can be very effective. Students are given specific problems to solve, but are divided into impromptu teams in order to solve those problems. Each team comes up with an answer to the problems as well as a step-by-step scenario of how to solve the problems.

For example, the groups can be given the same basic problem with a variation in data. This will mean that each group may come up with different answers, but with workable processes regardless of data. This method takes advantage of the fact that students often learn the most difficult processes and concepts from each other.

In a group setting, students who have a good grasp of the concepts will assist those students who do not, often using different (perhaps simpler) language than the instructor is apt to use. This provides students with a different perspective and explanation and often helps to add to the instructor's approach. Also, the collaborative aspect helps students learn to approach problems. Students can benefit from emulating other successful students.

A, G, VE, SE, P

Strategy 7
Cooperative Learning

Almost all group work involves collaborative learning between students. To foster collaborative learning, the instructor can set up permanent learning teams, taking care to place "high status" or gifted students evenly throughout the groups and to avoid concentrating problem students in any one group.

The instructor gives problems to the learning group throughout the course and requires the group members to help each other to work out the problems. In some cases, individual problems are assigned, but the students are instructed to get assistance from their learning group when necessary. The learning group members make certain that each group member can work out *each* problem.

A similar approach is to provide an ongoing series of problems that the learning group then works out in a team fashion. The products of the teamwork are then graded individually, or by team, depending on the approach to the task given in the directions.

Collaborative learning groups will probably require some explanation of the collaborative process at the outset because the traditional classroom norms require that students *do not* work together, but rather, work independently, in competition with each other. To change this paradigm and to get students to accept a different norm for collaborative learning requires some training in group process, and, at the very least, some explanation giving students permission to talk to each other, to help each other, and to collaborate. Of course, evaluation of a collaborative effort should be a group evaluation as any success or failure is due to the group process and not individual members. In fact, it's possible that the group itself might discourage certain individuals from participating [Cohen].

G, VE, SE, P

Strategy 8
Team Decisions

This strategy is used to give students practice in making decisions using the collaborative approach. It varies from Strategy 6 in that it doesn't set up a problem to be solved but rather sets up a scenario that requires some type of decision. In the workplace, few major decisions are made by individuals—most require a collaborative effort. An important tool to use for team decisions is the published case study. For example, in a human resource management course, the team could be given a scenario depicting a certain discipline problem displayed by an employee on the job and then be asked to decide how to handle the employee.

For a photography class, students could be given the same set of 50 black and white photographs and be asked to choose the ten photos to be displayed at an opening.

In an emergency medical technician course, students could be given symptoms and be asked to decide which ailment is most likely the cause of the symptoms.

This strategy requires some explanation by the instructor regarding the various types of decision-making methods such as the Benjamin Franklin method. (Refer to Critical Thinking Strategy 31.)

A variation of this approach is to establish a chain of decision authority in which individual students play roles and work together within those roles to make decisions. Students might play the roles of shop worker, shop foreman, middle manager, and executive manager. Students either can make a decision about the case or ask for insight from those in other roles. This provides a very real learning experience because it gives students practice in choosing what decisions to make and how to ask for assistance. This approach can be used with practically any discipline. The instructor simply needs a written case study requiring a decision and some type of organizational chart from a representative work situation.

To be valuable, the instructor should critique the decisions and process by which the decisions in the exercise were made. If the case study is an actual one, the instructor can research to find out what the final decision was and whether that decision proved to be sound.

G, P, A, DE, SE, VE

Strategy 9
Understanding Roles

Many students have not yet had an opportunity to work on a team. Some may have been involved in team sports, but team sports do not provide the same kind of challenge as teaming at work. For one thing, team sports often segregate males from females, and for this reason, the personal skills in teaming at work are more challenging.

Learning to be responsible for individual components of a project for which one has a special expertise and then learning to listen to and respect others as they enhance, critique, and add to that expertise requires very different personal skills.

One method that can enhance the abilities of students to work together is to create a team task for a scenario of roles. The task is then conducted with students playing initial roles. A product or outcome is produced and this then is critiqued and evaluated. The task is then repeated with different students playing the roles, which will give students insight into the emotions, stress levels, and constraints of various team roles and will often lead to better solutions or task products.

For example, in a Principles of Advertising course, the class can be divided into roles where one half of the class plays the role of the account services team, making demands, giving information, and setting deadlines, while the other half takes the role of the creative team, with creative director, writer, and layout artists. Once a solution to the task has been developed by the first role playing scenario, the students reverse roles. This gives each student understanding of the different, but still important, demands of various roles and demonstrates how perception changes due to the role one is in.

VE, G, SE, P

Strategy 10
Conflict Resolution

This strategy uses a case study as a basis for creating a conflict situation that must be resolved within the team. The content material can be chosen from any discipline. The key is to choose a case study scenario that is controversial, using appropriate content material. For example, a fashion design class could develop a case study presenting a controversy of whether to design clothes using fake fur or real fur. The team should be developed (and team members carefully chosen) so that a conflict would arise in the process of task completion. Students would have to resolve the conflict in order to produce the final outcome, that is, the design.

The group process should be carefully observed by the instructor to pinpoint the conflict resolution process. In some cases, students will resolve the conflict easily. In others, the instructor might have to step in to demonstrate techniques of conflict resolution (see Leadership, Strategy 7).

The most important factor of success for this strategy is to identify those behaviors that detract from or add to the ability of the team to deal with the conflict. This strategy provides students with a life experience because they must resolve the conflict in order to be successful. This will provide them with an incentive to "work things out" because they know they will be graded on the project's outcome. By observing and discussing those behaviors that led to conflict resolution, as well as methods for solving conflict, the instructor can better prepare students for situations of conflict on the job. In addition, this method is excellent for bringing out differing perspectives in a controversial issue within a discipline.

VE, G, DE, SE, P

Strategy 11
Coordination

This method is similar to Strategy 9 in that several groups are set up and given tasks that are interrelated. In this strategy, the instructor develops tasks that can be accomplished independently or with collaboration, but which can be achieved easier and faster through collaboration. An individual within each group has responsibility for bridging the groups. The emphasis is placed on concurrent groups that assist each other through the liaison of one or two individuals.

The strategy might be used in a Principles of Marketing course in this way. The class would be divided into four groups with two individuals assigned to be coordinators. These groups would be given a case study involving the facts about a new product. Each group would analyze product, price, promotion, or place (distribution) and develop strategies for these elements. The role of the coordinator would be to coordinate information between each team to be sure that the total marketing plan was appropriate and all elements work well together.

VE, SE, DE, G, P, A

Strategy 12
Meeting Role Play

This strategy helps develop students' abilities to use team meetings for planning and coordinating team activities. As with other strategies, the teams are set up for three to six people. An important first step in developing a team is to have an idea developing and planning session in which a student assumes the role of facilitator and facilitates discussion and planning activities for the team. This strategy puts the emphasis on role playing so that students can get a sense of the importance of planning specific team tasks and using appropriate content material from a discipline. The facilitator is given instructions in idea generation, such as nominal group technique, Delphi technique, programming, and Crawford blueslipping techniques. The team is given information on planning techniques and the facilitator then uses 30 to 40 minutes of class time to help the team create a plan for completing a task.

For example, a data processing class might plan the steps involved in programming names and numbers into a database; a technical writing class might plan the steps involved in writing and producing a technical proposal; and a photography class might plan the steps involved in photographing a wedding.

Ideally, the next step would be for the team to have the opportunity to use another strategy from this book to complete the task according to their plan. But the plan itself can be considered a product of the group and the process of planning will teach students to value planning as they work in teams. Many students have been thrown into group situations in the past in which no emphasis was placed on planning the team effort for the best, most efficient results.

VE, SE, G, P, A

Strategy 13
Team Scheduling Exercise

Similar to Strategy 12, this strategy emphasizes division of labor in accomplishing a task. It requires a team to work together on a group task and to develop a step-by-step schedule for completion in which each team painstakingly plans out which task must be accomplished, by whom, and when. For this strategy, however, it is imperative to build in time for groups to accomplish their tasks using their own schedules. Part of the important lesson for this strategy is to show students the importance of delineating tasks, meeting deadlines, communicating, and negotiating for materials and for time. Students will see how a schedule can be used as a guideline, but contingency planning must always follow.

Usually, there will be some problems with students not completing their tasks on time, not providing exactly what was assigned, misunderstanding directions, etc. These mishaps are a necessary part of the learning experience because they stress to students the importance of taking on responsibility for the team and of meeting individual deadlines for the team effort.

VE, SE, DE, P, G, A

Strategy 14
Goal Setting

This strategy is similar to Strategies 12 and 13 in that it emphasizes the importance of planning, but it uses management by objectives techniques (attributed to Peter Drucker) to demonstrate to students that teamwork evolves from objectives and goals. Ideally, the student team would use a session such as that described in Strategy 12 and would start with larger over-all objectives, segmented by smaller goals. These objectives and goals would be designated by criteria for fulfillment, and members would be assigned the responsibility of achieving them by specific deadlines. Students would then be evaluated according to what percentage of the objectives and goals was reached based on value ratings per goal.

This method can use content material from any discipline for tasks such as debates, report writing, presentations, and case study solutions. It emphasizes planning by objectives in a team context and helps students to value setting objectives and accomplishing team goals.

VE, G, P, SE

Strategy 15
Learning Centers

This strategy involves separating the class into three or four groups in different areas of the room. For best results, these groups should be permanent groups that will be involved in collaborative learning throughout the course. The instructor provides each group with appropriate resource materials, information, and support to complete a series of related tasks. In effect, each group becomes a "learning center" that supports the learning efforts of its members [Cohen, p. 39]. Team spirit and cohesiveness is intensified using this method. The main emphasis is to geographically separate the teams, providing them with appropriate resources, and then nurture them as they grow together in each nucleus.

VE, SE, G, P

Strategy 16
Group Tests

Most students have already participated in group projects during their scholastic careers. They are familiar with the implications and demands of group work for doing long-term ongoing, in-class projects. Few, if any, have probably participated in group tests. A group test is conducted in much the same way as an individual test. Students are each given essay exams to complete within a class period, but they are assigned to three- or four-person groups. They are allowed to discuss the answers to the exams without using any notes or books. Each student formulates and writes an answer to each question.

While students are allowed to converse about the topics of the exams, the final responsibility for the answer lies with the individual student. They are allowed to discuss answers, to listen, and to evaluate the worth of the answers of their fellow students, but ultimately, they must choose the answers they believe to be most correct. This requires as much preparation as an individual exam, perhaps more. Students not only need to know the content, they must exercise good judgment in what to accept and what not to accept based on their classmates' answers.

This method can be surprisingly helpful in fostering a healthy team attitude among students. It also exposes those students who have not prepared adequately. The peer pressure of the team situation helps to motivate the straggling students to work harder.

VE, SE, G, P, D

Strategy 17
Observer Scoring Sheet

Group work, if designed to enhance teamwork, depends extensively on participation. Participation is influenced by how the group members view other group members. The academic or social status of an individual can often seriously impede the progress of a group. Group members can greatly benefit from an observer's objective assessment of the participatory interaction of the group. To achieve this, the observer can use a scoring sheet such as that recommended by Cohen [pp. 120–121]. This scoring sheet serves as an evaluation of the group process as well as the group task because it includes such sections as

1. Orientation to the group work
   a. Are instructors clear?
   b. Are visual aids used?
   c. Are assignments and roles clear?
2. Student participation
   a. Are all students assigned to a group?
   b. Are students working on task?
   c. Are students confused about task?
3. Instructor
   a. Is the instructor delegating?
   b. Is the instructor helping students?
   c. Is the instructor asking questions?

In another example [Jaques, pp. 21–22], the observer maps out the group situation and then uses notation to show the interaction of the group members.

The instructor can either choose to teach the course using a team teaching approach or can develop a collaborative relationship with another instructor and ask the other instructor to sit in on the group assignment for the purpose of observation. This will not only enhance the ability of the instructor to refine the group task, but will also demonstrate participatory patterns to allow the instructor to encourage more participation from individual students.

Another excellent method for observing is to videotape the session and ask a collaborative instructor or set of instructors to view the video and mark down thoughts and insights. A video scoring sheet can be developed with a Likert scale to facilitate its use during video sessions. A sample scoring sheet follows.

VE, SE, G, P, A

Sample scoring sheet

	strongly agree	agree	not observed	disagree	strongly disagree
1. Does the instructor provide an orientation to the group work session?	1	2	3	4	5
2. Are the instructions clear?	1	2	3	4	5
3. Does the instructor provide written documentation of the instructions?	1	2	3	4	5
4. Is the role of facilitator clearly defined?	1	2	3	4	5
5. Are the roles assigned to group members clearly defined?	1	2	3	4	5
6. Are students working on assignments?	1	2	3	4	5

	strongly agree	agree	not observed	disagree	strongly disagree
7. Are students actively discussing?	1	2	3	4	5
8. Do students seem to be confused about what to do?	1	2	3	4	5
9. Are there any conflicts?	1	2	3	4	5
10. Are any students dominating their groups?	1	2	3	4	5
11. Are any students not participating?	1	2	3	4	5
12. Is the teacher stifling the group by being too involved?	1	2	3	4	5
13. Is the teacher providing enough assistance?	1	2	3	4	5
14. Is the teacher asking provoking questions?	1	2	3	4	5
15. Overall, is this group project effective?	1	2	3	4	5

Strategy 18
Team Guidelines

"Probably the most important rule to teach when training students to discuss, to make decisions, and to do creative problem solving is the norm for equal participation" [Cohen, p. 45]. Establishing norms or guidelines for a team is imperative, especially if the team will be required to break new ground, respond in an innovative fashion, or set new standards.

For more complex tasks, the list of norms may be quite in-depth. An excellent approach, at least the first time that a particular group task is used, is to ask students to develop a list of one to ten norms that are important enough to be included. In multi-attribute projects, the list of norms could include a variety of elements, such as the following:

1. Be tactful when critiquing someone else's ideas.
2. Participate by providing your own ideas.
3. Research the role(s) you have been given so that you can understand the approach to take when playing the role.
4. Provide evidence for any idea or theories you expound.
5. Meet every negotiated deadline.
6. If you think you might not meet the deadline, renegotiate the deadline.
7. Refrain from criticism based on stereotypes or personality.
8. Never interrupt anyone who is sharing ideas.
9. Use active listening.
10. Be open to changing your mind.

Once the group has chosen the norms for that work group, the norms can be posted prominently for the group to see. The facilitator can then refer to the established norms should a group member infringe upon them. If the facilitator, for example, overhears a group member interrupting another, he or she can tactfully remind the offender that the norms specify no interruptions will be made. If nothing else, publicly displayed norms serve as a reminder of acceptable behavior within the group.

VE, SE, G, P, DE

Strategy 19
Multimedia Tasks

A challenging method for using group work is to require the groups to develop multimedia class presentations. The use of three to five different media per group helps to enhance transferability as well as the learning process regardless of learning style. Requiring students to analyze the project and develop acceptable methods for completing the group task using video recording, color graphics, audio recording, photography, print media, or artwork, assures that students think through the process of finalizing that group task.

In advertising, for example, a group might be given the task of developing an image campaign for the manufacturers of children's wear. This might involve writing the campaign report, writing ads, using an audio cassette recorder to tape the idea for the commercial, using a video recorder to tape ideas, commercials, using graphics and photography to design ads.

This multimedia approach stimulates the senses as well as the creative imagination. Another example is an instructor in history could require a team to write a script about Custer's last stand and to research five articles published directly before and after the incident and to use audio recorders to provide the American Indian viewpoint and the Army view point. The students might then be required to choose a film from the library that best exemplifies the facts as documented by leading historians. This multimedia approach requires students to think, to integrate materials, and to use all their senses in the learning process.

VE, SE, P, A, G

Strategy 20
Short-Term Discussion Groups

The short-term discussion group probably predominates the classroom when group work is involved. This strategy can be used easily by dividing the class into groups of fours and assigning each group questions such as those that often appear in the discussion sections at the back of chapters. The assignment of questions can be handled in various ways depending on the objectives of the material and the goals of the instructor. Each group, for example, might be asked to discuss one question and to develop an "official" answer to the question that is a collaborative result of the group discussion. All groups would be given the same question to discuss. This would provide material for a lively discussion and/or debate on which group's answer is most correct. Another method would be to assign a different question to each group so each group would present ideas and discussion to the class and at the end of the project any information would be covered via class discussion. This method allows for a greater diversity of discussion among groups.

For content material that is controversial or for which the instructor wants to foster empathy for various viewpoints, one question can be posed to the group and each group could develop a solution. The solutions would be presented and then students would be reshuffled into new groups and given the same question once again. Then students would renegotiate and let go of any psychological attachment they might have had for their first group and first solution. These new groups would then develop new solutions consisting of the best ideas from their first solution.

Another method would be to ask the groups to develop the solutions they think are not feasible and then to pass the answers around to individuals in other groups. These individuals would then write ideas about why the solution might or might not work, how the solution could be improved, as well as any questions that might come to mind. This method would allow each group to benefit from the thought processes of the individuals. Because the ideas would be given anonymously, individuals would not be as reluctant to point out faults as they would be in open discussion.

VE, SE, G

Strategy 21
Collegial Model

One way to achieve interaction is to develop a task using a collegial model in which the products are individual but the members of the group are resources for each other (such as Strategy 16).

For this strategy, each group member is required to develop an individual piece of work—a plan of some sort, or a written brief, or a case study. The group members are allowed to assist each other by giving help, advice, or suggesting resources.

Labor can also be divided in large tasks to provide a simulation of real world activity. If, for example, a computer class was given the task of debugging a program, individual group members could be given individual pieces of the program to develop and be asked to provide a total package composed of all individual efforts. Members can be given roles such as client, programmer, and manager and be asked to work through the problem of debugging a program so that all parties would be satisfied. This kind of task teaches more than the mechanics of debugging a program. It provides students with the human teamwork experience of getting the job done.

Tasks to be developed using the collegial approach (with division of labor) need to have clearly definable parts, detailed instructions, and requirements for pulling the individual components together into one product.

I, G, DE, VE, SE, P

Strategy 22
Facilitation Techniques

For group work to successfully prepare students for work unit teamwork, the instructor must delegate authority to students so they can lead themselves, solve their own disputes, come up with their own ideas, generate discussion, and evaluate and change their solutions based on the input from the group. The instructor must provide a "trial by fire" experience yet maintain final control through evaluation of the final product.

As part of this delegation process, the instructor could identify a student facilitator for each group or for the class as a whole. If possible, the tasks associated with the facilitator's job can be written in a handout or placed on a chart where everyone can view them. This helps to show that the facilitator is fulfilling the tasks of his/her role as directed by higher authority.

In addition, if facilitators can be identified in advance, the instructor can develop a short training session for them so they can see the various responsibilities required for facilitation—leadership, coaching, harmonizing, and disseminating information.

Sometimes it may be advantageous to train the whole class in the role of facilitation, especially if student facilitators are to be used instead of teacher-led lecture material. This allows everyone to understand the responsibilities and challenges of facilitation and to "buy-in" to the idea of using student facilitators.

VE, SE

Strategy 23
Team Score for Evaluation

This strategy is based on the idea that all group work should be evaluated in part using group products. Because the group process is dynamic, there may be reasons why one student is excluded more or included more in the development of a project.

Students should be informed in the orientation that they will receive only a collaborative group evaluation and that they must work to assure that all members of the group participate and contribute.

SE, G, DE, P

Strategy 24
Debate Teams

Almost any discipline has components that are controversial and can lead to lively debate. Consumer behavior classes, for example, can debate the viewpoints of marketers vs. consumers, emergency medical technician preparation classes can debate methods of care, and electronics classes can debate designs of circuits. Almost any discipline can provide the raw material for debating. Debate teams often require several things from participants:

1. Participants must research the material thoroughly covering issues from both sides.
2. Participants must prepare oral and visual presentations that enhance their communications ability.
3. Participants must be able to appreciate the viewpoints of both sides as they may not know which side they will represent.
4. Participants must learn to listen actively in order to formulate appropriate rebuttals.
5. Participants must "think on their feet" in order to answer rebuttals, which helps to develop critical thinking skills.

To organize a debate, divide the class into an even number of teams. One topic of controversy can be assigned to a whole class or one topic can be assigned to each set of two groups. The students are given the topic and assigned to the group before the actual debate in order to fully research the topic. The day of the debate, the groups flip coins to decide which of the viewpoints they will be representing. For two competing teams, the agenda might read:

Team 1 (10 mins)—Opening statement and contention
Team 2 (10 mins)—Opening statement and contention
Team 1 (10 mins)—Rebuttal
Team 2 (10 mins)—Rebuttal
Team 1 (5 mins)—Conclusion
Team 2 (5 mins)—Conclusion
Instructor summary (15 mins)

The teams often get so involved in the debate that the instructor has to step in to be sure that the discussion doesn't get heated. An important component of this learning activity is the summary conducted at the end of the debate by the instructor. This provides the class with any key points that might have been missed in the research or glossed over during the debate. It allows the instructor to compare and contrast the viewpoints and then to canvas the class on their feelings about a particular issue. The exercise is valuable to team development because it allows students to work together to develop evidence and to support the contentions of team members as well as to work together to think through the premises of the other team and to counter them. The actual division of the class into competing teams seems to enhance team support and team spirit as well.

VE, SE, A, G, P

Strategy 25
Group Investigations

This strategy uses division of labor to divide the class into teams that go off by themselves to research a specific topic and then present the results to the class. The emphasis here is on the investigation of content material or on different viewponts such as those in Strategy 24 (Debate). Group investigation uses a variety of skills, all of which are important to teamwork: reading comprehension, summarizing, research skills, time management skills, use of resources, evaluative skills, analysis, integration of ideas and information [Cohen, p. 87].

This technique can be used to provide: 1) additional information not given in the text, as in the case of investigating methods for designing fabrics in courses such as fashion design; 2) answers to case study questions, such as in the case of investigating the Federal Trade Commission ruling about a company discussed in courses such as business; 3) current information from industry, as in the case of interviewing the top five real estate firms to determine their criteria for success; and 4) information on events in history, such as the life histories of those killed in the sinking of the Titanic for courses in history.

The applications for this approach are many, but the number of activities generated using the strategy must be tempered with the long lead times required for research to get maximum benefit from the technique.

VE, SE, G, P, A

Strategy 26
Team Experimentation

Similar to group investigation (Strategy 25), this strategy divides the class into groups and provides each group with an experiment to perform in a collaborative manner. Usually, the group is required to do some research and some planning in addition to the actual experiment. The group will be evaluated on the outcome of the experiment. Electronics classes, for example, may be given a circuit to design within specific variables, a fashion design class might be given an evening gown to design based on certain principles, a marketing class might be given a survey using three different approaches to creating an ad, or a photography class might be given an experiment using different kinds of chemicals.

In order to achieve success based on the criteria of evaluation given by the instructor (which should include group or teamwork criteria), the process group must effectively research, plan, use time, schedule work, divide tasks, and accomplish them.

One variation of this approach is to give each group the same experiment and let the groups compare and contrast each other's approaches. Another variation can be developed by giving each group slightly different input, data, criteria, or materials so that the groups can see the different outcomes created by having slightly different inputs.

VE, SE, P, G

Strategy 27
Conceptual Model Building

This strategy divides the class into groups of three to six. Each group is given a verbal description of a process involved with the discipline. For an advertising course, the description could be the steps involved in developing an ad campaign; in computer programming, it could be the steps involved in creating a directory; in electronics, the description could be the steps involved in troubleshooting a circuit. Students are asked to come up with a graphic representation of the process (unlike anything shown in the text). Students are allowed to create flow charts, cartoons, three-dimensional representations, or whatever, as long as the final product represents a "model" of the process.

This strategy helps students work together on collaborative critical and creative thinking. Often the groups divide the labor tasks into segments concerned with the development of ideas and then with the graphic execution of those ideas.

VE, SE, P, A, G

Strategy 28
Concrete Model Building

This strategy, similar to Strategy 27, requires student teams to design and/or build actual physical models of processes or objects associated with a discipline. Students might create their physical models out of soda cans, for example, or they might use children's linkage toys, or cardboard cutouts, or modeling clay. Students can be highly creative, using almost any type of easily obtainable material.

Whether it's a computer process, a physical process, or object being modeled, this strategy helps students to visually integrate concepts in their minds. It also provides exceptional fun for the teams. Innovative companies, such as Boeing, have used this strategy to develop new products and services.

VE, SE, G, P, A

Strategy 29
Multiability Tasks

Cohen stresses the use of multiability projects in her book, *Designing Groupwork*. Group activities should be developed that integrate discussion, expressing and defending points of view, logic, critical thinking, experimentation, role playing, and model building, etc. Tasks that are developed using several of these approaches can help students to see that learning involves all of these dimensions and more (not just memorization).

The instructor can choose three to four of these dimensions and create a task certain to include criteria for each dimension in the evaluation.

"More students will attain intellectual goals if the range of the goals is broader; individuals will use multiple intellectual routes to the attainment of goals" [Cohen, p. 149]

VE, DE, A, P, G

Strategy 30
Team Roles

For long-term group work, it may be beneficial to teach teaming techniques and to delineate possible team roles to be experienced throughout the project. Roles may differ substantially based on the type of discipline. Students in classes in advertising might be assigned to roles like account manager, creative director, account executive, and copywriter. Students in EMT (Emergency Medical Technician) classes might choose roles such as scene supervisor, leading EMT; students in electronics classes might divide into design and technician groups.

Not all team roles need be as specific as these. Erb and Doda [p. 22] suggest possible generic roles that could be identified for any group. These include:

- Team leader
- Communicator
- Recorder
- Esteem builder—sees to the issue of building self-esteem, not tearing it down.

Once the roles have been negotiated and set, job descriptions should be developed for each role and clearly posted for team participants to remind them of the roles they and other team members are playing.

VE, SE, G, P

Strategy 31
Team Evaluation

Erb and Doda [pp. 61–69] suggest that teams be required to set aside time for evaluation of internal effectiveness, using some kind of self-administered questionnaire to evaluate the dynamics of the team. This type of systematic evaluation provides checkpoints throughout the project to help bolster team effectiveness. If the evaluation results are low, all members of the team will become aware of the problem and can work to get the group process back on track.

An effective team evaluation tool might be to ask questions such as:

1. Do you think your group is using its time effectively?
2. Are all members of your group contributing to the work product?
3. Are all members of your group contributing to the discussion?
4. Is your project progressing toward completion in an appropriate manner? Why? Why not?
5. Should your group evaluate your schedule in order to meet the deadline?
6. Is your project of the kind of professional quality expected by the instructor?
7. Are there any noticeable conflicts that need to be resolved? Which ones are they?
8. Is any one person taking too much of a leadership role?
9. Does your group have enough information to complete the task?
10. Does your group work together (collaborate) well enough?

VE, SE, G, P, DE

Strategy 32
Building Identity

Providing the groups in a classroom with a process for developing team identity can give students the experience of working on an identifiable team. Team identity helps bond the group and builds morale, team effort, and self-esteem. To build identity for long-term group projects, the instructor can use the following process.

1. Ask students to talk together about the team project and to develop a set of one to five realistic goals for the group.
2. Ask students to discuss possible names for the group and to choose a name that best exemplifies the "spirit of the team."
3. Ask students to reevaluate their goals and to restate them in terms of measurable outcomes.
4. Ask students to plan celebratory events that will be conducted once individual goals have been met.
5. Provide team "scoring" sheets prominently displayed so team members can see how the teams are doing.

VE, SE, G, P, DE

Strategy 33
Interdisciplinary Curriculum Units

Interdisciplinary curriculum units (ICUs) are units of instruction that are multiability (see Strategy 29) as well as interdisciplinary. An ICU is an integrated set of objectives that combines into a single piece of instruction such skills as group process, critical thinking, writing attitude, oral and written communication, and self-efficacy. In a fashion design project, for example, the instructor might require a group task (group process skills), design fashion (design and arts), a marketing plan for selling the design (marketing, business), and a written component forecasting success and future sales (mathematics).

An exciting way to breathe life into an ICU is to request that other instructors in different disciplines prepare material tailored specifically to the project and act as a guest speaker for the class. Their viewpoints and expertise can assist students in seeing how each discipline can be integrated into one project. They can also contribute specific criteria from their discipline to the final evaluation instrument. Like Strategy 29, the evaluation of an ICU must include all components of the project.

VE, SE, DE, G, P

Strategy 34
Group Contract

To ensure that students get the optimal benefit from a particular project, a special learning contract can be developed to set forth the evaluation criteria for a group project. A learning contract [Knowles, 1984, pp. 25–30] should cover the following items:

- learning goals
- strategies and sources
- evidence of accomplishment
- criteria
- means of measuring accomplishment

"It makes sense, for a group project to be assessed according to criteria that demand a cooperative effort and that these criteria should be clearly negotiated with the group near the start of the project, or at the very least, before irrevocable decisions are made" [Jaques, p. 114].

By using a learning contract (and including the development and negotiation of that learning contract as part of the evaluation process), the group can be involved in the total learning experience of establishing criteria, setting goals, setting measurement, working toward goals through the group process, and making the final evaluation of the success of both individual and group efforts.

VE, SE, DE, G, P

Strategy 35
Team Board Games

Board games can be used successfully to foster both a sense of excitement and of team affiliation within a short time frame.

"A game," according to Jaques, "is usually taken to describe a group exercise in which players cooperate or compete towards a given end within a regime of explicit rules. Players behave as themselves" [p. 116]. The primary attribute of games is that the actions in games are generally governed by the artificial structure of the game rules, whereas in a simulation, the scenario itself provides that the common sense rules of life govern the action of the players. There is evidence to indicate that for developing teamwork, it is best to use cooperative instead of competitive games.

Board games created by the instructor or adopted from readily available board games can help balance cooperation and competition in the classroom. Typical games that can be adopted (depending on the discipline) to group cooperative games are:

1. Monopoly
2. Chinese checkers
3. Discipline - based Trivial Pursuit
4. Scruples

The most important component of games as a learning tool comes at the end of the game—the "debriefing" or the summary of the game given by the instructor.

During the debriefing the instructor can ask a variety of questions such as [Jaques, p. 118]:

1. How are you feeling?
2. What is going on in the game?
3. Who is "winning"?
4. Why do you think they are "winning"?
5. Who is achieving what?
6. What are you (their) perceptions of what has happened?
7. Did the games reveal any specific applications to the discipline? Why or why not?
8. Can the group identify causes for group failure or success?

VE, SE, G, P

Strategy 36
Team Simulations

When a game is used in conjunction with some type of scenario, it becomes a role play situation, a replication or representation of life. This is a simulation. The biggest difference between a game and a simulation is that while the players of a game are given distinct, artificial rules to play by, the players of a simulation have only their knowledge of the subject and common sense. The rules of a simulation are unwritten "rules of life" and the players often play characters other than themselves.

For a marketing or business instructor, the possible scenarios for simulation are endless. The students can play roles such as:

• The ad agency creative team
• The marketing client
• The owner/operator of a retail establishment
• The local banker
• The developer

Simulations, in one form or another, are also used extensively in health care courses with the student playing roles of patients, caregivers, etc. As with games, a period of debriefing should follow the simulation that analyzes the student's work and role playing.

Typical debriefing questions for simulations include:

1. What did you think of your role?
2. How did you feel in it?

3. Did you relate differently to people than you would have as yourself?

4. Did you feel comfortable? Why or why not?

5. Did you think the others played their roles well?

6. What did you learn about yourself as a result?

VE, SE, G, P

Strategy 37
Critical Panels

This strategy places students in the role of experts in material that is discipline-oriented. Students are given some aspect of the discipline to study at length (a week or more). To be most effective, the instructor should choose a topic that is controversial or one in which there can be many viewpoints represented.

A group of three to four students is assigned individual components of a subject viewpoint while three or four other students are assigned aspects of the opposite (or any contradictory) viewpoint. At a prescribed time in the classroom agenda, the two groups make up a critical panel and are required to respond to questions developed by other groups of students. Of course to prevent any competitive problems, it is advisable to let all groups know that everyone will have a chance to ask questions. (Those serving on the panel during this week's session will be allowed to ask questions of others who will serve on the panel later.)

Each of the evaluators (who could include a business mentor selected by students or an instructor) can evaluate the effectiveness of the groups and individuals involved in the panel discussion.

The purposes of a critical panel discussion can include

- Representing each viewpoint.
- Providing details concerning each viewpoint.
- Forcing students through debate to think critically about what they need.
- Creating important discussion to give students practice in thinking, speaking, and analyzing.
- Providing a broad overview for a school of thought.

As in games and simulations, a key aspect of using critical thinking panels is to provide a debriefing at the end of the exercise to point out to the students areas such as:

- Good use of data
- Good use of quotes
- Excellent reasoning
- Good ability to communicate "off the cuff"
- Thorough coverage of material
- Fallacies of logic
- Lack of insight
- Inability to apply facts as necessary

It is recommended that each team or group be debriefed privately so that (in terms of grading) those who perform last do not have an unfair advantage of having seen the critiques of the first groups.

VE, SE, DE, A, P, G

Strategy 38
Cooperative Games

It is important for members of any society to learn how to cooperate. Our educational systems provide us with a foundation of aggressive competitiveness that threatens our adulthood. We must develop methods of teaching that place an emphasis on cooperation instead of competition.

In planning classroom activities, the instructor can develop games and role plays that allow for reversal of roles, democratic orientations, and collaboration. Placing the emphasis on collaboration can assist adults in tempering their competitive behavior in situations where cooperation is more productive.

SE, VE, G, P, DE

Strategy 39
Group Diaries

If the project is being used to enhance the ability of students to work in teams (using group processes), a valuable strategy would be to require a group log or diary. A group diary is simply a meeting-by-meeting log that outlines who said what and who did what to accomplish group goals. The diary is kept methodically throughout the project. The group elects a diarist (or secretary) to record all events and even quotes from members. Every significant conversation or decision is logged into the book. At the end of the project, the project itself is evaluated as well as the group process skills reflected by the writings in the diary. An exceptional evaluation tool is to ask students to prepare an essay reflecting their thoughts on the group process as depicted in the diary entries.

SE, VE, DE, G, P

Strategy 40
Group Essay

For this exercise, the class is divided into groups of three people. Each group is required to develop a response to a controversial topic such as abortion, marketing ethics codes, the true causes of World War II, or whatever topic is appropriate for the discipline. The groups meet together and develop a conceptual response to the problem. Once the group members have outlined the concepts they perceive as important, the task is to write an essay collectively that reflects the overall thinking of the group.

The essential element is to write collectively. The instructor should not allow the group members to write the essays (or even parts of the essays) individually, but must require each line of the final essay be written collectively. This will mean that each line must be negotiated between the group members until it is satisfactory to all. This exercise will not only teach the content material associated with the essay, but will illustrate for students the issues involved in group process and the difficulties associated with negotiation.

VE, SE, DE, G, P

CLASSROOM STRATEGIES FOR LEADERSHIP

1. Role Play—Authoritarian
2. Role Play—Permissive
3. Role Play—Participative
4. Meeting Planning
5. Discussion Leaders
6. Conducting a Meeting
7. Handling Conflict
8. Experiential Training
9. Decision Making
10. Leader of Long-Term, Large Group
11. Leader of Short-Term, Large Group
12. Leader of Long-Term, Small Group
13. Leader of Short-Term, Small Group
14. Lessons in Followership
15. Debate on Leadership
16. Role Play—Employee vs. Production Orientation
17. Skit—Sources of Power
18. Interview with a Great Leader
19. Report on Theories of Leadership
20. Panel Discussion on Leadership
21. Leadership Self Assessment
22. Leadership Peer Assessment
23. Code of Ethics
24. Leadership Game
25. Risk Taking Game
26. Leadership Journal
27. Programmed vs. Nonprogrammed Decisions
28. Individual Theory of Leadership
29. Self Assignments
30. Mentor Program
31. A Leader a Day
32. Leadership Poster
33. Changing Leaders
34. Essay—Leaders Are Born
35. Essay—Leaders Are Made
36. Substitutes for Leadership
37. Presentation—Charismatic Leaders
38. Group Project—Power
39. Leadership Grid
40. Path Goal Theory Role Play

The debate has long been waged over whether leaders are born or are made. Can leadership as a skill be taught in a training or academic setting? Whether charismatic leadership can be taught is still debatable, but it is clear that the subskills of leadership (decision making, judgment, ethics, risk management, use of power) can be taught and their uses improved on the job by training.

Leadership is somewhat of an ambiguous term. When the ASTD study was conducted, leadership emerged as a major heading over a wide variety of skills that could be considered leadership subskills. Leadership as exemplified by employers varies from industry to industry and from company to company. Indeed, employers want leadership skills and traits that contribute to their own firm's goals. Individuals who are charismatic leaders may actually have problems in entry-level jobs if their leadership skills do not mesh well with the firm's goals. The skills employers want in an entry-level employee are those skills that contribute to the effectiveness of the employee as well as the organization. These include decision making, gaining the respect of others, learning to work with and through others, developing a goal orientation, and acquiring a reputation for dependability, reliability, and ethical standards.

The strategies in this section can be divided into three major categories. The first contains strategies designed to provide insight into the uses of power and leadership styles that demonstrate how those styles and uses affect others in the work setting. These strategies use role playing activities extensively to demonstrate major leadership styles, sources of power, and orientation. In addition, several content modules are included to briefly introduce concepts associated with leadership into any curriculum. These include modules on leadership, followership, contingency theory, and leadership theory.

The second category of strategies focuses on subskills required for training leadership, such as those for handling conflict, planning, leading discussions, decision making, and making programmed and nonprogrammed decisions.

Finally, several strategies for experiential leadership training are included, such as the four types of leadership training activities for small and large groups, long-term and short-term projects. There are several content-oriented tasks to provide experiential learning, such as developing a code of ethics, debates, essays, and reports involving leadership.

The strategies outlined here can be effectively used with the projects and activities listed under Teamwork.

Strategy 1
Role Play Authoritarian Style

This strategy relies on role play group activities to provide students with opportunities to experience an authoritarian leadership style. An autocratic leader gives followers little voice in decision making and makes decisions for them. "Autocratic leadership depends on the formal power of the leader's position and the ability to administer rewards and punishment" [Costley, Todd, p. 237].

The followers are evaluated on the basis of whether they "do what the boss wants." Autocratic leaders frequently use fear as a foundation of power. The strength of this style lies in the fact that tasks can be accomplished quickly and consistently, but this must be tempered with low motivation.

Autocratic leadership

Pros	Cons
Consistency	Low motivation
Rapid decisions	Low creativity/innovation
Centralized control	Avoidance of responsibility
Effective crisis management	Miscommunication

[Costley Todd, p. 238]

The classroom is divided into three or four small groups to complete a discipline-oriented task. (See Critical Thinking and Teamwork Strategies). One student in each group is given instructions that he/she is the leader and all decision-making authority lies with him/her. The student leaders are told in written instructions to make decisions for the group and to maintain control. The class is informed that these leaders are chosen by the instructor and are the "boss" of the group. The students are also told that they are responsible for the work of the group, and they must perform.

The group task (emphasizing content material) should be designed to take from 10 to 15 minutes. After that allotted time, the instructor should take up the projects for immediate evaluation (ideally) and then direct evaluation comments to the leaders, as if the other members were not involved. Once the evaluations of the task have been discussed, the instructor would pass out an evaluation sheet asking questions such as:

1. How did you enjoy the project?
2. What was your input?
3. Did you enjoy the leadership style of your leader? Why or why not?
4. Did you feel uncomfortable at any time during the project?
5. Did your leader use two-way or one-way communication?
6. How did you feel about it?
7. What would you do to improve the leadership style of your leader?
8. What kind of leader do you usually enjoy working for?

Note: If only one leadership role play can be used, Strategy 3 should be used. This strategy should not be used alone. It should be given along with Strategy 3 to show the differences between the two.

LC, DE, SE, G, P

Strategy 2
Role Play Permissive Leadership Style

This strategy uses role play to provide students with the experience as a leader and a follower of permissive leadership style. A permissive leader is one who does not attempt to influence or control the group, but leaves the group members essentially alone and waits for them to complete the task. "Permissive leadership depends on the group to establish its own objectives and solve problems as they arise. This approach can work effectively if group members are highly motivated to achieve group objectives and will assume responsibility for leadership functions" [Costley, Todd, p. 236].

The permissive leader may serve as the liaison between the group and outside groups, but provides little, if any, real direction. "The widespread use of permissive leadership in an organization can lead to confusion or even chaos. Organizations have few leadership situations in which the manager can leave decisions entirely to a group of employees" [Costley, Todd, p. 236].

The class is divided into three or four groups and given a group project associated with content material in the discipline. A leader is designated for each group. The leader receives written instructions that he/she is the leader of the group and is responsible for the outcome of the group project but must refrain from trying to influence group members and must allow group members to work independently. The class is simply told to complete the project and is given the name of the student leader.

Permissive leadership

Pros	Cons
Independence for followers	Lack of coordination
Fosters creativity/innovation	No focus on group objectives
Flexibility	Lack of control
Open/direct communication	Little cooperation

[Costley and Todd]

The group task is then evaluated by the instructor and discussed as to its merit relative to the discipline. This discussion should be directed more at the group than the leader. After the evaluation and discussion of projects, the instructor would provide a questionnaire such as the following:

1. How did you enjoy the project?
2. What was your input?
3. How did you like the leadership style of your student leader?
4. Briefly describe how you view the student leader's leadership style?
5. Did you feel uncomfortable at any time during the project? Why or why not?
6. Did your leader use one-way or two-way communication?
7. How did you feel about your leader's communication style?
8. What would you do to improve your leader's style?
9. What kind of leader do you usually like to work with?

Ideally, this role play exercise would be given after Strategy 1. The use of Strategies 1, 2, and 3 will provide students with opportunities to experience these styles as followers and as leaders.

Note: If only one leadership role play can be used, Strategy 3 should be used. This strategy should be used in conjunction with Strategy 3 and not alone.

LC, DE, SE, G, P, VE

Strategy 3
Role Play Participative Style

This strategy, similar to Strategies 1 and 2, uses role play exercises to allow students to experience participative leadership style. Participative leaders share both authority and responsibility with the group. Group members are given opportunities to be involved in planning and decision making. "Participative leaders do not reject the responsibilities of leadership and attempt to be just another member of the group. They are active leaders in making decisions, using the input of group members. They focus on achieving objectives and direct the flow of communication to provide group members with adequate information" [Costley, Todd, p. 239].

Participative leaders rely on individuals to evaluate their own activities and to work to achieve their own goals so that the leader does not have control over their activities.

Participative leadership

Pros	Cons
High individual motivation	Time consuming
Use of knowledge of group members	Individuals may dominate the group
Commitment to goals	Compromise can lead to ineffectiveness
Two-way communication	Unclear responsibilities

[Costley, Todd, p. 240]

The class is divided into three or four groups and given a discipline-oriented group task (see Critical Thinking and Teamwork Strategies). A leader is identified for each group and given instructions to share responsibility for decision making and to allow all members to share input. In fact, the leader should be told to encourage the group members to participate fully.

About 10 to 15 minutes should be allowed for accomplishing the task. Once the task has been accomplished, the instructor should evaluate the results, directing the evaluation at all the members of the group. The instructor should then hand out an evaluation questionnaire such as the following:

1. How did you enjoy the project?
2. What was your input?
3. Briefly describe how you viewed the student leader's leadership style?
4. Did you feel uncomfortable at any time during the project? Why or why not?
5. Did your leader use one- or two-way communication?
6. How did you feel about it?
7. What would you do to improve the leader's leadership style?
8. What kind of leader do you usually like to work with?

Ideally, this exercise should be given after Strategies 1 and 2 have already been conducted so that students can compare and contrast the different leadership styles.

Note: This is the only leadership role play exercise that can be given as a stand-alone strategy.

LC, DE, SE, P, G

Strategy 4
Meeting Planning

One of the major functions of a leader is to be able to plan and conduct a meeting. Students can be given a discipline-oriented assignment that requires them to learn this skill. (see strategies for Critical Thinking and Teamwork).

The major decisions to be made by the student leader concern items such as [Stech and Ratliffe, pp. 270–271]:

1. Goals and tasks for the meeting
2. Membership and attendance
3. Time and length of meeting
4. Location and facilities
5. Arrangements and equipment
6. Documents and materials needed
7. Methods and procedures

In addition, the leader must also accomplish other important activities to ensure the meeting is productive such as [Stech and Ratcliff, pp. 275–277]:

Pre-meeting Activities

1. Arrange for meeting place.
2. Issue an announcement of the meeting.
3. Prepare agenda.
4. Develop necessary materials and bring them to the meeting.

Meeting Activities

1. Open meeting. Use a friendly welcome and information about goals and tasks of meeting.

2. Set tone for meeting. Set the tone as friendly, down-to-business, creative, or whatever is appropriate.
3. Describe procedures for group work. Suggest procedures and ask for a vote.
4. Maintain control. Formally recognize members, maintain balance of control between members.
5. Deal with conflict. Step in and mediate if there is a crisis or conflict.
6. Close meeting. Assess meeting and bring it to a close.

Post Meeting Activities

1. Prepare minutes of meeting.
2. Followup on persons assigned tasks during meeting.
3. Compile data from postmeeting reaction sheets.

Students can be given responsibility for planning a group activity meeting (using group work as described under Teamwork). The instructor might assign permanent work groups and allow students to take turns planning the group meetings as the groups prepare their content-oriented materials. An evaluation form like that described in Strategies 1 through 3 can be developed for use.

VE, SE, G

Strategy 5
Discussion Leaders

Throughout a semester or class, students should be given opportunities to lead the class in formal discussions. If this function is traded off from class to class (or each half hour or so), each student can get experience in opening the discussion, balancing input from different members, drawing out reluctant members, tactfully discouraging members from dominating the discussion, managing conflict, and helping elicit generalizations and conclusions based on the discussions.

Student leaders can be appointed for the class as a whole, given an assigned date and time for leading their discussion and the topic to be covered during their session. It will be more meaningful if students are given a set of guidelines on how to lead the group.

Guidelines

1. Set the tone for the discussion by opening the discussion in a warm yet serious tone.
2. Review what is to be discussed with the group.
3. Begin with a point drawn from your own interpretation of the material.
4. Ask for additional input.
5. Be sure to get input from everyone in the group.
6. Pick out exceptionally good comments and comment on them.
7. Pose questions to get the audience to respond to the comments.
8. Close the discussion at the appropriate time.

VE, G, SE

Strategy 6
Conducting a Meeting

Similar to Strategy 4, this strategy is designed to teach students to conduct meetings. According to Stech and Ratcliffe, leadership responsibility in terms of running meetings includes the following:

1. Opening the meeting
2. Setting the tone for the meeting
3. Describing procedures
4. Maintaining control
5. Dealing with conflict
6. Closing the meeting

This strategy is a continuation of Strategy 4. Students would be given responsibility for running a group meeting that had already been planned by another student. (See Strategy 4. The two strategies can also be combined into one activity.) The instructor can assign syndicates (permanent work groups) or temporary groups. An evaluation form similar to that shown in Strategy 1 can be administered after the session to provide feedback to the student to help him/her with his/her skills.

VE, G, SE

Strategy 7
Handling Conflict

A major role of any leader is to be able to handle conflict for the good of the work group. Even in group work such as that described under Teamwork and Critical Thinking, some kinds of conflict are likely to arise. "Sometimes a leader has to step in when a dispute or conflict arises. Members cannot always get themselves out of such situations" [Stech, Ratliffe, p. 276].

Two basic kinds of conflict will need to be handled. They are substantive conflict and personality clashes.

Substantive Conflict

Substantive conflict is conflict over content, ideas, or policies. This kind of conflict can be resolved by using voting, or getting consensus, or by brainstorming.

Personality Clashes

Personality clashes are deep emotional disagreements based on strong conflicting values. These conflicts may NOT be resolvable. Sometimes the leader must be content to try to mediate so that no one appears to "lose" and everyone seems to gain.

In managing conflict, the leader must learn to recognize confirming responses—messages that express value as opposed to those that do not express value. According to Ronald Adler in *Communicating at Work* [p. 93], a leader can learn to recognize several kinds of disconfirming responses:

- Impervious responses. The person does not acknowledge the other person's attempt to communicate.

- Interrupting responses. One person will not let the other person finish a point. The implication is that "I'm not interested in what you have to say."

- Irrelevant responses. A person brings up topics that are unrelated to what the other person has said.

- Tangential responses. A person acknowledges the message and then brushes it off and steers the conversation in another direction.

- Impersonal responses. A person displays superficial reactions as if the person's feelings and ideas are not important.
- Incongruous responses. A person provides obscure, hard-to-understand responses.

Leaders also need to be able to use confirming, positive language to keep the discussion flowing [Adler, pp. 96–100]:

- Use "I" language. Be careful of evaluative, attacking statements.
- Focus on solving problems. Try not to control or force someone to do something. Solve problems in ways so that everyone "wins." Describe results, not how to do the job.
- Be honest. Never manipulate anyone. Honesty helps keep people from being defensive.
- Show concern for others. Having empathy for others will help develop and maintain positive interaction.
- Show an attitude of equality. Never act superior to the participants in the discussion. No one likes to be made to feel less valuable.
- Have an open mind. Be open to new ideas. Most people have knowledge you do not have due to their life experience.

In addition, leaders must learn to redirect conflict between members of a group by calming individuals who seem to be reacting with conflict to situations or statements presented. Leaders have to learn to "raise delicate issues" even if a conflict may ensue. To introduce possible conflict issues, the leader can use one of the following techniques [Adler, pp. 103–104]:

1. Identify goals
2. Choose the best time
3. Rehearse a statement to diffuse conflict
4. Pinpoint a specific problem
5. Pinpoint reactions to a problem

The instructor can provide student leaders with handouts on these issues before allowing the students to lead a discussion. This preliminary training may help students deal with conflict later on the job.

In some cases, the instructor might want to "plant" some mild conflict into the discussion (enlisting the assistance of a student) to allow for actual practice in identifying and redirecting conflict. If the leadership evaluation form is used, the instructor can add a question relating to conflict management such as:

1. Did your student leader successfully resolve any conflicts that occurred during the discussion?
2. How successful was he or she?
3. What was the leader's most successful behavior in terms of managing conflict?

VE, DE, G, SE, A

Strategy 8
Experiential Leadership Training

One of the most controversial training methods for developing leadership traits is to use experiential learning courses to develop crisis management skills for leaders. These programs have their origin in World War II when the German U-boats were sinking British vessels by the scores. Ironically, the older, more experienced sailors outlived the younger and stronger sailors. Kurt Hahn, a German educator and an expatriate, studied the situation and decided that "the younger men lacked the self-reliance, confidence and compassionate bond with their fellow crew members that was so essential to meeting the challenge of the crisis" [Broderick, p. 78]. Hahn set up a program called "Outward Bound" designed to instill these special leadership qualities—spiritual tenacity, will to survive, self-reliance, and confidence—in British seamen.

Another Outward Bound program was developed in the U.S.A. in 1961 in which wilderness training was used. ". . . the concept of building a training program around physically and psychologically challenging outdoor experiences has been adopted by all sorts of enterprising people and offered to corporations as a way to instill team spirit, leadership skills, full-fledged self actualization" [Broderick, p. 78].

Some of these programs include jumping from cliffs (with appropriate cables attached), crossing rivers, and scaling walls. Of course, this kind of approach would be out of the question for most secondary and college classes. There are, however, experiential learning courses that have been developed using much less strenuous or dangerous methods, such as falling off chairs into the arms of coworkers or students, allowing someone (whom you do not know) help you walk through mazes, hugging classmates, and visioning.

Programs such as these can often be found through the chamber of commerce or universities. An extracurricular field trip developed as a final activity for a program could greatly enhance the leadership abilities of students. Even if such a program is unavailable or simply not feasible based on the other requirements of the curriculum, an exercise such as walking through a maze can be easily incorporated with a followup describing experiential learning and its benefits. This type of exercise can be discipline-based if it is used in conjunction with a group project based on the discipline in which students are required to build up their "team spirit" as they complete a project.

VI, DE, SE, G

Strategy 9
Decision Making

Students need practice in making decisions, no matter what discipline they plan to study. On future jobs, each student will be asked to make decisions. Managers, executives, and nonmanagerial personnel make decisions every day, even if the decision is as simple as when to go to lunch.

Decision making is a reaction to a problem or opportunity and relies on people's perceptions regarding what constitutes an opportunity. This strategy provides students with three models or methods of making a decision [Robbins, pp. 95–106]:

Model 1: Optimizing Decision Model. This is "a decision making model that describes how individuals should behave in order to maximize some outcome" [Robbins].

Steps in Optimizing Decisions:

1. Ascertain need for a decision
2. Identify the decision criteria
3. Allocate weights to the criteria
4. Develop alternatives
5. Evaluate the alternatives
6. Select the best alternative

The optimizing decision model is based on the concept of rationality—that the decision maker is objective and logical. The optimizing model assumes there are no conflicts over goals, that all options are known, that alternatives are clear and constant, and that the final choice should maximize outcomes.

Model 2: Satisfying Model. This is "a decision-making model where a decision maker chooses the first solution that is 'good enough,' that is satisfactory and sufficient" [Robbins].

The satisfying model requires that problems be reduced to a level at which they can readily be understood, because human beings simply cannot process and understand all information necessary to optimize a decision. Decision makers create simple models of situations requiring a decision and then try to make a rational decision based on those models. Decisions made using this model are based on a few obvious choices that are easy to identify (not on all the choices available). The decision maker reviews the choices until he/she finds one that is sufficient and satisfactory. The decision maker does not continue to search until he/she has found the optimum solution.

Model 3: Implicit Favorite Model. This is "a decision making model where the decision maker implicitly selects a preferred alternative early in the decision making process and biases the evaluation of other choices" [Robbins].

Individuals solve complex problems by developing simplified models, in this case, by not continuing to search for alternatives to evaluate. An alternative is identified as a "favorite" and rather than being objective, the decision maker simply chooses the favorite instead of going through the painstaking process of identification and evaluation of complex alternatives. ". . . the decision maker is often unaware that he or she has already identified an implicit favorite and that the rest of the process is really an exercise in prejudice [Robbins]. According to Robbins, the implicit decision model is used more than the others and the decision process is influenced more by intuition than rationality.

For this strategy, students would be given a discipline-oriented case study requiring a specific decision to be made. The class would be divided into three groups. One group would be told to use the optimizing decision model, another group the satisfying model, and another group the implicit favorite model.

Students would then share their decisions with the class as well as their feelings and experiences using a particular decision making model. For many students, the model assigned to them will be significantly different from the model they use in everyday decision making. An introduction to different decision making models within the context of their major will provide them with structures for decision making on their jobs.

Examples of decisions:

- Whether to develop a program for a color or monochrome monitor.
- Whether to use print ads or radio ads.
- Whether to work in pediatrics or trauma for clinical practice.
- Whether to use black and white or color shots for photographing graduation.
- Whether to use natural or man-made materials for a dress design.
- Whether to attribute the cause of World War II to economics or politics.
- Whether to use ABSTAT or another program for statistics.

VE, A, G, DE, SE, P

Strategy 10
Leader of Long-Term, Large Group Project

Many of the strategies have used group work as a basis for teaching content as well as team work. Group work can also be used extensively to develop both leadership and followership skills in students. For the group projects, as described in Teamwork and Critical Thinking, a student leader can be identified as the group leader for long-term projects.

Setting up a student leader allows students to relate to each other in a "boss—employee" format, allows student leaders to practice those leadership skills over time, and allows student followers to relate to a leader (as they would a boss). The true-life struggles of such relationships will inevitably surface: students will be unhappy with decisions, students will not complete their portion of the work, students will have to work harder to make up for the inactivity of their peers, and students will lack coordination and planning. The importance of this strategy is that students will learn to cope with situations such as these and relate to them. These assignments provide both the experience and pressure of leadership responsibility in a relatively low risk situation, and these skills can be transferred to the job later.

An important aspect of a large, long-term group project is to provide each student (especially the leader) with a short, one-page description. An example description follows:

Student Leader—Advertising Campaign Project

The student leader will be responsible for

- Coordination of activities of public relations account executive, advertising account executive, research manager, creative director, and account executive.
- Direction of activities of those sections above including scheduling work, making assignments, filling out evaluation sheets for each product and each intermediate student leader.
- Liaison with instructor via a meeting once per month.
- Liaison with client via a meeting once every two weeks.
- Development of final report and presentation through coordinated work of the student group.
- Quality review and control of the work.

A job description puts the leader's duties for the project in clear terms so the leader knows what he/she will be graded on. Of course, in a long-term project where each student has a different "job" and different job tasks, evaluation for each student will have to be made based on that student's duties, as well as, in part, on the overall success of the project.

An important point to be made with regard to this strategy is that it allows only one student to practice the leadership skills required to lead the entire group, but subgroups can be developed (see Strategy 12) to allow more students to practice leadership skills.

VE, G, SE

Strategy 11
Leader of Short-term, Large Group Project

Similar to Strategy 10, this strategy allows a student to hold the position of student leader for a large group project, but only for a group project which lasts one class period. Using a group project as described in Critical Thinking or Teamwork, the instructor develops a content-oriented task or plan to be developed and chooses a student leader to lead the class in accomplishing that assignment. The student is given a one- or two-paragraph job description similar to the one that follows.

Student Leader—CPR Exercise

- Monitors the group as they attempt to provide CPR to the mannequin, being sure that they accomplish the task using exactly the appropriate procedures.
- Corrects any group member who is not correctly administering the CPR (after checking with the instructor to be sure the student is performing incorrectly).
- Directs the activity of the group as they move the mannequin on the stretcher to the "ambulance" after CPR is declared successful.
- Fills out an evaluation form on the progress of each group member including him/herself.

One advantage of using this strategy is that (unlike Strategy 10) every student in a class could get practice in leadership, if the class structure allows for one or two of these exercises to be conducted per class period.

VE, G, SE

Strategy 12
Leader of Small Group, Long-term Project

In some long-term group projects (as outlined in Critical Thinking and Teamwork), the group may have a student leader who has overall responsibility for the coordination of a project, but also has intermediate student leaders who lead small subgroups within the large group. This scenario is helpful because it more closely resembles the working environment. Students are required to concurrently develop and maintain relationships with a hierarchy of student leaders. The small group student leaders also practice dealing with both a manager (student leader) and followers and can begin to understand the complexities of middle management or middle leadership role.

As in Strategy 10, the large group is divided into several task-oriented work groups and each group is assigned a leader who reports to the overall student leader. These intermediate student leaders are also given job descriptions similar to the one that follows.

Student Leader—Public Relations Manager

- Responsible for directing small group work in developing a public relations campaign.
- Responsible for coordinating work of a project team so that the campaign will be effective and efficient within budgetary constraints.
- Responsible for scheduling work assigned to the public relations group of the larger student group.
- Responsible for liaison between the overall student leader and members of the public relations group.
- Responsible for presenting final public relations campaign to client.
- Responsible for presenting final public relations campaign to instructor.
- Responsible for filling out evaluation forms for each member of the group.

Student Leader—Economic Systems Comparative Study of the Free World

- Responsible for splitting larger group into sections representing each major economic system in the free world.
- Responsible for directing group work involved in developing in-depth presentation concerning history, strengths, and weaknesses of those economic systems of the free world.
- Responsible for scheduling work assigned to each subgroup.
- Responsible for reviewing final document for accuracy and completeness.
- Responsible for redirecting individual student members who may need assistance in developing their portion of the work.
- Responsible for liaison with overall student leader and student leaders of the group covering economic systems of communist and socialist countries.
- Responsible for final editing and production of report.
- Responsible for planning and developing class presentation using team members.
- Responsible for filling out evaluation forms for each member of the group.

This strategy provides important leadership experiences (which are both positive and negative) that these students probably will not receive any other way until they have an entry-level position and perhaps have been on the job two to three years. From this experience, they will learn how leadership feels, how it can be difficult, yet rewarding, stressful, yet stimulating. This is valuable training for life situations to come.

VE, SE, G

Strategy 13
Leader of Small Group, Short-term Projects

Similar to Strategy 11, this strategy requires the instructor to develop short-term group projects and to assign student leaders to each project. Even though the time frame is short, an overall leader can be identified and then subgroups identified with intermediate leaders who report to him/her. Using group projects such as those identified under Critical Thinking and Teamwork, the instructor develops a group task designed to teach content and adds the leadership roles as a means of instilling leadership.

Student Leader—Product Marketing Plan Exercise

- Responsible for leading small group in developing name, features, packaging, labeling of a new product that is currently not on the market.
- Responsible for liaison with student leaders for the price, place, and promotion subgroups.
- Responsible for final presentation of product to the class.

Student Leader—Price Marketing Plan Exercise

- Responsible for leading group in developing pricing strategies based on the product developed by the product group.
- Responsible for liaison with student leaders for product, promotion, and place.
- Responsible for final presentation of price to the class.

Student Leader—Place Marketing Plan Exercise

- Responsible for leading group in developing distribution strategies based on product and price developed by product group and price group.

- Responsible for liaison with student leaders for product, price, and promotion.
- Responsible for final presentation of place to the class.

Student Leader—Promotion Marketing Plan Exercise

- Responsible for leading the group in developing a promotion plan, including strategies for advertising, public relations, selling, and sales promotion, based on the product developed by the product group, price developed by the price group, and distribution developed by the place group.
- Responsible for liaison with student leaders in product, place, and price groups.
- Responsible for final presentation of promotion plan.

All of these intermediate small group leaders would then coordinate with the overall student leader who would be responsible for managing the overall effort of the class.

The difference between this and Strategy 12 is that this exercise requires less time. The instructor can develop plans or activities to be accomplished within one or two class periods. This strategy can be adopted for any discipline in which research projects can involve similar and related parts (history, psychology, sociology) or for which there is a process that can be broken down into parts. It allows students to experience the rewards and difficulties of leadership roles.

VE, SE, G

Strategy 14
Lessons in Followership

Part of learning good leadership skills is to also learn to be a gracious and cooperative follower. Most leaders, in fact, lead their respective groups of people or organizations but also have significant responsibilities for following as well. Learning to be a good follower is oftentimes more difficult than learning to be a good leader. For this reason, it is advisable to introduce exercises designed to enhance leadership skills with an introduction on the virtues of "followership." Those who learn to follow, yet are professional and display leadership where appropriate, make important contributions and will greatly enhance any organization. Good followers are likely to transform into excellent leaders.

In developing an introduction on "followership," the instructor can develop a handout such as the one that follows.

Ten Commandments of Followership

1. You should not follow blindly.
2. You should give opinions when appropriate.
3. You should work as hard as possible even if you don't agree with the leader's decision.
4. You should be loyal to your leader (even if you don't always agree with him/her).
5. You should bring concerns directly to the leader and not talk about his/her leadership style.
6. You should not be a "yes" person who always tells the leader what he/she wants to hear.
7. You should always contribute your share of the work.
8. You should respect deadlines.
9. You should learn to handle valid criticism.
10. You should not criticize without having input for a solution.

VE

Strategy 15
Debate on Leadership

There are three major theories of leadership that can explain leadership behavior:

Theory 1: Great Leaders Are Born. This theory is based on the idea that leadership skill is genetic, that leaders are born leaders. According to this theory, if an individual is not born with leadership skill, no amount of development or training can transform that individual into a leader.

Theory 2: Trait Theory. This theory uses personality characteristics of leaders as a basis for leadership success with the idea that leadership can be predicted if one has a quantifiable set of traits. In a study conducted by Kouses and Posner in *The Leadership Challenge,* a thousand leaders were interviewed and a list of five common attributes were developed:

1. Leaders challenge existing processes, seek opportunities, and take risks.
2. Leaders inspire new visions and prompt new goals by their employees.
3. Leaders support followers, collaborate, and make commitments.
4. Leaders model leadership. They set examples.
5. Leaders reward their followers by recognizing individual achievement.

Theory 3: Behavioral Theory. This theory is based on the idea that leadership develops out of the interaction between the leader, the followers, and the environment. In other words, leadership is contingent on the interaction of these three components. In his book *The Leadership Factor,* Kotter outlines six attributes that individuals can foster to achieve leadership success. They are:

1. Knowledge of environment and organization.
2. Relationships in industry and organization.
3. Strong reputation and track record of success.
4. Thinking ability, good judgment, analytical ability, strategic thinking, interpersonal ability.
5. Respect for everyone.
6. High energy and strong desire to lead.

Students will also have their own opinions of what makes a good leader. This assignment should be developed using examples from the discipline. Students would be divided into three groups. Each group would be assigned a leadership theory and asked to research leaders in the discipline that seem to reflect the theory as well as research information about the theory itself. Once all groups have completed their research, the class could hold a three-way debate with each group expounding its theory. It is an effective tie-in to communication to require that the debate use formal debate style. Each group would give an overview of its position, then each group would provide rebuttals to the other groups, and finally each group would develop a conclusion using comments and examples from research based on the leaders and leadership roles in the specific area of study.

VE, SE, A, G

Strategy 16
Role Play—Employee Versus Production Orientation

An excellent strategy is to develop a group project (see Teamwork, Critical Thinking, Motivation) that will introduce some kind of new project or task to be accomplished.

The class is divided into four groups. Each group selects a student to serve as the leader of the group. The instructor asks the leaders to pick an index card. Two of the cards show people orientation and provide instructions to the student to role play an executive who is concerned primarily with the welfare of the group members, while the other two cards show task orientation and provide instructions to the student to role play a leader whose only concern is getting the task done.

Once the tasks have been completed, the instructor would evaluate the tasks per the content-oriented criteria and then administer the leadership questionnaire shown in Strategies 1 through 3. The objective is for students to compare and contrast their own feelings and motivation levels under each style.

G, SE, A, VE

Strategy 17
Skit—Sources of Power

Leaders must learn to use power widely and constructively. Power comes in many forms and allows the leader to achieve his/her goals (and the group's goals) based on the source of power and how that power is used. Several types of power are described below.

Expert power. "This power comes from the group's recognition of a member's expertise in a certain area. . . . In a manufacturing firm, for example, a relatively low ranking engineer could influence management by using her knowledge to declare that a new product wouldn't work" [Adler, p. 189].

Referent power. "Referent power refers to the influence members hold due to the way others in the group feel about them, their respect, attention, or liking. It is here that the greatest difference between nominal leaders and true influence occurs. An unpopular boss might have to resort to his or her job title and the power to coerce and reward that come with it to gain compliance, while a popular person can get others to cooperate without threatening or promising even without a leadership title" [Adler, p. 198].

Legitimate power. "Legitimate power . . . is the ability to influence that comes from the position one holds. We often do things for the boss, precisely because he/she holds that title. While legitimate power usually belongs to nominal leaders, lesser positions sometimes possess it depending on the circumstances" [Adler, p. 198].

Coercive power. "Coercive power is the power to punish. . . . We often follow another's bidding because failure to do so would lead to unpleasant consequences. Nominal leaders do have coercive power; they can assign unpleasant tasks, deny pay raises and even fire us. Other members have coercive power, too, though it is usually subtle" [Adler, p. 198].

Reward power. "Reward power is the flip side of coercive power. Nominal leaders have the most obvious rewards: pay raises, improved working conditions, and the ability to promote. But . . . other members can give their own rewards. These come in the form of social payoffs, such as increased goodwill and task-related benefits like voluntary assistance on a job" [Adler, p. 198].

Information power. "Some members influence a group due to the information they possess. This information is different from knowledge . . . defined as expert power. Whereas an expert possesses some form of talent based on training or education, an information rich group member has access to otherwise obscure knowledge that is valuable to others in the group" [Adler, p 198].

Connection power. "In the real world . . . member's influence can often come from the connections he or she has with influential or important people outside or inside the organization. A classic example of this is the son or daughter of the boss" [Adler, p. 198].

This strategy requires the student groups to use their knowledge of each of the individual types of power to develop a short 10- to 15-minute skit that depicts the effective use of each of the types of power. The instructor can divide the class into seven groups and have each group develop a skit on one type of power or, each group can develop a skit that represents the use of at least three types of power. The skits could be developed in the context of the discipline area. The objective is to make the students aware of the kinds of power at the disposal of leaders and the proper ways to use power.

VE, SE, G

Strategy 18
Interview With a Great Leader

For this strategy, the instructor would require students to interview someone who exemplifies a "leader." Students identify the individual with whom they would like to conduct an interview and then they develop a series of questions to ask the individual. Students review their questions with the instructor prior to the interview so the instructor can provide insight and information.

Students write an account of the interview in the form of an article about the leader, similar to the ones in popular magazines. Students interested in photography might also want to take pictures of their leader.

Students should be coached to take note of nonverbal communication, such as the physical appearance of the leader, his/her expressions, his/her laugh, and other communication that might give insight into the attitudes of the leader.

The interviews can be shared in class and then "packaged" into a notebook so that students can get a broad view of feelings, behaviors, and concerns of a broad range of leaders.

This strategy will have more impact if leaders are chosen from the area of study or discipline. Some examples might be as follows:

- An interview with the mayor (political science, government)
- An interview with an astronaut (aerospace engineering, engineering technology, etc.)
- An interview with the president of a major corporation (business)
- An interview with an author (English, literature)
- An interview with an historian (history, social science)
- An interview with a programmer (computer science)

VE, I, SE

Strategy 19
Report on Theories of Leadership

This strategy can be used as an adjunct assignment to classes in most disciplines. It requires students to research and report on the following theories of leadership (see Strategies 37, 39, and 40):

1. Great person theory
2. Path-goal theory
3. Managerial grid

The examples concerning leadership should be related to the discipline of the class.

The report should be approximately 1,000 to 1,500 words (4 to 5 typewritten pages) and should be developed in the style of a typical research paper (see Communication). This assignment will provide students with an overview of leadership related to their area of study and yet will not take up too much class time.

VE

Strategy 20
Panel Discussion on Leadership

This strategy is similar to Strategy 15. The following leadership theories are assigned to a student to research, review, and relate to the discipline (see Strategies 37, 39, and 40):

1. Great person theory
2. Path-goal theory
3. Managerial grid

After each student has had a week or two to review and research, students conduct a round table panel discussion based on their findings. The discussion that ensues will help them to clarify their opinions and beliefs and to see the differences among the theories.

SE, G, VE

Strategy 21
Leadership Self Assessment

Students can use a fundamental self-reporting questionnaire to determine if they are a leader (in their opinion). A questionnaire such as the one that follows can be developed for the class. This type of questionnaire is subjective. There is no set formula to determine that a person is or is not a leader. The purpose of this questionnaire is simply to get students to think about their own leadership styles and potential.

Leadership questionnaire

Answer the following questions in short answer essay form:
1. Do you consider yourself to be a leader? Why? Why not?
2. What are the qualities that you think are most important in terms of leadership?
3. Rate the following in terms of its importance in leadership:

	Never important	Usually not important	Undecided	Sometimes important	Always important
energy	1	2	3	4	5
intelligence	1	2	3	4	5
judgment	1	2	3	4	5
decisiveness	1	2	3	4	5
knowledge	1	2	3	4	5
fluency of speech	1	2	3	4	5
creativity	1	2	3	4	5
integrity	1	2	3	4	5
self confidence	1	2	3	4	5
drive	1	2	3	4	5
responsibility	1	2	3	4	5
ability to get things done	1	2	3	4	5
cooperativeness	1	2	3	4	5
popularity	1	2	3	4	5
diplomacy	1	2	3	4	5
sociability	1	2	3	4	5

4. Rate the following in terms of whether each characteristic is present in you:

	Never important	Usually not important	Undecided	Sometimes important	Always important
energy	1	2	3	4	5
intelligence	1	2	3	4	5
judgment	1	2	3	4	5
decisiveness	1	2	3	4	5
knowledge	1	2	3	4	5
fluency of speech	1	2	3	4	5
creativity	1	2	3	4	5
integrity	1	2	3	4	5
self confidence	1	2	3	4	5
drive	1	2	3	4	5
responsibility	1	2	3	4	5
ability to get things done	1	2	3	4	5
cooperative- ness	1	2	3	4	5
popularity	1	2	3	4	5
diplomacy	1	2	3	4	5
sociability	1	2	3	4	5

5. Based on your answers to questions 3 and 4, what areas do you see need improvement in order for you to become a better leader?

6. Write an action plan below for improving these items. Take each item and develop at least three courses of action that will help you to improve it.

I, VE, SE

Strategy 22
Leadership Peer Assessment

This strategy can be used in conjunction with group projects (see Critical Thinking, Communication, and Teamwork). It can be used to assess the perceptions of group members as to the leadership skills of student leaders. Instructors should use this strategy with caution however. It involves the use of questionnaires (similar to Strategy 21) for assessing perceptions of students toward student leaders. The questionnaire responses should

never be given directly to the students to review. The instructor should gather the responses and develop a tactful, diplomatic summary of the responses (providing the instructor agrees with them). The instructor's judgment should prevail. Even though students are entitled to their opinions, as Jaques points out in *Learning in Groups,* there may be hidden agendas involved and social mores that make students either popular or unpopular [Jaques, 1984]. The instructor should review the responses and then summarize them to be sure there is nothing said that could potentially damage anyone's self-esteem.

Instructors can use this questionnaire to assess student views of student leaders. A questionnaire such as the one that follows can be developed. This kind of questionnaire is subjective. There is no set formula to determine whether or not any student is a leader. The purpose of this questionnaire is to provide student leaders with feedback on how their behaviors are seen by their peers.

Leadership questionnaire

Answer the following questions in short answer essay form:
1. Do you consider (student leader's name) to be a leader? Why? Why not?
2. What are the qualities that you think are most important in terms of leadership?
3. Rate the following in terms of its importance in leadership:

	Never Important	Usually Not Important	Undecided	Sometimes Important	Always Important
energy	1	2	3	4	5
intelligence	1	2	3	4	5
judgment	1	2	3	4	5
decisiveness	1	2	3	4	5
knowledge	1	2	3	4	5
fluency of speech	1	2	3	4	5
creativity	1	2	3	4	5
integrity	1	2	3	4	5
self confidence	1	2	3	4	5
drive	1	2	3	4	5
responsibility	1	2	3	4	5
ability to get things done	1	2	3	4	5
cooperative- ness	1	2	3	4	5

popularity	1	2	3	4	5
diplomacy	1	2	3	4	5
sociability	1	2	3	4	5

4. The following characteristics are present in (student leader's name) leadership behavior.

	Never Important	Usually Not Important	Undecided	Sometimes Important	Always Important
energy	1	2	3	4	5
intelligence	1	2	3	4	5
judgment	1	2	3	4	5
decisiveness	1	2	3	4	5
knowledge	1	2	3	4	5
fluency of speech	1	2	3	4	5
creativity	1	2	3	4	5
integrity	1	2	3	4	5
self confidence	1	2	3	4	5
drive	1	2	3	4	5
responsibility	1	2	3	4	5
ability to get things done	1	2	3	4	5
cooperative- ness	1	2	3	4	5
popularity	1	2	3	4	5
diplomacy	1	2	3	4	5
sociability	1	2	3	4	5

5. Based on your answers to questions 3 and 4, what areas do you see need improvement in order for (student leader's name) to become a better leader?

6. Rate (student leader's name) overall in terms of his/her leadership ability:

1	2	3	4	5	6	7	8	9	10
Poor Leader				**Mediocre Leader**				**Excellent Leader**	

7. Rate how well you work with (student leader's name).

1	2	3	4	5	6	7	8	9	10
Poorly				**Neither poorly nor well**				**Very well**	

8. What strengths did you see in (student leader's name)'s performance?

9. What weaknesses did you see in (student leader's name)'s performance?

10. What advice would you give to help him or her improve his/her leadership abilities?

This questionnaire can be given for each student leader with the instructor summarizing the total results into an action plan of items for improvement as well as items that the student performs particularly well that will enhance self-esteem.

G, VE, A, DE

Strategy 23
Code of Ethics

This strategy requires students to draft a "code of ethics" for themselves as they become leaders. It is best to use this strategy in conjunction with a strategy that provides an overview of leadership theory and leadership responsibility such as Strategies 15, 16, 18, 21, or 22.

This code of ethics may include ideas such as the students' views on:

- honesty
- trust
- compassion
- work ethics
- values
- integrity

A code of ethics describes the general values of the students and defines their life goals so that they can use this code of ethics as a standard by which to make decisions when they do become leaders.

I, SE, VE

Strategy 24
Leadership Game

This game is similar to other popular games that require students to make decisions about future behavior based on scenarios. The instructor writes each situation on an index card. Students are asked to pick a card and then tell what they would do in a specific situation.

Card 1. Your boss has informed you that there may be budget cuts and you will have 30 days to decide which of your three employees will have to be cut. What procedure would you use to make this decision?

Card 2. You are the manager of a resource group that prepares proposals for clients. Your boss has just handed you a proposal that must be completed by 7:30 a.m. tomorrow. It is now 2:30 p.m. You know that in order to complete this proposal, several of your coworkers will have to stay overnight. What will you do?

Card 3. You have recently been promoted to supervisor of your section. When you worked as part of the "team," John was a good friend of yours. You and John shared thoughts, work ideas, and frequently went out to lunch together. Now that you've been promoted, John's work behavior seems to have changed. He is frequently coming in late, taking long lunch breaks, and not finishing assigned work on time. What do you think is the problem? What will you do about it?

Card 4. One of your coworkers has recently been coming to work late and seems to be very withdrawn. You have noticed her crying when she thinks she is alone. She seems to be having trouble controlling her emotions. What would you do?

Card 5. You are a computer programmer involved with installing special highly technical computer programs for clients. Your boss has promised a small business owner that you can have a specific computer software installed in half the time it normally takes. You are not sure that you and your coworkers can accomplish the task even if you work 12- to 14-hour days. What will you do?

Card 6. Your company has just signed a very prestigious, very exclusive contract with a major computer manufacturer. This contract will bring in millions of dollars over a five-year time frame. The new contract, however, also means that you and your department will have to work 14- to 18-hour days over the next two months in order to complete negotiations and proposals for the work. What will you do?

Card 7. Your boss has told you that your company will be selling a piece of highly complex instrumentation equipment to a major client. The client was very cost conscious and wanted the cost to remain below a certain fixed amount. In order to maintain your company's desired profit level, your boss decided to sell the instrumentation package without the normal two-week training package that accompanies it. You believe that the use of this equipment without the proper training could be very dangerous both to the operators as well as to the workers of the plant and to the general public. What will you do?

Card 8. You have just been told that you and two associates who work for you will have ten working days to complete a photography project at five locations. Describe your ideas for ways you could schedule the work.

Card 9. You have a recalcitrant employee who grumbles about almost every task assigned to him. Since you were hired about three months ago, he seems to have become more and more uncooperative. You have heard rumors that he applied for your job but was turned down due to his inability to cooperate and get along with people. What will you do?

Card 10. Your department has been very busy filling orders for retail items. You have been handling all of the reorders yourself and letting the first time orders go to your two employees. Now, however, due to a problem with the product, there are three times as many reorders as first time orders. You're quickly getting behind and you need help, but you do not want your two employees to feel that you're giving them your job to do. What will you do?

There are no wrong or right answers, just answers that seem to fit within the individual student's leadership style. Students can defend their "solution" to the scenarios while their peers offer suggestions and comments.

Some possible solutions are as follows (Cards 1 through 10):

1. Decide whose performance is best.
2. Discuss the problem and ask for volunteers and stay yourself.
3. Talk to John about his performance. Be a leader, not a friend.
4. Talk to your coworker and find out what is bothering her.
5. Ask for the contract help and ask for volunteers. Schedule overtime.
6. Talk to workers, explain importance, ask for volunteers.
7. Explain dangers to the boss. Get the boss to talk to the client or talk to the client yourself.
8. Schedule two days per location or split out by time and send individuals.
9. Talk to employee and try to enlist help or start disciplinary action.
10: Talk to employees and delegate the work.

LC, G, VE

Strategy 25
Risk Taking Game

This game requires student players to be risk takers—they must share their thoughts about what they would do in risky situations. Each student pulls a card from a stack and then tell how he/she would react in a risky situation.

Card 1. You are employed at a company that has a long track record of success. You enjoy your job immensely. You like the people you are working with and you've developed a reputation as a "star" employee. Then, you get a call from a friend who says there is a job opening at his company that would pay 40 percent more. The job has an impressive title, but you have not heard very good things about the company. What would you do?

Card 2. You have just completed training to be an Emergency Medical Technician. You have had your certification for only one week when you happen on an accident on the freeway. You can see that one victim is bleeding and the other may need CPR. What will you do?

Card 3. You have been looking for a job in marketing for six months. Now, suddenly you have two offers. One is for a company that needs someone to sell industrial chemicals. It is a very exciting job with a great deal of travel. It pays commission only, but the average earnings are $50,000 per year. The other job is as an inhouse staff coordinator. It's less exciting but seems to be more stable. The set salary for this job is $30,000 per year. Which job would you take and why?

Card 4. You are a blossoming amateur photographer. You keep your camera with you at all times. One day, by chance, you drive past a building that is on fire. You get an excellent photograph of a fireman leaping from a flame-filled window with a young blonde girl in his arms. You know the shot is good, but you don't know if the local papers or any other publication would publish it. You've never tried to get anyone to buy your photographs, and you don't have a portfolio to show them. All you have is the one timely photograph in your film canister. What will you do?

Card 5. You are a computer programmer. You are working on a new sound program for a sophisticated client who wants to use your program to develop his own computer-based training. You have discovered a way that your client's employees can "program" sound just by typing out the words on the keyboard. You know this is an advance that will be of great benefit to him, but you also know that software with this capability will cost 40 to 45 percent more than the price you quoted him. At the time you quoted him, you were unaware that you would develop such a breakthrough. Will you ask for more money? Why or why not?

Card 6. You are a fashion designer. You've been observing what the buyers of department stores are buying for next year. You have an idea for a line of clothes—all of which will be totally black, a color your colleagues seem to think is not a good color for the next fall season. What will you do?

Card 7. You have an employee who used to perform excellently. Over the last three months, her performance has declined substantially. You know that she has been afflicted severely by some personal tragedies in her life. Suddenly she calls in sick and does not come to work for four weeks. She does call in every day and she does have cumulative sick time to cover her absences. Your boss tells you to "get rid of her" because she is "dead weight." He doesn't know this employee like you do. You know that before her problem, she was an excellent employee. What will you do?

Card 8. You have recently been employed by a technical firm that has retained a public relations firm to assist in promotion. After looking over the records showing the amount of work achieved by the firm and the high cost of the retainer fee being charged by the firm, you do not think your company is getting its money's worth. Although your background is communications, you do not have much experience in public relations. You think you could do a better job on your company's public relations and you would like the opportunity to take over this responsibility and develop the public relations programs yourself. This idea is risky. You have not been with the company long enough to gain everyone's confidence and if you fail, you're likely to lose your job. Yet, you feel strongly that your company needs to stop spending money for public relations firm fees that are not accomplishing the company's goals. What do you do?

Card 9. You are working on a team that is doing a proposal for a large multibillion dollar contract. In the past, this organization has approached large-scale contracts in a very disorganized way. Most of the people in the organization think that the "old" way is the only way. You would like to use some different techniques to get the work organized so that no mistakes will be made and the proposal will be completed on time. You've written a schedule that you think would work. It would mean that all workers involved would have to be committed to completing their assignments on time. Will you suggest your schedule to the boss knowing the new system will make you "unpopular"?

Card 10. You have been asked to develop the budget for next year's promotion campaign. Your boss says to use the percentage of sales method that takes last year's sales, multiplies it by a percentage, and then gives an easily identifiable and containable figure·for the budget to work with. You prefer to think of promotion as an investment in the future. You would rather use the objective/task method of budgeting. This method requires the budgeter to set goals for the company, to decide how much promotional monies must be expended to reach those goals, and then to budget for the amount of estimated expenditures needed to achieve the goals. This method is much more risky because no one knows for sure if the promotion will work, and this method usually ends up costing more than other methods. In addition, the budget figure is not nearly as "containable" using this method. What will you do?

Students share their solutions to these scenarios and decide whether they are risk adverse. The scenarios provide excellent beginning points for exploring individual orientations to risk.

LC, G, VE, A

Strategy 26
Leadership Journal

The leadership journal strategy is developed in conjunction with one of the strategies that require students to be group leaders for long or short-term projects (see Strategies 10 through 13). Throughout the group process, the leader is required to keep a journal of his/her thoughts as decisions are made, ideas developed, conflicts resolved, and work accomplished.

This journal is shared with the entire class at the end of the group work. The leader reads certain portions of it to explain thoughts or feelings that might have occurred during the course of completing the work. The journal will give the student additional insight into his/her reactions to the group and to the problems faced during the group process. The requirement to write down the problems, challenges, and solutions will force the student to clarify his/her thoughts and to observe his/her own behavior with regard to solving those problems.

The journal will be more effective if the instructor provides comments and guidance to the student leader at the end of the project and helps the student leader relate the issues to the thoughts and behaviors reflected in the journal.

Possible journal topics are:

- Choosing individual assignments
- Resolving conflict
- Evaluating individual assignments
- Coordinating the total project
- Scheduling
- Guiding individuals
- Coaching
- Accountability techniques used

I, VE, SE

Strategy 27
Programmed Versus Nonprogrammed Decisions

A programmed decision is one that occurs frequently enough that a leader can develop a systematic approach to the problem. If the company overspends its budget, the manager can have a line of credit established with a bank to solve the problem. If the chemist needs to neutralize a liquid chemical solution, he/she can use a specific formula to do so. If a retailer allows customers to return unwanted items, he/she will have a procedure for refunding money. Decisions such as these can be carefully planned ahead to minimize time spent in developing solutions.

Nonprogrammed decisions require "tailor made" solutions that can be used only once. When the astronauts prepare for a trip on the space shuttle, each mission is different, so the training for each mission must be uniquely designed. What to include in this training is a nonprogrammed decision because it must be unique. Similarly, if a company finally overspends its budget to the point where it goes bankrupt, the decision about what process to use to go bankrupt is a nonprogrammed decision because it is unique and not likely to occur again.

For this strategy, the instructor develops a list of 20 to 25 decisions based on the subject area. There should be a variety of programmed and nonprogrammed decisions. Students are placed in groups of four, and each student group is required to create a graphic model of possible solutions and label each decision as a programmed or nonprogrammed decision. For each decision, students should be able to identify factors that show that the decision is programmed or nonprogrammed and should be able to provide some kind of graphic representation of solutions. At the end of the exercise, the instructor should be able to point out the similarities between the graphics configured for the programmed decisions (many of which will require the same process for solution) and nonprogrammed decisions (which will probably be reflected by totally unique designs that do not seem to match the designs of any of the other decisions). As a point of discussion, the instructor can observe the groups and point out when they are naturally using a programmed decision process by using the graphic models developed previously as starting points for new decision models.

A, G, VE, SE

Strategy 28
Individual Theory of Leadership

This strategy requires students to write a one- to two-page essay expounding their individual theories of leadership. This essay should include the characteristics students think are important for leaders, the behaviors leaders should exhibit, the training leaders should have to develop their leadership potential, and the style of leadership students are most comfortable with.

It is important to have students write the essay in class because the assignment should be used as a foundation for discussion on leadership as well as a means for assisting students in clarifying their thoughts on leadership. It will be more effective if it is used before any modules or material concerning leadership is introduced. If students develop their essays first, their original thinking will not be influenced by the material introduced in class. Then, they can see how closely their theories match the theories that have been developed by social scientists and managerial experts. The assignment should be fun for students, requiring them to use their imaginations to develop new theories of their own. They can share their theories with the class and then compare and contrast their original theories with the theories introduced.

SE, VE, A, I

Strategy 29
Self Assignments

This strategy uses group work as in Strategies 10 through 13. For this strategy, the class is divided into groups of four. Members of each group are required to get to know each other and to choose a leader. Once a leader has been identified for each group, the instructor then presents a list of several comparable group projects that could be accomplished by the group for a grade. The leader from each group chooses which of the assignments his/her group will accomplish. (The class is not informed beforehand that the leader will have this power.) The student leader can get information from other group members, but he/she cannot "call for a vote." The decision and responsibility for the choice are the leader's.

This assignment creates the problem for the leader of making the decision (which probably will not please all group members) and then of leading his group to completion of the task. He/she must rally support of his/her decision just as a manager or supervisor must do in the workplace. The leader will have to deal with conflict over the decision, uncertainty, and perhaps regret if the decision is unpopular.

If possible, this can be used several times during the course of a semester for in-class projects to allow different students the opportunity to experience the responsibility of leadership.

VE, SE, G, P

Strategy 30
Mentor Program

For this strategy, students are required to identify a leader in the field for which they are studying who will agree to serve as their mentor for a semester and hopefully beyond the semester or end of the course. The student would approach the leader and explain the requirements for being a mentor for a semester (see Strategies for Motivation to Learn).

Requirements for Students

- Identify the mentor
- Interview the mentor
- Write an article on the mentor

- Get advice from the mentor on:
  - How to break into the field (see Career Development)
  - How to get a job in the field
  - How to keep a job in the field
  - How to be a good leader
  - How to grow professionally
- Get input from the mentor on projects for class
- Obtain a letter of recommendation from the mentor

Requirements for Mentors

- Make time for student
- Agree to interviews
- Give solid advice on:
  - How to break into the field
  - How to get a job in the field
  - How to keep a job in the field
  - How to be a good leader
  - How to grow professionally
- Comment on class projects
- If acceptable, provide a written letter of recommendation

This assignment requires a great deal of salesmanship on the part of the student because the mentor in this situation gets little in return except the satisfaction of helping a student. (Most true leaders, however, make time for students, and students should find ample mentors.)

VE, LC, G

Strategy 31
A Leader a Day

Students are constantly exposed to information concerning leaders. From magazines to newspapers, to sports programs and other media, students have ample opportunity to recognize leadership. This strategy requires students to seek out "a leader a day," to find an article, a video, or some reference to a leader in their chosen field and bring it to class each day. The discoveries are shared with the class and articles (or summaries of videos or books) are kept in a spiral notebook for students to peruse throughout the semester.

The assignment should be clear (based on the discipline) concerning the type of individuals who constitute "leaders" in the field, but always flexible enough, of course, to reflect students' viewpoints. Students may view someone as a leader who the instructor would not. The important point is to provide a vehicle for students to seek out and identify with leaders in the field.

VI, VE, LC, I, EE

Strategy 32
Leadership Poster

This strategy requires students to develop a poster-size graphic depicting a leader in their discipline. The poster should be written similar to an advertisement and should include a statement starting with the words "A LEADER IS . . . ."

This assignment will require students to research leaders in their field and then summarize their ideas about leadership in a succinct, clear way. The graphics can be developed using photographs, magazine photographs, original drawings, or paintings. The statement is the most important element of the assignment because it briefly captures the students' thoughts.

The posters can be displayed during class time and/or posted if there is permanent space.

LC, VI, SE, G, I

Strategy 33
Changing Leaders

This strategy uses group work (see Critical Thinking and Teamwork) as the basis for experiential learning in leadership. The class is divided into groups of four and given a long-term task to accomplish. The task should require four separate hours to complete. The instructor asks each member of the group to fulfill the leadership role during a particular segment of the task.

After the task is complete, the instructor evaluates the content-specific work and then asks each group to answer the leadership questionnaires (see Strategies 21 and 22). The styles of each leader would be compared and contrasted as well as the feelings and experiences of each leader. This exercise gives students practice in learning to adapt to differing leadership styles (a situation that happens frequently in the workplace) and gives each student practice in using leadership skills.

VE, G, SE, A

Strategy 34
Essay—Leaders Are Born

"'Universalist trait' or 'great person' theories of leadership contend that certain individuals such as Martin Luther King, Jr. or Indira Gandhi possess traits that set them apart as leaders, regardless of the situations in which they find themselves" [Northcraft, Neale, p. 403].

This strategy relies on the essay (see Communication strategies) as a vehicle for students to explore their own beliefs concerning leadership. The essay can be of 200–250 words in length and should require students to research the discipline area for examples of leadership within their field. Using appropriate evidence to support their theses (see Critical Thinking strategies), students can take a stand for or against the theory that "leaders are born."

Essays can be written in two different ways—inductive or deductive. The deductive approach starts with a thesis statement that is developed in the first paragraph. This statement is then explained more fully in the body paragraphs, which develop proofs or pieces of evidence to support the main thesis. The main thesis is reinforced in the beginning of the concluding para-

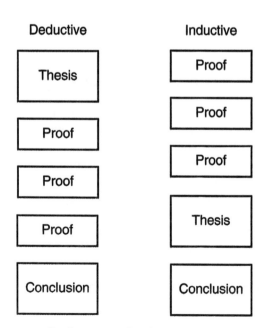

Deductive and inductive logic.

graph which ends with a generalization statement regarding the main thesis.

An inductive approach sets the evidence or proof out in the beginning, going from one piece of evidence to another in order until all points tie in to a thesis statement and then a conclusion. The main thesis is developed in the paragraph preceding the concluding paragraph and a generalization regarding the main thesis follows in the concluding paragraph.

These basic guidelines for developing essays can be used for essays on any topic including this leadership topic.

VE, I, SE

Strategy 35
Essay—Leaders Are Made

Behavioral theories developed after World War II when

> ... leadership research in the late 1940s began to focus on behaviors of leaders rather than their personality and demographic characteristics. Thus, rather than attempt to use personal characteristics to separate leaders from followers, this stream of research attempted to determine exactly which leader behaviors resulted in follower satisfaction and high performance.
>
> The focus on leader behaviors rather than on leader traits has a number of advantages. First, examining behaviors rather than traits allows us to consider formal as well as informal leaders. . . . Second, if critical and effective leader behaviors can be identified, our ability to train leaders will be enhanced [Northcraft, Neale, p. 412].

This strategy (like Strategy 34) relies on the essay (see Communication) as a vehicle for students to research leadership theory and to voice their own beliefs concerning leadership. The essay can be 200–250 words in length and should require students to research the discipline area for examples of leadership within their field. Using appropriate evidence to support their theses (see Critical Thinking), students can take a stand for or against the theory that "leaders can be made."

Essays can be written either using deductive or inductive approaches.

VE, I, SE

Strategy 36
Substitutes For Leadership

This strategy uses a module of training to introduce certain characteristics that Northcraft and Neale [p. 432] suggest can be substitutes for leadership.

Substitutes for leadership

Worker	Worker's Task	Organization
Ability	Repetitiveness	Formalization
Experience	Ambiguousness	Inflexibility
Training	Methodological task	Specific advisory functions
Knowledge	Intrinsic satisfaction	Closely knit work group
Professionalism	Feedback	Reward system
Independence		
Indifference		Distance

This strategy is based on the idea that some factors can neutralize a leader's influence. An individual leader's ability to make these substitutions can be helpful or harmful to him/her depending on his/her "fit" with the total organization.

This strategy uses a class discussion of these and other hindrances and helps that can be important factors in the leadership focus of a particular organization. This assignment can be given as an adjunct to other leadership assignments, especially in vocational and technical programs.

VE

Strategy 37
Presentation—Charismatic Leaders

This strategy requires students to choose a charismatic leader (hopefully within their discipline area) and report on that person's style and outlook. It requires a secondary research project using at least five different sources and covering a famous charismatic leader's life.

Possible subjects include:

• John F. Kennedy
• Martin Luther King, Jr.
• Gandhi

- Indira Gandhi
- Robert Kennedy
- Ronald Reagan
- Bill Clinton
- Prince Charles
- Admiral Zumwalt
- John Glenn
- Dr. Debakey
- Susan B. Anthony

The presentation should include the following information:

- Birth date, city, state, country
- Background through high school (or equivalency)
- Background from high school to maturity or death
- Major accomplishments
- Major beliefs
- Major philosophy of leadership
- Death circumstances (if applicable)
- Incidents of note that may have influenced the subject
- The effect the subject's attitudes and accomplishments have on the student

The presentation should deal more with qualitative beliefs, attitudes, and thoughts rather than simple events in the subject's life. A typical report and ten-minute presentation would be 10 to 15 pages typed and double-spaced. The last section would ask the student to relate this newly researched philosophy to his or her own life and would be the most important part of the assignment.

I, VE, SE

Strategy 38
Group Project—Power

This strategy involves the comparison of the seven types of power—expert, coercive, information, legitimate, reward, connection, and referent power (refer to Leadership, Strategy 17). The class is divided into seven groups. Each group is given one day in the library to research one of the types of power. The research should include such information as definition, examples, short descriptions of famous people within the discipline who display this kind of power, uses of power, and strengths and weaknesses of use. The students then present their findings to the class and each group prepares a chart discussing each type of power. The charts are taped to a wall, and all seven types of power are compared and contrasted in the class.

VE, SE, G

Strategy 39
Leadership Grid

Blake and McCanse's Leadership Grid can provide an excellent self-analysis tool for students. The Leadership Grid identifies five leadership styles using production orientation coupled with people orientation.

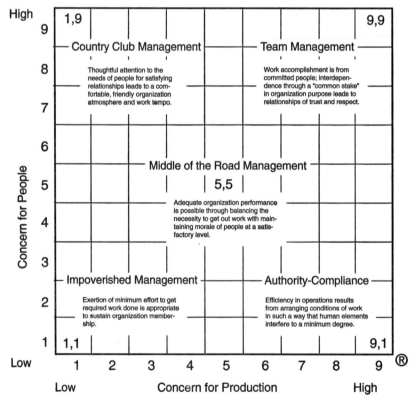

The Leadership Grid®. (The Grid® designation is the property of Scientific Methods, Inc. and is used here with permission.)

These leadership styles can be roughly summarized as follows:

Country Club—High concern for people/low concern for task. People are happy, but production is low.

Impoverished—Low concern for people/low concern for task. People are unhappy and dissatisfied and the production is low.

Middle of the Road—Medium concern for people/medium concern for task. Leader is not highly enthusiastic about motivating people or about production. The work unit does not excel under such conditions.

Task Centered—Low concern for people/high concern for task. Production is accomplished usually to the detriment of the people. Morale is low and there is high turnover.

Team Oriented—High concern for people/high concern for task. This is the ideal style. Not only is production high, but the people are highly satisfied and motivated.

This is a very effective tool (even for students who are in nonmanagerial courses) for students to begin to understand their own orientation toward work [Blake and McCanse, 1991].

VE, VI, I

Strategy 40
Path Goal Theory Role Play

The Path Goal Theory was developed by Robert House and is a contingency model of leadership that sees the role of the leader as one of assisting his/her followers in the achievement of goals by providing necessary support and direction [House, pp. 321–338]. According to the theory, a leader's behavior is acceptable to followers if it provides satisfaction to them, and it is motivational if it taps into the subordinate's needs and provides that subordinate with support both in resources and in psychological reassurance through coaching and guidance. House identifies four leadership behaviors.

- **Directive leader.** Tells subordinates what to do, how to do it, schedules work, gives guidance on specifics.
- **Supportive leader.** Shows concern for people and needs of subordinates.
- **Participative leader.** Asks for input of subordinates and uses suggestions on final decision.
- **Achievement-oriented.** Sets goals and expects the subordinates to perform at their highest level.

The classroom is divided into four groups of students who are given content-oriented projects based on a specific discipline. The student leaders of the groups are asked to role play a specific style of leadership. After the tasks have been accomplished, the instructor first evaluates the tasks based on the content requirements (see strategies in Critical Thinking and Teamwork).

Next, the instructor administers the leadership questionnaire (see Strategies 1–3) and then reveals the role playing assignments to the class. The questionnaires can then be used as a basis for thorough discussion of leadership styles based on House's four leadership behaviors.

This kind of role play will provide students with the experience of leading and following and will help them recognize certain leadership styles in others as well as provide them with models for practice.

G, SE, VE

Bibliography

Adler, Mortimer J., *How to Read a Book,* New York, NY: Simon and Schuster, 1940.

Adler, Ronald B., *Communicating at Work,* New York, NY: Random House, 1989.

Alessandra, Anthony, Phil Wexler, and Rick Barrera, *Non-Manipulative Selling,* Englewood Cliffs, NJ: Prentice Hall, 1987.

A Manual of Style, Chicago: The University of Chicago Press, 1982.

Anderson, Rolph, *Professional Personal Selling,* Englewood Cliffs, NJ: Prentice Hall, 1991.

Ary, Donald, Lucy C. Jacobs, and Asghar Razavieh, *Introduction to Research in Education,* Fort Worth, TX: Holt, Rinehart and Winston, Inc., 1990.

Associated Press Stylebook & Libel Manual, Reading, MA: Addison-Wesley Publishing Co., 1987.

Blake, Robert R. and Ann Adams McCanse. *Leadership Dilemmas—Grid® Solutions,* Houston, TX: Gulf Publishing Co., 1991. Copyright by Scientific Methods, Inc.

Bloom, Benjamin S., *Taxonomy of Educational Objectives,* New York, NY: David McKay, Inc., 1956.

Boone, Louis E., and David L. Kurtz, *Contemporary Business,* Chicago, IL: The Dryden Press, 1990.

Broderick, Richard, "Learning the Ropes," *Training,* (Vol. 26, No. 10, pp. 78–86), October, 1989.

Carnavale, Anthony, Leila J. Gainer, Ann S. Meltzer, *Workplace Basics: The Skills Employers Want,* Alexandria, VA: U. S. Department of Labor Employment and Training Administration and American Society for Training and Development, 1989.

Chaffee, John, *Thinking Critically,* Boston, MA: Houghton Mifflin Co., 1988.

Cohen, Elizabeth, *Designing Groupwork,* New York, NY: Teachers College Press, 1986.

Costa, Arthur L., *Developing Minds,* Roseville, CA: Association for Supervision and Curriculum Development, 1989.

Costley, David and Ralph Todd, *Human Relations in Organizations,* St. Paul, MN: West Publishing Co., 1991.

Crawford, C. C., "How You Can Gather and Organize Ideas Quickly," *Chemical Engineering,* New York, NY: McGraw-Hill, July 25, 1983.

Cross, K. Patricia, and Thomas A. Angelo, *Classroom Assessment Techniques,* Ann Arbor, MI: National Center for Research to Improve Postsecondary Teaching and Learning, 1988.

Daft, Richard L., *Management,* Chicago, IL: The Dryden Press, 1991.

De Bono, Edward, *Lateral Thinking for Management,* New York, NY: American Management Association, 1971.

Drucker, Peter F., *The Practice of Management,* New York, NY: Harper and Brothers, 1954.

Engel, James F., Roger D. Blackwell, and Paul W. Miniard, *Consumer Behavior,* Chicago, IL: The Dryden Press, 1990.

Engstrom, Ted W., and R. Alec MacKenzie, *Managing Your Time,* Grand Rapids, MI: Zondervan Publishing House, 1967.

Erb, Thomas and Nancy M. Doda, *Team Organization,* Washington, D.C.: National Education Association, 1989.

Fieldler, Fred. E., Martin M. Chemers, and Linda Mahar, *Improving Leadership Effectiveness,* New York, N Y: John Wiley and Sons, 1976.

Franck, Frederick, *The Zen of Seeing,* New York, NY: Vintage Books, 1973.

Gibson, James, John Ivancevich, and James H. Donnelly, *Organizations,* Plano, TX: Business Publications, 1982.

Gregg Reference Manual, 6th ed., Willaim A. Sabin, ed., New York: McGraw, 1985.

House, Robert J., "A Path Goal Theory of Leader Effectiveness," *Administrative Science Quarterly,* 16, 1970.

Jaques, David, *Learning in Groups,* Beckenham, Kent: Croom Helm, Ltd., 1984.

Johnston, William B., *Workforce 2000: Work and Workers for the 21st Century,* Indianapolis, IN: Hudson Institute, 1987.

Kearns, David T. and Denis P. Doyle, *Winning the Brain Race,* San Francisco, CA: Institute for Contemporary Studies, 1988.

Knowles, Malcolm, *Andragogy in Action,* San Francisco, CA: Jossey-Bass Publishers, 1984.

Knowles, Malcolm, *The Adult Learner: A Neglected Species,* Houston, TX: Gulf Publishing Co., 1990.

Kolb, D., *The Learning Style Inventory,* Boston, MA: McBer and Co., 1976.

Kotter, John P., *The Leadership Factor,* The Free Press, Division of Macmillan, Inc., New York, New York, 1988.

Kurtz, David L. and Robert H. Dodge, *Professional Selling,* Homewood, IL: Irwin, 1991.

Luft, J., *Group Process: An Introduction to Group Dynamics,* Palo Alto, CA: National Press, 1970.

Mayfield, Marlys, *Thinking for Yourself,* (Draft of chapter nine revision given at 1989 Critical Thinking Conference in Sonoma, CA), Belmont, CA: Wadsworth Publishing Co., 1987.

McKeachie, Wilbert J., *Teaching Tips: A Guidebook for the Beginning College Teacher,* Lexington, MA: D. C. Heath and Co., 1978.

Merrill, David W. and Roger R. Reid, *Personal Styles and Effective Performance,* Radnor, PA: Chilton Book Co., 1982.

Michalski, Ryzzard, Jaime Carbonell, and Tom N. Mitchell, *Machine Learning:* San Mateo, CA: Morgan Kaufman Publishers, 1983.

Morrisey, George, *Getting Your Act Together: Goal Setting for Fun, Health and Profit,* New York, NY: John Wiley and Sons, 1980.

Northcraft, Gregory and Margaret A. Neale, *Organizational Behavior,* Chicago, IL: The Dryden Press, 1990.

Ogilvy, David, *Ogilvy on Advertising,* New York: Random House, 1985.

Pascale, Richard T., and Anthony G. Athos, *The Art of Japanese Management,* New York, NY: Simon and Schuster, 1981.

Paul, Richard, *Critical Thinking,* Rohnert Park, CA: Center For Critical Thinking and Moral Critique, 1990.

Pena, William, *Problem Seeking,* Washington D.C.: AIA Press, 1987.

Prentice Hall Handbook for Writers, 11th ed., Glen Leggett *et al.,* Englewood Cliffs, N.J.: 1990.

Pride, William, M. and O. C. Ferrell, *Marketing,* Boston, MA: Houghton Mifflin Co., 1989, 1991.

Robbins, Stephen P., *Organizational Behavior,* Englewood Cliffs, NJ: Prentice-Hall, 1989.

Rogers, Carl R., *On Becoming A Person,* Boston, MA: Houghton Mifflin, 1961.

Russon, Allien and Harold R. Wallace, *Personality Development for Work,* Cincinnati, OH: Southwestern Publishing, 1981.

Shaughnessy, Mina P., *Errors and Expectations,* Oxford, England: Oxford University Press, 1977.

Stech, Ernest, and Sharon Ratliffe, *Effective Group Communication,* Lincolnwood, IL: National Textbook Company, 1987.

Stodgill, R. M., "Personal Factors Associated With Leadership," *Journal of Psychology,* 25, 1948.

Swartz, Robert J. and D. N. Perkins, *Teaching Thinking: Issues and Approaches,* Pacific Grove, CA: 1990.

Tobias, Sheila, *Overcoming Math Anxiety,* New York, NY: W. W. Norton and Co., 1978.

Timm, Paul, Brent Peterson, and Jackson Stevens, *People at Work,* St. Paul, MN: West Publishing, 1990.

Tyner, Thomas E., *Writing Voyage,* Belmont, CA: Wadsworth Publishing Co., 1985.

Winston, Stephanie, *The Organized Executive,* New York, NY: W. W. Norton and Company, 1983.

Zemke, Ron and Thomas Kramlinger, *Figuring Things Out: A Trainer's Guide to Needs and Task Analysis,* Reading, MA: Addison-Wesley Publishing Co., 1989.

Zinsser, William, *Writing to Learn,* New York, NY: Harper and Row, 1988.

INDEX